U.S.S. NEW JERSEY
CAPTAIN E.H.THOMSON
COMMANDING
20 APR 1946

BATTLESHIPS

BATTLESHIPS

PAUL STILLWELL

MetroBooks

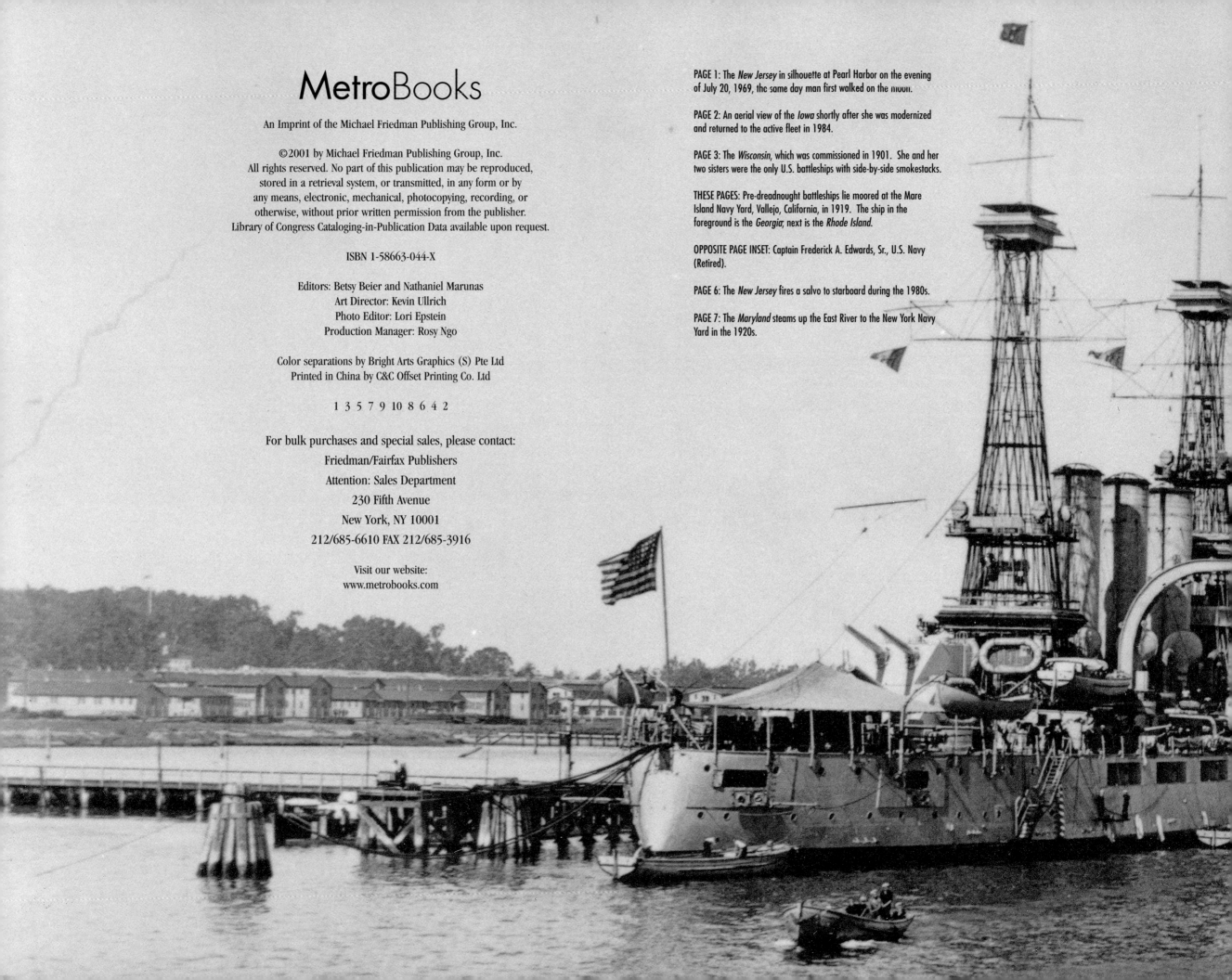

MetroBooks

An Imprint of the Michael Friedman Publishing Group, Inc.

ISBN 1-58663-044-X

Editors: Betsy Beier and Nathaniel Marunas
Art Director: Kevin Ullrich
Photo Editor: Lori Epstein
Production Manager: Rosy Ngo

Color separations by Bright Arts Graphics (S) Pte Ltd
Printed in China by C&C Offset Printing Co. Ltd

1 3 5 7 9 10 8 6 4 2

For bulk purchases and special sales, please contact:
Friedman/Fairfax Publishers
Attention: Sales Department
230 Fifth Avenue
New York, NY 10001
212/685-6610 FAX 212/685-3916

Visit our website:
www.metrobooks.com

PAGE 1: The *New Jersey* in silhouette at Pearl Harbor on the evening of July 20, 1969, the same day man first walked on the moon.

PAGE 2: An aerial view of the *Iowa* shortly after she was modernized and returned to the active fleet in 1984.

PAGE 3: The *Wisconsin*, which was commissioned in 1901. She and her two sisters were the only U.S. battleships with side-by-side smokestacks.

THESE PAGES: Pre-dreadnought battleships lie moored at the Mare Island Navy Yard, Vallejo, California, in 1919. The ship in the foreground is the *Georgia*; next is the *Rhode Island*.

OPPOSITE PAGE INSET: Captain Frederick A. Edwards, Sr., U.S. Navy (Retired).

PAGE 6: The *New Jersey* fires a salvo to starboard during the 1980s.

PAGE 7: The *Maryland* steams up the East River to the New York Navy Yard in the 1920s.

Dedication

To Captain Frederick A. Edwards, Sr., U.S. Navy (Retired)

In early 1992, Captain Fred Edwards and his wife Lydia summoned me to their apartment in a retirement community in Annapolis. He was then ninety years old and terminally ill. He told me that he had been collecting material for many years with the intention of creating a book on the history of battleships. He now realized that he would not be able to write the book and asked me to do so. At the time I was not able to take on the project, but I did persuade Captain Edwards to do an oral history about his own career, for he had served in seven different battleships and had many other interesting duties in the Navy. As we did the interviews in his office, a large, framed photo montage was on the wall. It was made up of pictures of all the ships in which he had served. We proceeded down the rows of photos and discussed one ship after another. He displayed a lively memory and an eye-twinkling sense of humor—as evidenced by the stories in the narrative that follows. Captain Edwards and I developed a warm friendship during the course of the oral history project. When he died later that year, I inherited the photo montage, which now hangs outside my office at the U.S. Naval Institute. Captain Fred Edwards was a naval engineer and probably would have written a more technical account than I have, but I am confident that this book fulfills the spirit of his vision.

Acknowledgments

A number of people have made valuable contributions in the development of this book. I thank coworker Eric Mills of the Naval Institute for recommending me and Roger Cirillo, and Sharyn Rosart, who initiated the book at the MetroBooks end.

Dr. Jack Sweetman, Robert Kaplan, and Ed Calouro, all of them longtime friends of mine, read an early draft of the manuscript and made valuable suggestions. Rebecca Bundy Brown and Heidi Bundy Brown generously allowed me to use material from their book *The "Mighty A" and the Men Who Made Her Mighty*, a tribute to their father and his shipmates on board the USS *Alabama* in World War II. Several others made their memoirs available for use: Rear Admiral Edgar Batcheller, Captain Doug Merritt, Captain John "Bud" Gore, Chief Quartermaster Herb O'Quin, and the late Captain Albert Pelletier. Mrs. Edgar Hull Forrest gave permission to use her husband's memoir. Captain Edward L. "Ned" Beach, famous as the author of *Run Silent, Run Deep*, allowed me to use his father's manuscript autobiography, and Chuck Hartman provided a copy of his shipmate Paul Barnes's recollections of service in the *Mississippi*. Chris Nardo, curator for the *Massachusetts* memorial in Fall River, shared the results of oral history interviews with former crewmen from the ship.

The oral history collection of the U.S. Naval Institute was the source of a number of memoirs by former battleship men; a list of those is contained in the bibliography. Dawn Stitzel, John Urlock, and Sarah Moreland were helpful in providing many of the photographs in the book from the Naval Institute's large photo archive. Betsy Beier of MetroBooks supplied valuable editing skills and an endless supply of perceptive questions that helped make the text clearer. When Betsy left for a sabbatical in Greece, Nathaniel Marunas picked up the reins and guided the project to completion. Lori Epstein did a masterful job of rounding up illustrations, and Kevin Ullrich used them well in executing the book's superb design.

As always, I am thankful for the support of my family. Sons Joseph, Robert, and James provide a father with a bountiful supply of pride through their manifold achievements. My wife, Karen, has been tolerant of the many hours I've spent talking about battleships and has encouraged my telling of the ships' stories in the following account.

CONTENTS

INTRODUCTION

From the time the first U.S. battleship was commissioned in 1895 until the last left active service in 1992, ships of this type played a variety of roles on the world stage. In wartime, the projectiles from their guns sank enemy ships, shot down airplanes, bombarded invasion beachheads, and protected friendly troops. In peacetime, the ships served as mobile ambassadors, symbolizing the nation's power and representing its interests far from home. Indeed, when diplomats of the world powers met in the early 1920s to try to prevent future wars, they sought to do so by limiting the size and numbers of battleships.

Ironically, battleships seldom achieved in combat the expectations that were held for them at the time of construction. In the Spanish-American War, they did what they were designed for, though they were matched against an inferior opponent. In World War I, they formed part of a fleet prepared to fight the Germans in a sea battle that never came to pass. In World War II, the opportunities for gunnery duels were few, and even those

encounters came in restricted waters rather than on the high seas as expected. Even so, battleships performed well in the new missions of antiaircraft protection for carriers and shore bombardment. In subsequent wars, their role was limited almost completely to firing against targets on land.

These majestic, ruggedly built warships captured the public's fancy with their big guns, heavy armor, and handsome lines. But they were more than just collections of machinery. They were floating cities that served as homes and workplaces for several generations of American Navy men and Marines. For these thousands of individuals, the term "battleship sailor" carried with it a great deal of pride. The account that follows is based largely on the recollections of the officers and enlisted

men who served on board battleships in peace and war. Through their eyes, one sees advances in technology and living conditions, along with the events, large and small, that marked the interaction of men and machinery. Though they no longer steam on the world's oceans, several battleships still remain in various parts of the country for visits by tourists and others who want to recapture the mystique of these great ships. Though reason suggests that battleships are and were inanimate objects, the heart has other ideas. Many who served in their crews believed they had souls as well, and those souls are still with us.

Captain Edward M. Thompson (with his officers in a gun tub just left of center) gathers with the ship's crew on board the *New Jersey* at Bremerton, Washington, in April 1946.

U.S.S. NEW JERSEY
CAPTAIN E.H.THOMSON
COMMANDING
20 APR 1945

FIRST STEPS

ABOVE: On the eve of the twentieth century, Secretary of the Navy Benjamin Franklin Tracy, a Civil War veteran, played a key role in providing the United States with oceangoing battleships. OPPOSITE PAGE: Sailors and civilians mingle on the forecastle of the *Kentucky*. When battleships visited port cities, citizens were often welcomed aboard to see what their Navy had to offer—and to build support for the construction of more ships in the future.

In a considerable manifestation of irony, a man who made a substantial contribution to the building of the nation's new steel navy in the late nineteenth century had served as a Confederate Army officer during the Civil War. In 1877, Hilary A. Herbert joined the U.S. Congress as a representative from Alabama and subsequently became chairman of the House Committee on Naval Affairs. There, he exerted considerable skill

in revitalizing a U.S. Navy that had sunk into disrepair following the war in which he had fought on the other side.

First in the "new Navy" were steel-hulled protected cruisers. Then, urged on by Herbert, an 1886 act of Congress authorized the construction of several warships, including two that were eventually designated as second-class battleships. The design for the first battleship, *Texas*, came from Britain. The second ship, *Maine*, was designed in the United States. The fledgling steel industry took three years to produce the armor that would protect them. By the time they entered the fleet in the summer of 1895, both were already outmoded by newer battleships that went into commission shortly afterward. Secretary of the Navy Benjamin Franklin Tracy, a Union Army general in the Civil War, pushed strongly for those more capable ships and encouraged the creation of a large fleet of battleships.

When the *Maine* was commissioned at the New York Navy Yard on September 17, 1895, Hilary Herbert was the Secretary of the Navy. Because of his naval contributions while in Congress, he had been asked to join the Cleveland administration in 1893. For the ceremony on board the *Maine*, the members of the initial crew came aboard from the wooden-hulled receiving ship *Vermont*, a veteran whose construction had begun in 1818 when she was intended as a seventy-four-gun ship of the line. Seventeen-year-old Apprentice Ambrose Ham was one of 346 enlisted men lined up in ranks on the port side of the quarterdeck; to starboard were thirty officers. The thirty-first was the skipper, Captain A.S. Crowninshield, who presided as the forty-five-star American flag was raised and the ship joined the fleet. As he looked about him, Ham saw a ship that had a white-painted hull, black guns and searchlights, and a superstructure that was buff,

or tan, in color. At 319 feet (97m) long, she was considerably shorter than a destroyer of World War II vintage, for example, but her armor made her heavier, with a displacement of 6,682 tons (6,062t). She was slightly larger than the *Texas*, commissioned a month earlier.

ROLE OF BATTLESHIPS

Back in the late 1880s, when Herbert was still in Congress, the nation was divided over what purpose its Navy should serve. Some believed that it should be for the defense of the nation's shores, so the ships need not be capable of wide-ranging operations. This school of thought advocated coast-defense ships. The other group believed that the best way to keep America's shores from harm was by subscribing to the philosophy that the best defense is a good offense. In keeping with this was the idea that the nation needed ships that could steam out and defeat an approaching enemy on the deep blue ocean. The latter concept received a good deal of support from Captain Alfred Thayer Mahan, a naval officer who wrote influential works on the value of sea power. Tracy and Herbert also believed strongly in the second school of thought and contributed greatly to the naval debates in 1890 that approved the construction of three new battleships which were intended to take on the best that a potential enemy had to offer. The language of the legislation directed the building of "three sea-going coast-line battle ships designed to carry the heaviest armor and most powerful ordnance." The term "coast-line" was a sop to those who still believed in a defense-only approach. Their real character was described well by the rest of the sentence.

Two on the Same Day

As timing would have it, a commercial shipyard in Virginia launched the hulls of two new battleships the month following the sinking of the *Maine*. In fact, the event occurred on the same day—March 24, 1898—the only such twin launching of battleships in U.S. Navy history. The Newport News Shipbuilding and Dry Dock Company had also laid the keels for both on the same day—June 30, 1896. In the patriotic impulse that followed the loss of the *Maine*, more than twenty thousand spectators, brought in by excursion trains and chartered steamers, had gathered at the shipyard on the crisp Thursday morning of the launching.

The first launching was of the *Kearsarge*, the only U.S. battleship not named for a state of the union. Her name honored the 1,550-ton (1,406t) screw sloop that had defeated the Confederate raider *Alabama* in a celebrated Civil War battle off Cherbourg, France, in June 1864. That *Kearsarge* had, in turn, been named for a mountain in Merrimack County, New Hampshire. The new battleship displaced 11,540 tons (10,469t), standard for her time but minuscule in comparison with today's largest warships. Six battleships of *Kearsarge* dimensions could be lined up, bow to stern, in two parallel rows on the flight decks of the Nimitz-class aircraft carriers that the Newport News shipyard would turn out a century later.

The sponsor for the 1898 *Kearsarge* was Mrs. Herbert Winslow, daughter-in-law of Captain John Winslow, who had commanded the *Kearsarge* that had sunk the Alabama in the Civil War. Mrs. Winslow broke a bottle of champagne across the bow of this new ship before the hull went sliding backward down the building ways into the James River. Her counterpart for the sister ship *Kentucky*, the second ship launched that day, was Christine Bradley, whose father was Virginia Governor William O. Bradley. But this young woman was a member of the Women's Christian Temperance Union and had no use for a bottle of alcohol, even if it was to be splashed against the hull of a ship rather than consumed by humans. Miss Bradley's fluid of choice, contained in the cut-glass decanter she swung, was water from a spring in Kentucky. Many of the Kentuckians present for the event did not take kindly to this use of water, particularly since superstition suggested that it was unlucky for the ship. To be safe, they tossed small bottles of Kentucky whiskey at the hull to give it a bourbon bath before it slid into the river.

The two battleships had been commissioned within a few months of each other in 1900, and both were members of the Great White Fleet that circumnavigated the globe several years afterward. Still later, both saw token service as training vessels in World War I, by which time they were far outmoded as prime fighting ships. Then their careers diverged dramatically. The *Kentucky*—she of bourbon and water birth—was scrapped in 1924 as part of an international disarmament treaty. The superstructure of her sister was cut off, and a giant crane fitted in its place. As a self-propelled crane ship, *Kearsarge* (renamed *Crane Ship Number 1* in 1941) had many more years of life. Among other jobs, her 250-ton (227t) crane put material such as guns, turrets, and armor into place during the construction of the World War II battleships *Alabama* and *Indiana*. She continued to serve until she was finally struck from the Navy list in 1955 and sold for scrap.

LEFT: March 24, 1898, was an auspicious day at Newport News, Virginia. In this painting the hull of the *Kearsarge* hits the water upon launching; the *Kentucky* will follow soon after. RIGHT: In this photo taken in the early 1900s, after she was completed, the *Kearsarge* receives a replacement for a damaged 13-inch (33cm) gun.

The initial group of first-class battleships included the *Indiana*, commissioned in 1895, and her sisters *Massachusetts* and *Oregon*, which joined the fleet the following year. As was common in battleships of that era, they carried more than one size of major-caliber gun; they had turrets for both 13-inch (33cm) and 8-inch (20cm) guns, as well as some smaller ones. Lieutenant Commander Seaton Schroeder, executive officer of the *Massachusetts*, was one of many who observed the problem of mutual interference. When the 8-inch (20cm) guns were fired, for example, the blast effect could be dangerous to officers in the sighting hoods atop nearby 13-inch (33cm) turrets. The ships had to organize their firing so that those positions were not occupied when guns were to fire close by. Schroeder was also uncomfortable with the torpedo tubes located slightly above the waterline at the bow. He was concerned that if a torpedo fell short when launched, the *Massachusetts* might run into it and set off an explosion. His recommendation to remove the tubes was soon put into effect, and the crew's head (bathroom) was enlarged into the extra space made available.

In the ensuing years, the new battleships gained more and more sea experience and held gunnery practice to prepare for whatever eventualities lay ahead. They also visited a number of port cities to

ABOVE: Off-duty fun, including the opportunity to dress up in decidedly non-regulation costumes, was part of shipboard life. Here, a group of crewmen from the second-class battleship *Maine* demonstrate a variety of styles for a minstrel show.

THIS PAGE, TOP: In order for the United States to build capable battleships, the domestic steel industry had to build up its facilities. The photo at right was taken around 1900 in the ordnance shop of the Bethlehem Iron and Steel Company, Bethlehem, Pennsylvania. The shop contains large lathes to work on gun barrels like the one suspended in the center of the picture.
THIS PAGE, BOTTOM: The view looking forward from the quarterdeck of the second-class battleship *Texas*. Her mainmast, superstructure, and single smokestack are in the background. In the left center of the photo, an awning is furled while not in use. Low on the ship's starboard side, a turret contains a single 12-inch (30cm) gun. The ship had a similar one-gun turret forward on the port side. The designer of the *Texas* was William John, a British naval architect; all subsequent U.S. battleships would be designed by Americans.
OPPOSITE PAGE: The scale of the *Texas'* crewmen, at work cleaning her starboard side, makes clear how small the U.S. Navy's first battleship was. Commissioned on August 15, 1895, the *Texas* was 309 feet long and 64 feet in the beam (i.e., her width). This photo was taken at the New York Navy Yard August 3, 1898, with the ship still in war paint following a July battle off Cuba. Note the torpedo tube just above the waterline on the ship's bow.

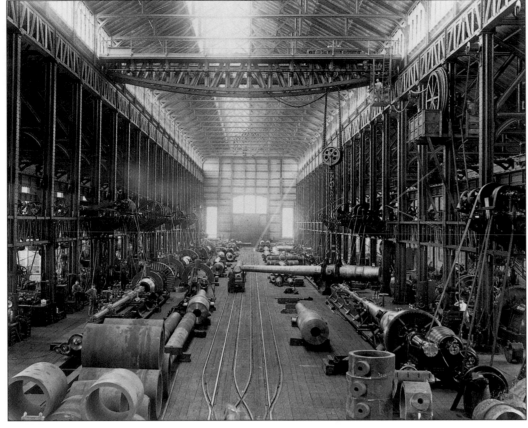

show the American citizens what congressmen had bought on their behalf. In November 1895, for instance, the *Maine* visited the city of Portland in the state for which she was named. She entertained visits from dignitaries, and her officers received from the citizens of the state the gift of a silver service that comprised a soup tureen and two side dishes. Many ships of the era also received a punchbowl and goblets, but Maine's gift did not include such silver items because state law prohibited alcoholic beverages. When the North Atlantic Squadron visited Bar Harbor, Maine, in the summer of 1897, the flagship issued a signal that read, "Give the men all the liberty they want; there is no rum in this state." The enterprising crewmen soon found otherwise. Teams from the *Massachusetts* and the armored cruiser *New York* later played a baseball game that was followed by reports of drunk and disorderly sailors ashore. Chaplain Harry Jones of the *Texas*, another ship present for the visit, later wrote, "I have never, during my experience in the Navy, seen so many drunken sailors as I saw there in that prohibition port."

"REMEMBER THE *MAINE*"

At the beginning of 1898, the United States faced the possibility of going to war with Spain. The Spanish controlled Cuba at the time and imposed a harsh regime on the Cuban citizens. That in turn led to revolutionary activities by Cubans who were unhappy with the status quo and sought independence. Back in the United States, President William McKinley was in favor of some sort of autonomy for Cuba rather than complete independence. Meanwhile, U.S. practitioners of what was then known as yellow journalism were not at all hesitant about arousing war sentiments because such sensationalism helped sell newspapers. Across the Atlantic, Spain's government believed that failure to fight would produce problems in domestic politics in that nation.

The *Maine* had been standing by in Key West since mid-December, ready to steam to Cuba in the event she was summoned by U.S. Consul General Fitzhugh Lee. When the other battleships reached Key West, the *Maine* joined them and went to the fleet anchorage in the Dry Tortugas, a group of islands sixty miles farther west. She was there on January 24 when a quartermaster on the ship's bridge observed red and green rockets ascending in the night sky as a

signal to the *Maine*. Her commanding officer, Captain Charles Sigsbee, prepared his ship to get under way for what the State Department intended as a display of friendship. On January 25 she steamed in past Morro Castle, a fortification high above Havana's harbor entrance. Though the crew was not at battle stations, the men were near their guns in the event the Spanish fired on the ship, which they did not.

While some of his shipmates were concerned about the excitement of the occasion, Seaman Mike Flynn took it in stride, later explaining, "I was the kind of lad who didn't bother much. I just went along." He figured that those wearing gold braid should do the worrying. Captain Sigsbee made a round of calls on various local dignitaries, and he took some of his officers to watch the big game in town—the bullfights. The enlisted men were not permitted liberty and went ashore only on official business. On the evening of February 15, the crew ate supper as usual, followed by a sweep down. Ambrose Ham and some of his shipmates gathered to listen to accordion music. In a nearby turret, a sailor with a mandolin entertained his shipmates.

The music ended when C.H. Newton, a Marine bugler, played the call for men to sling their hammocks for the night. When he had done that, Seaman Ham reported to the poop-deck aft, where he was to stand signal watch from 8:00 until midnight. At about the same time, Lieutenant John J. Blandin took over as the ship's in-port officer of the deck. Captain Sigsbee spent the evening writing letters. During the course of composing a letter to his wife, he heard Bugler Newton sound taps at 9:10 and was struck by the flourishes the Marine added in his playing. Throughout the ship, men fell asleep in their hammocks.

At 9:40, while Captain Sigsbee was pushing his wife's letter into an envelope, Apprentice Ham looked forward from the poop deck and saw a plume of flame shoot up near the bow of the ship and heard a roaring explosion. A second explosion came soon after the first. Then he was hit by a piece of flying debris and for a time knocked unconscious. The bulk of the crew had berths up forward, and some 250 of them were killed outright; the explosion tossed a number of bodies into the air. The officers slept near the stern of the ship and thus fared better. Several crew members, including Marine Sergeant

RIGHT: Commissioned a month after the *Texas* on September 17, 1895, the *Maine* is shown here in her peacetime color scheme. The hull is white, the superstructure a buff or tan color, the gun barrels black, and the ornamental scrollwork on the bow gold. The *Maine* was fitted with four 12-inch (30cm) guns, twice as many as in the *Texas*. The starboard turret is seen here; the other turret was farther aft on the port side, creating a staggered arrangement. The old-fashioned anchor is housed on the side, aft of the bow.

BOTTOM LEFT: The *Maine*'s officers take their ease in the wardroom. Their wicker chairs sit atop a decorative carpet.

BOTTOM RIGHT: This 1896 photograph shows the *Maine*'s chief petty officers in their quarters with two curtained bunks at right. The same unabridged dictionary is a prop in both photos.

Michael Meehan were blown overboard and into the water. Many of the survivors were injured. They escaped the wrecked *Maine* in whatever manner they could. Sigsbee was reluctant to leave as long as crewmen were still on board. When the executive officer, Lieutenant Commander Richard Wainwright told him that the roaring fires near a powder magazine made a further explosion possible, Sigsbee finally abandoned ship. In the ensuing days, the death toll rose as injured men died ashore.

In the United States, the shock was electric, aided by the jingoistic newspaper articles of the day. "Remember the *Maine*" became a national rallying cry. A subsequent investigation determined that the ship had been destroyed by an external mine, and the Spanish were blamed. Others suggested the cause was an internal explosion, set off by spontaneous combustion in a coal bunker that overheated a nearby powder magazine. In the more than a century that has passed since then, the cause has been the subject of a great deal of speculation and forensic investigation. Both sides have strong-minded proponents, but neither has proved its case with certainty. For the people of the United States, however, already worked up to a war fever by news reports, the loss of the *Maine* was taken as evidence of Spanish treachery.

In the aftermath of the sinking of the *Maine*, the task of serving as president of the ensuing court of inquiry fell to Captain William T. Sampson, commanding officer of the *Iowa*. The stenographer during the early sessions was Yeoman Fred Buenzle, who was Sampson's clerk on board the battleship. He had a particular interest because several of the *Maine*'s crew members had been his shipmates years earlier. In particular, he had developed a bond with John R. Bell, a black man who had joined the Navy during the Civil War as an officers' servant and had served in essentially the same capacity ever since.

Now that the *Maine* was at the bottom of Havana Harbor, Buenzle went to see the wreck, part of which was above the surface. He saw the tangle of wood and metal that had once been a warship. He saw a main deck hatch that had become a death trap for the men below. A wooden ladder for the hatch had come loose, floated to the surface, and blocked the entrance; it had served to imprison the men below. In that tangle of dead sailors, arms and legs moved in concert with the ebbing and flowing of the

The *Maine* lies at anchor in Bar Harbor, a resort town in the state for which the ship was named. Her port 12-inch (30cm) turret hangs over the side of the ship on a sponson. In an awkward setup, the turrets could fire across the ship's main deck when trained inboard. One of the ship's boats hangs from davits, below the large American flag. It carries oarlocks for the crew to use when rowing. All the way to the left is a gangway, now usually known as an accommodation ladder, for the crew to use when entering or exiting boats.

Two 13-inch (33cm) guns protrude from the after turret of the *Oregon*. With the advent of the first-line battleships (the *Indiana* and her sisters) 13-inch (33cm) guns became the norm for battleships' main batteries. Beyond the turret is the ship's afterbridge, which was connected by a centerline walkway to the forward bridge, thus permitting quick movement between the two. A capstan and pair of bitts for line handling are in the foreground; a spare anchor lies on the deck.

tide. An arm extended through a hole in the deck. It bore a tattoo of an arrow piercing a heart and a single word: "Beatrice." Those who explored the wreck never found the body of John Bell. In 1912, the hulk of the *Maine* was raised from the harbor bottom and towed to sea to be scuttled. In the process, someone found a gold watch with the name "Bell" engraved on its cover. To Buenzle, it was "the only relic of the presence aboard of any of the men who had died without warning on that fatal night."

VOYAGE OF THE *OREGON*

On the faraway West Coast, the *Oregon* was in the navy yard at Bremerton, Washington, when the *Maine* blew up. Having neither fuel nor ammunition on board, she was not combat-ready. She finally obtained enough coal to get under way on March 6 so she could proceed to San Francisco to take on a full load of coal, powder, and projectiles. Because of her skipper's ill health, Captain Charles Clark took over command on March 17, and the ship departed San Francisco two days later for Callao, Peru. It was to be a remarkable trip because there was no Panama Canal in those days, and the *Oregon* had to steam around South America. As she neared the equator, the temperature in the engineering spaces was typically more then one hundred degrees Fahrenheit (38°C), and fresh water had to be rationed for drinking so that the boilers would have an adequate supply.

The *Oregon* did not proceed all the way around Cape Horn but steamed instead in the face of gale-force winds through the Strait of Magellan, near the tip of South America. Upon arrival in Rio de Janeiro, Clark learned that the United States and Spain were officially at war. Captain Clark had heard reports that Spain had sent a fleet toward America and was concerned that he might encounter them. With little intelligence to go on, he pushed on northward and checked in at Jupiter Inlet, Florida, for instructions. En route, the crew tore out the mahogany pilothouse and other wooden items that might prove fire hazards in battle. The men also turned the buff-and-white color scheme into one of dark gray—war color. Once he reached Florida, Clark was ordered to join up with the squadron of ships at Key West. In her voyage from Bremerton to Jupiter Inlet, the *Oregon* had covered 14,500 miles (23,331km) at an average

LEFT TOP: After the Febuary 15, 1898 explosion that sank her, the shattered *Maine lay* on the bottom of Havana Harbor for more than a decade. In August 1910, Congress authorized the removal of the ship, and work began in December of that year.

LEFT BOTTOM: These enormous cylinders were filled with mud and gravel to form a cofferdam around the ship. Once the cofferdam was pumped out, the hull was made watertight.

RIGHT: The ship came afloat on Febuary 13, 1912, covered with the shells and barnacles shown at far right. The Navy towed her to sea, sinking her in deep water on March 16, 1912.

ABOVE: In this painting, the cruiser *Olympia*, flagship of Commodore George Dewey, heads a column of American warships in the victorious Battle of Manila Bay on May 1, 1898. A significant triumph for the ships of the new Steel Navy, it was also a forerunner of the successful Battle of Santiago, which took place on July 3.
RIGHT: This painting from a 1900 Du Pont Powder Company calendar shows one of the U.S. battleships using the company's product during the battle off Santiago. The illustrations along the sides in the bottom section of the calendar show individual pellets, or grains, of molded gunpowder. The substance inside powder bags was not actually powdery.

speed of 11.5 knots. The amazing voyage dramatically demonstrated that she was indeed a true seagoing battleship.

Still more preparation for war came in late March when the *Texas* was directed to suspend coaling at Newport News, Virginia, and report to the New York Navy Yard for modernization of her 12-inch (30cm) guns turrets. Lieutenants Francis Haesler and Mark Bristol had submitted to the Navy Department a suggestion for improving the rate of loading the turrets. When the ship was commissioned, the projectiles and powder bags could be rammed into the guns only by hydraulic rammers located outside the turrets, which restricted the positions the turrets could be in during loading. The two officers suggested a scheme whereby the turrets would be equipped with internal telescoping rammers that would enable the loading of the guns no matter which direction the turrets were trained. The department approved the suggestion and the ship went to New York to implement it. Another sign of things to come was the repainting of the *Texas* in dark gray war color while she was in Brooklyn. On April 6, after Chaplain Harry Jones said goodbye to his wife and two children in Brooklyn, the ship got under way to face whatever might lie ahead.

WAR WITH SPAIN

On April 11, because Spain had not acceded to an ultimatum that it grant independence to Cuba, President McKinley asked Congress for the authority to intervene in the conflict. Congress passed a declaration of war on April 19, McKinley signed it, and it went into effect on the 21st. The next day, the President proclaimed a blockade of Cuba, and recently promoted Rear Admiral Sampson's North Atlantic Squadron set forth from Key West, less than one hundred miles (161km) from Havana, to set up shop off the Cuban coast. On the other side of the world, Commodore George Dewey's Asiatic Squadron, led by the cruiser *Olympia*, engaged the Spanish in the Battle of Manila Bay in the Philippines. It was the first resounding victory in a war that would turn largely on U.S. naval superiority. Despite the blockade, on May 19, a squadron of Spanish cruisers and destroyers under the command of Rear Admiral Pascual Cervera y Topete managed to slip into the protected harbor of Santiago on the south coast of Cuba, near the eastern end of the island. The Spanish ships became the focus of considerable attention from the Americans, who set up heavy ships in a semicircular blockade pattern a few miles off the harbor entrance.

In early June, Admiral Sampson decided to take offensive action rather than remain in the passive

blockade stations off the coast. He ordered a bombardment of the forts, Morro Castle and Socopa, that guarded Santiago's harbor entrance. Men on board the U.S. warships would now have an opportunity to avenge the *Maine*. They would also be facing their own potential mortality in the event return fire hit their ship. Several sailors came to Chaplain Harry Jones of the *Texas*; they brought him letters and other keepsakes to deliver to their families in the event they were killed.

Because Santiago had commanding gun positions at both sides of the entrance channel, it was too heavily fortified for an assault from the sea. Thus, on June 22, the army began an unopposed landing of soldiers at the village of Daiquiri, sixteen miles (26km) eastward down the coast. The troops made their way ashore in ships' boats. No water craft were available for the horses and mules that accompanied the Army in that era. The animals were thrown overboard on the premise that instinct would guide them to swim ashore, but it did not. An imaginative bugler ashore played the assembly call, which turned the horses around and led them to swim to land. The mules—characteristically stubborn—ignored the bugle and continued swimming seaward until they drowned.

In conjunction with the landings, the battleships and armored cruisers bombarded Santiago. On board the *Indiana*, Midshipman Daniel Mannix was at his battle station in the conning tower. His role was to listen to information from a shipmate named McDowell, who was operating a range finder. Mannix set the range indicator to communicate with the rest of the ship's guns. After the *Indiana* had fired for a bit, he had a hard time seeing because the brown powder used as a propellant at the time produced a good deal more debris than the smokeless powder adopted later. The air filled with clouds of smoke, dust, and solid matter that bothered his eyes and left a layer of saltpeter on his uniform. The guns also hurt his ears, even though they were stuffed with cotton.

Incoming rounds poured in from the Spanish shore battery. Mannix heard a buzzing sound like that of a giant bumblebee and then a large splash of water sprang up near the ship as a projectile made contact. Then he encountered McDowell, who sported a bright red bullet hole in each side of one of his

calves. In the excitement of measuring ranges to the target, he had dropped his revolver, which then shot him when it hit the deck. On board the *Texas*, an incoming round exploded after entering the bow on the gun deck. It literally blew F.J. Blakely to pieces and wounded a number of others. Shipmates had the grim duty of picking up the scattered fragments of Blakely's body. A sailmaker then sewed the remains into the dead man's canvas hammock, along with an armor-piercing 6-inch (15cm) projectile to ensure that the body sank when it was buried at sea.

As the American soldiers advanced on Santiago, the ships continued their patrol offshore. Part of the routine included one battleship going to general quarters from midnight to 2:00 A.M. so the crew could shine a searchlight at the harbor entrance. This enabled them to detect any Spanish warships that sought to escape in the darkness. In that era before radio, picketboats sat just off the harbor entrance, prepared to fire warning rockets if the Spanish left their landlocked sanctuary. They were

This artistic depiction shows the *Oregon*'s superstructure deck, the level that connected the forward and afterbridges. At right, a boatswain's mate has a long white lanyard leading to the pipe that is a tool of his trade; his shipmates were quite familiar with the different calls signaling events in the ship's routine. Above his head, a row of light 6-pounder guns can be seen. The light guns were used for close-in fire against an approaching enemy; they derived their designation from the six-pound projectiles they fired. Overhead, the bottoms of the boats that carried crewmen between ship and shore can be seen.

Naval Battle of Santiago,
July 3rd 1898.

Taking considerable artistic license, a contemporary lithograph shows the U.S. ships (right) as they chase the fleeing Spanish squadron during the Battle of Santiago. The most prominent ship in the foreground is the armored cruiser *New York*, which played only a small part in the overall battle. At the bottom of the print, portraits of the admirals and commanding officers of the Spanish and American warships are arrayed.

also ordered to fire at any torpedo boats that came out to attack the battleship that lay just a mile (1.6km) offshore.

Weeks passed as the U.S. ships remained arrayed outside the harbor entrance. The *Indiana*'s crew was coaling on the morning of July 1 when it received news of a combined U.S. land and sea attack on the port of Santiago. That sped up the refueling operation, which lasted until midnight. The ship arrived off Santiago at 4:00 A.M. on July 2. At daybreak, the U.S. blockade force began an even more violent bombardment than before, and it drew fire from ashore. Midshipman Mannix observed that the *Indiana*'s equipment suffered from the violence when the ship's own guns fired. The concussion knocked the range-transmission device out of

operation, so the crew had to send messengers to the gun crews on the range to use when firing.

The next day, which dawned with picture perfect weather, was expected to be a peaceful Sunday of personnel inspection and church. Admiral Sampson, in command of the blockading force, was on board the armored cruiser *New York*. At 8:45 A.M. the ship departed to the east so Sampson could confer with his Army counterpart, Major General William T. Shafter, on the best means of capturing Santiago. Left in charge of the blockading force was Commodore Winfield Scott Schley in the armored cruiser *Brooklyn*. While Captain Henry C. Taylor of the *Indiana* was inspecting a division on the ship's quarterdeck, his activity was interrupted by the sound of gunfire from the *Iowa*. Admiral Cervera and his

squadron were steaming forth to attempt an escape. Captain Taylor ordered his bugler to sound general quarters. As the sailors ran to their battle stations, members of gun crews flung off their inspection-ready neckerchiefs, jumpers, and undershirts so they would be bare-chested as they fired the guns. As Midshipman Mannix later surveyed the crews of the 8-inch (20cm) guns, he saw that they were on gratings above the deck and had no protection against incoming fire. To Mannix, the well-muscled, shirtless gunners resembled the Roman gladiators of old.

With the capture of Santiago apparently imminent, Governor General Ramon Blanco, the senior representative of the Spanish government in Cuba, had ordered Cervera to put up a fight for the sake of national honor, rather than surrender. The admiral's

flagship, the cruiser *Infanta Maria Teresa*, emerged first, and headed toward Commodore Schley's flagship, the *Brooklyn*, then turned toward the west. In the wake of the flagship came the armored cruisers *Almirante Oquendo*, *Vizcaya*, and *Cristobal Colon*. About all the *Cristobal Colon* could do was follow, since her turrets of 10-inch (25cm) guns had not been installed before she joined the rest of the squadron in steaming from Spain to the Caribbean.

The ships of the two nations were so close to each other that the Americans had a good view as the flash of Spanish gun blasts erupted against the black-painted hull of the flagship. Soon afterward, the fast-moving projectiles arrived nearby and, at about the same time, the sounds made by the enemy guns. The Spanish destroyers *Pluton* and *Furor* emerged, but they did not follow the cruisers. Instead, they steamed directly toward the American ships and came under fire from all four battleships. A projectile from one of the *Indiana*'s 8-inch (20cm) guns knocked out the *Pluton*, and the converted yacht *Gloucester* dispatched the *Furor*. (The skipper of the aggressive *Gloucester* was Lieutenant Commander Richard Wainwright, who had been executive officer of the *Maine* at the time of her sinking.)

The main batteries of the American battleships pounded away at the fleeing Spanish, who responded in kind. At times the powder thrown up by their own gun smoke forced the 13-inch (33cm) turrets to cease fire for a while until the gun pointers gained a clear view of the targets. On board the *Texas,* the pall of smoke was so heavy that Captain John Philip said he might as well have tried to see with a blanket over his head. When it did clear a bit, he saw the cruiser *Brooklyn*, which had turned to avoid the

Spanish flagship, bearing directly toward his ship. The skipper ordered the engines of the *Texas* reversed and just barely missed being rammed by the *Brooklyn*'s prow, which would have done considerable damage. The projectiles from the U.S. ships found their mark on the flagship *Infanta Maria Teresa*, and flames spread rapidly aft from her bow. As American sailors raised a cheer, the helmsman of the Spanish ship put the rudder to starboard and ran his ship aground at 10:15 A.M.

The *Vizcaya* and the *Cristobal Colon* continued their run to the westward, chased by incoming shells from the *Oregon*, *Texas*, and *Brooklyn*. The *Iowa* and *Indiana* concentrated fire on the *Almirante Oquendo*, which caught fire and also opted for beaching, running aground at 10:35. When an explosion tore through the burning ship, the men on board the *Texas* shouted in their happiness. Captain Philip responded by saying, "Don't cheer, boys; the

poor devils are dying." The *Oregon* poured rounds of both 13-inch (33cm) and 6-inch (15cm) projectiles into the *Vizcaya*, and the Spanish ship's crew drove her toward shore shortly after 11:00. On board the *Oregon*, Captain Clark did not feel the sense of pleasure he expected. Like the skipper of the *Texas*, he thought of the victims and imagined the situation if his own ship's decks had dying men on them. In several of the cases, the fires on the Spanish ships were particularly devastating because their upper decks were made of wood, not wood-covered steel, as was the case for the Americans.

The *Indiana* headed for the grounded Spanish ships and joined the *Iowa* and *Gloucester* in providing boats to go rescue their crews. Now that the Spanish crews had surrendered, they were no longer the enemy; they were fellow mariners. Midshipman Mannix was in charge of one of the rescue boats. He saw the desperate Spaniards jumping into the water

so they could escape their flaming ships and try to swim ashore. As soon as they made it, they came under fire from Cuban insurgents who emerged from the jungle. Now the Americans became the defenders of the defeated sailors and rushed out to beat off the marauders.

The last of the Spanish ships still in action was the modern cruiser *Cristobal Colon*, which was named for a previous visitor to the Caribbean, Christopher Columbus. As the other Spanish ships dropped out of the battle, she sought to escape to westward because her ten 6-inch (15cm) guns were no match for the pursuing Americans in the *Texas*, *Oregon*, and *Brooklyn*. The *Oregon* was best suited for the chase because she was the only battleship with all her boilers lit and ready when the battle began. Moreover, Captain Clark had saved his best coal for just such an occasion, and his ship was cranked up to sixteen knots. The Spanish cruiser had

BATTLE OF SANTIAGO

The newly minted U.S. battleship fleet got its first trial by fire in this July 3, 1898, confrontation off the south coast of Cuba. When Rear Admiral William Sampson, in the flagship *New York*, hauled off to the east of the harbor entrance for a conference, Rear Admiral Pascual Cervera y Topete's Spanish squadron emerged from the landlocked Santiago harbor and started steaming to the west. But the rest of the American ships were ready and waiting and set off in hot pursuit when the Spanish ships appeared. As the U.S. fleet bombarded the Spanish ships, the beleaguered vessels turned to starboard and beached themselves one after the other. For years afterward, controversy existed over which officer should get credit for the victory—Admiral Sampson, who was in overall command but not physically present, or Commodore Winfield S. Schley, who was at the scene of the action, on board the armored cruiser *Brooklyn*.

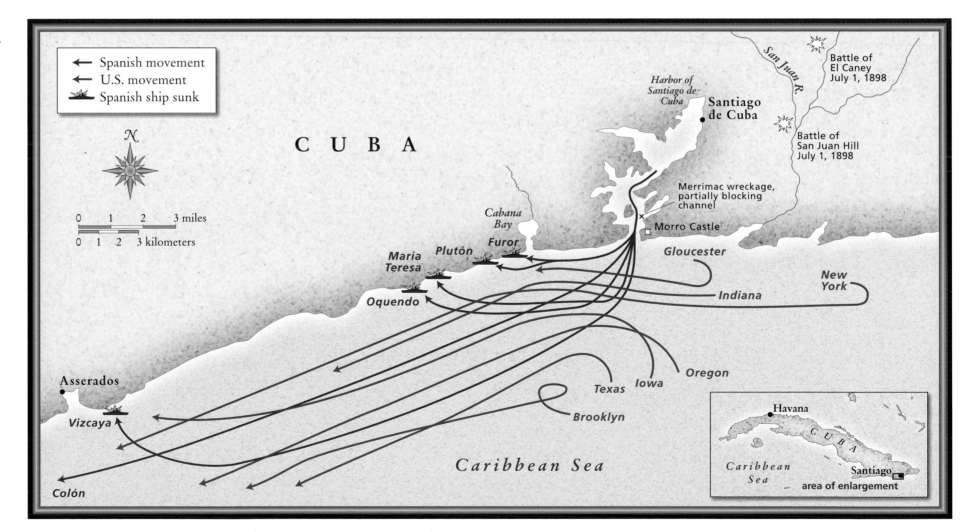

Through the Eyes of a Boy

When Ron Waudé was a grade school student in Portland, Oregon, in the 1930s, he was drawn to the famous battleship *Oregon*. Because of the attention she had gained during the Spanish-American War, especially for her dramatic race from Puget Sound to the East Coast, she had been spared the fate of her contemporaries, which were either scrapped or used as targets. As a result of an international disarmament treaty, she had been demilitarized in 1924, and in 1925 was lent to the state of Oregon for preservation as a memorial and floating museum.

As a boy, Waudé used the money he had earned from his newspaper route to pay the ten-cent admission price to visit the *Oregon*. He went aboard practically every other weekend in the late 1930s and early 1940s. The old ship was a veritable time capsule of technology and weaponry, far removed from the war that was then engulfing the world. For young Waudé, the ship was also a sort of playground. He explored the decks; saw the turrets with their 13-inch (33cm), 8-inch (20cm), and 6-inch (15cm) guns; and experienced the compactness of a ship that was, in her time, among the biggest in the fleet, though still only 351 feet (107m) long with 11,700 tons (10,612t) of displacement. In a museum on shore, next to the ship, he saw the uniforms, silverware, and other artifacts that had been used by the men of the *Oregon*. These were particularly appealing because they lent a human touch to the conglomeration of metal and wood that comprised the ship herself.

In his imagination, the youngster traveled back to the era when the United States was just beginning to emerge as a world power and was using naval forces as instruments of that emergence. In 1942, to the great dismay of Ron Waudé and many other citizens of the state, the Navy sold the *Oregon* so that her steel could be recycled to help fight World War II. The gesture was more symbolic than useful. In fact, after her superstructure was stripped off, the Navy reclaimed her armored hull, which it towed to Guam to serve as a dynamite barge. After the war, the corpse of the once-proud *Oregon* was in sad shape and was eventually scrapped in Japan in 1956.

Today, one of the old warrior's masts resides, intact, in Portland's Battleship *Oregon* Park. And the memories of her past glory are scattered throughout Waudé's Seattle home. He has a book on the Battle of Santiago, autographed by the author, who was in the ship's crew during the battle. On the walls are some three dozen framed photos of the *Oregon* and almost that many more unframed in his files. The highlight of his collection is a magnificent oil painting of the ship. He spotted it several years ago in an art gallery and knew instantly that he wasn't going to leave without it. Would that the government of the United States had cared about the *Oregon* as much as he.

TOP: Sightseers approach the stern of the *Oregon* at anchor off New York City; her crew is out on deck. The photo was taken in the summer of 1898, shortly after she played a part in the victory at Santiago. Her afterbridge is prominent above the 13-inch (33cm) turret and near an 8-inch (20cm) turret.
BOTTOM: The hull of the *Oregon* can be seen at Guam in the 1940s, after her service in World War II as a barge in which to store explosives.

only inferior coal left and began to slow. The pursuit lasted until early afternoon, when the *Oregon* launched 13-inch (33cm) projectiles at long range (somewhat damaging the guns by firing at a high angle), dropping them near the *Cristobal Colon*. The last, shot at a range of ninety-five hundred yards, fell ahead of the cruiser and convinced her that further flight was futile. *Cristobal Colon* surrendered and turned toward the beach at about 1:15 P.M. She had steamed some fifty miles west from Santiago since the start of the battle.

Admiral Cervera had abandoned his burning ship and swum ashore in his underwear. Commander Wainwright of the *Gloucester* provided him with civilian clothes to wear, and he was put into a boat, manned by oarsmen, for transfer to the *Iowa*. The men of the *Indiana* looked down as the boat approached their ship. In the water at the bottom of the boat was the body of a dead Spanish sailor. Cervera hung his head in dejection. Midshipman Mannix later wrote of the scene as Cervera's boat passed: "It made me feel as though I were in church. I was never so sorry for anyone in all my life." Down inside the *Indiana,* the ship's doctors ministered to Spanish seamen who had been wounded in the battle. Only one American was killed in the battle. A shell from the *Vizcaya* decapitated Chief Yeoman George Ellis on board the *Brooklyn*. Of the Spanish, 323 were killed, and 151 were seriously wounded.

AFTERMATH OF VICTORY

On the evening of July 4, as the Americans celebrated their victory, the *Massachusetts* again had searchlight duty off Santiago Harbor, scanning the water for any more Spanish ships that might try to escape. The men of the nearby *Indiana* went to general quarters shortly before midnight because of activity at the harbor mouth, where the Spanish tried unsuccessfully to block the channel by sinking the cruiser *Reina Mercedes*. Out of the night, two 8-inch (20cm) mortar shells, aimed by Spanish gunners at the searchlight of the *Massachusetts*, plowed, instead, into the *Indiana*. The first shell hit the ship's bow, and the second exploded when it hit the armored deck of the officers' quarters aft. The stern was wrecked, and the officers would have been killed had they not been at their battle stations. The mortar shell not only set the *Indiana*'s stern

afire, it ruptured a water main, letting loose a burst of water that extinguished the fire. Midshipman Mannix proclaimed it "the first time in history that a fire had been put out by an automatic sprinkling system!"

Soon after the Battle of Santiago de Cuba, Chaplain Harry Jones left the *Texas* and reported aboard the *St. Louis*, a passenger ship that had been chartered into the Navy. She took him back to New York for treatment of internal hemorrhaging he had suffered when a Spanish projectile exploded near him a few days before the big battle. Among the other passengers on board were Admiral Cervera and about eight hundred others from the defeated fleet who were being taken to the United States as prisoners of war. Jones took advantage of the occasion to question the admiral about why he had chosen to fight as he did. Cervera said he had been ordered to go, even though he had concluded that a fight at sea would be suicidal. He believed his best chance came on Sunday morning, when the *Massachusetts*, which he had mistaken for the *Oregon*, was away to fuel, and the flagship *New York* was missing as well. His plan was to rush by the *Texas*, ram the *Brooklyn*, and escape to sea. His

scheme was undone by one of the first projectiles fired by the American ships; it disabled his flagship and forestalled execution of his plan. He ordered the ship run aground to save what was left of the crew. And then, because he was not a good swimmer himself, he had stripped down to his underwear to make the trip easier as he went toward shore.

On August 19, the ships of the victorious American fleet arrived at New York City, where the local populace welcomed their crews as heroes. The ships were still wearing their dark gray battle paint and the wounds they had received off Cuba. They steamed up the lower Hudson River to the west of Manhattan, fired gun salutes to the tomb of former President Ulysses Grant, and then proceeded to their anchorages. For one junior midshipman on board the *Indiana,* there was a bit of awkwardness. When the Spanish mortar shell had destroyed the officers' quarters of his ship, he had been left with only one pair of trousers, and the seat was worn through. Whenever ladies came aboard for a tour of the battleship that had played such a part in the recent struggle, he had to remain in a chair or lean against a bulkhead—a small price to pay after a naval triumph.

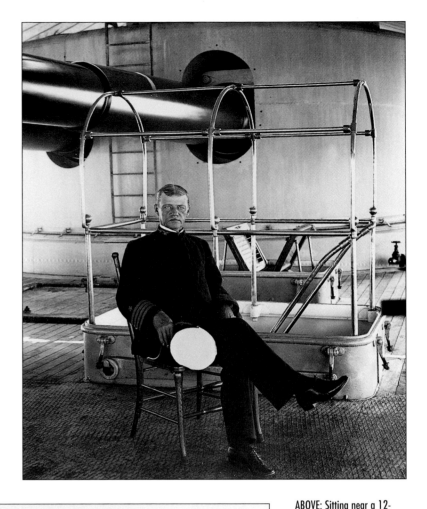

ABOVE: Sitting near a 12-inch (30cm) turret on the quarterdeck of the *Iowa*, which he commanded in the Battle of Santiago, Captain Robley D. "Fighting Bob" Evans displays a stern demeanor befitting his nickname.
LEFT: The *Iowa* is shown here near Tompkinsville, New York, in 1898. As a rear admiral, Evans would command the Great White Fleet ten years later. With her tall stacks and 12-inch (30cm) guns, the *Iowa* differed from her three Indiana-class sisters.

Chapter Two
THE BIG STICK

Thanks to his role as head of the Rough Riders, a cavalry outfit, in the Spanish-American War, Theodore Roosevelt was on the national ticket during the election of 1900. The following year, the former Assistant Secretary of the Navy became Vice President. In his new capacity, he spoke at the Minnesota State Fair and uttered a phrase that has been quoted many times since: "Speak softly and carry a big stick." Less well remembered but closely tied to that sentence was another remark: "Build and keep at a pitch of the highest training a thoroughly efficient Navy."

As the twentieth century opened, the U.S. Navy was still relatively primitive in terms of technology and war-fighting. Despite its victory over a not-very-impressive foe in the recent Spanish-American War, the Navy had much room for improvement. John Alden has done a superb job of explaining the developments that took place in the fleet one hundred years ago in his book, *The American Steel Navy*. One notable change was in the method used to aim the ships' big guns. In the late nineteenth century, the standard practice was for a ship and her guns to roll together when the target was off the ship's beam. A gunner fired his weapon when the gun sight intersected with the target at the top of the roll. The results of this sort of shooting were dramatically demonstrated in the Battle of Santiago. U.S. warships fired approximately 8000 rounds of ammunition but achieved only 123 demonstrated hits.

Lieutenant William Sims had served as a U.S. naval attaché in Paris late in the old century and had become acquainted with the more effective aiming methods used in Europe, particularly those developed by the Royal Navy's Captain Percy Scott. In essence, Scott advocated keeping the gun pointed at the target while allowing the ship to roll around it. This was known as the continuous-aim method, and Lieutenant Sims sought to introduce it to his own Navy. His criticisms of the status quo reached Theodore Roosevelt, who became President in September 1901 upon the assassination of William McKinley. Roosevelt, who had been Assistant Secretary of the Navy before heading the Rough Riders, encouraged Sims, who became Inspector of Target Practice for the Navy in 1902 .

The new method was more difficult to use than the old one, so Sims instituted a strong regimen of target practice throughout the fleet. The gunners fired at both short range (1,600 yards [1.5km]) and at the longer ranges (7,000–9,000 yards [6.4–8.2km]) expected in battle conditions. New optical range finders determined how far away a target was, and mechanical range keepers computed future positions of moving targets, much as a duck hunter leads the flying ducks with his shotgun. Sims's regimen paid dividends by dramatically improving gunnery accuracy during his tenure, which lasted until early 1909. In addition to his role with fleet gunnery, Sims served as naval aide to President Roosevelt from 1906 onward, and thus had strong support for his efforts.

FAR EAST DUTY
In 1903, after exercises around the United States, the almost-new *Wisconsin* steamed to the Far East. In Chefoo, China, she became part of the U.S. Asiatic Fleet, which represented the nation's interests in the region. The fleet was under the command of Rear Admiral Robley Evans, who had been skipper of the *Iowa* at Santiago. Soon her captain's boat was involved in a race with boats from the *Kentucky* and *Oregon* and the cruisers *New Orleans* and *Albany*. Such races were popular diversions for off-duty sailors and a great source of pride among winning ship's crews. During the *Wisconsin*'s long voyage out from the United States, Chief Boatswain's Mate O'Neill had been supervising the training of his oarsmen on a shipboard rowing machine. The *Wisconsin*'s boat won, accompanied by cheers from her crew and the blowing of steam whistles. The

ABOVE: Soon after the end of the Spanish-American War, the officers of the *Oregon* gather at their mess table with the remnants of a meal. The bulkhead behind them is covered in wood paneling, and curtains decorate the portholes. Overhead illumination is provided by a novelty—electric lights.
RIGHT: The *Oregon*'s chief petty officers pose for a formal portrait near a main-battery turret. Unlike today's CPOs, that era's wore their rating badges on the right sleeve rather than the left.

crew from the *Kentucky* posed a challenge for a five-mile (8km) race, which the rowers of the *Wisconsin* also won. The crew members of the *Wisconsin* pocketed an estimated $30,000 in bets from their rowing shipmates, so the victory was a boost not only for morale but also for individual finances. They stowed their winnings in ditty boxes, which was where men stored personal possessions, other than uniforms, before lockers came into vogue. On board the winning ship, Lieutenant Henry Wiley kicked ditty boxes at random and heard the clink of the silver dollars inside.

While new and improved battleships were emerging from American shipyards during Roosevelt's tenure, the older ones hung on in a variety of roles. After her triumph of 1898, the *Oregon* spent several years in the Far East. Her travels took her to China, Japan, the Philippines, and Hong Kong. One of the new crew members in 1905 was Seaman Charlie Fowler, who was not long out of recruit training at Goat Island near San Francisco. He was in his early twenties, a bit older than most recruits, and had a remarkable gift for observation and description. During an extended tour of the Orient, Fowler wrote long letters to his sister Clare. Thanks to Naval Academy Professor Rodney Tomlinson, who edited the letters to form the book *A Rocky Mountain Sailor in Teddy Roosevelt's Navy*, we have wonderful insight into the life of an enlisted man early in the century.

Readily apparent was the *Oregon*'s rundown condition following years without sufficient maintenance. At her best, the *Oregon* had been able to do seventeen knots. Now, following the steady degradation of her boilers and other equipment, she could manage no more than ten. Her small size, only 351 feet long (107m), posed another type of problem when her big guns, which were 13 inches (330cm) in diameter and nearly 40 feet (12m) long, were trained off the beam, perpendicular to her keel. The entire ship could list as much as five degrees in the direction the guns were pointed. Sometimes when the *Oregon* was taking on coal and bunkers filled up more quickly on one side, the guns were trained toward the other side to bring the ship back to an even keel. This problem would be eliminated in later battleships with the introduction of counter-balanced turrets.

Fowler also described to his sister the sleeping arrangements on board. The ship had four turrets of 8-inch (20cm) guns, and one of these provided a sleeping spot for Seaman Fowler. Berthing down inside the ship was uncomfortable, especially in the warm climates in which the *Oregon* operated. The first month or so he was on board, he slept on a piece of canvas laid on the steel roof of the turret. As he put it, "A fellow soon gets used to a hard bed." Later, he was able to rig his hammock over the forward port turret "with heaven as my roof, and, if anyone gets any more fresh air than I do, they are welcome to it." He also recognized the need for protection from the elements and from the cinders that were likely to come up the smokestacks from the coal-stoked boilers below. When there was a threat of rain or sea spray, the seaman spread a piece of canvas over the top of his hammock and tied it down. Long before the Navy made "habitability" a priority, Fowler did so on his own.

A GROWING FLEET

In May 1906, the USS *Virginia*, a ship of a new class, went into commission. Like the earlier Kearsarge-class, the ships of the Virginia class had superposed turrets, that is, an 8-inch (20cm) gun on top of a 12-inch (30cm) gun. The rationale was that this dual approach afforded more gun power to be fired in a given direction. The potential of this approach was reinforced by the success of the 8-inch (20cm) guns in the Battle of Santiago. There were drawbacks, however. If one of the dual turrets were knocked out in battle, the ship would have essentially lost half her big-gun capability all at once. And the arrangement lacked flexibility: since the turrets had to turn together, the guns couldn't be aimed at different targets. Captain Seaton Schroeder, first commanding officer of the *Virginia*, discovered another problem. The turrets of two different sizes interfered with each other, ironically because of an increase in the rapidity of fire. In the past, there might have been one shot per gun every three minutes; now it was possible to fire more than one round per gun in less than a minute. It took time for the smoke and gases to clear, so that a round might be loaded and ready in a 12-inch (30cm) gun, but in order to see well enough to aim the crew had to wait to fire until the residue from the 8-inch (20cm)

For generations, Bath Iron Works of Bath, Maine, has enjoyed a reputation as a builder of superb destroyers. Less well known is the lone battleship in the shipyard's legacy. Here, the *Georgia* sits on the building ways just before her launching on October 11, 1904. At right, dignitaries gather on a bunting-draped platform, while viewers with less clout stand below. A house flag bearing the shipyard's initials, B.I.W., flies from the mainmast. The *Georgia* went into commission in 1906 and was later a part of the Great White Fleet that steamed around the world.

At the turn of the twentieth century, cameramen from the Detroit Photographic Company produced a remarkable series of glass-plate negatives that depicted shipboard life in the Navy of the era. Men of the *Massachusetts*, a veteran of the Battle of Santiago, are portrayed on these pages.
RIGHT: Members of the Marine guard are outfitted with spiked helmets.
BELOW LEFT AND RIGHT: Crewmen lie in their hammocks on the berth deck while others eat in the petty officers' mess.

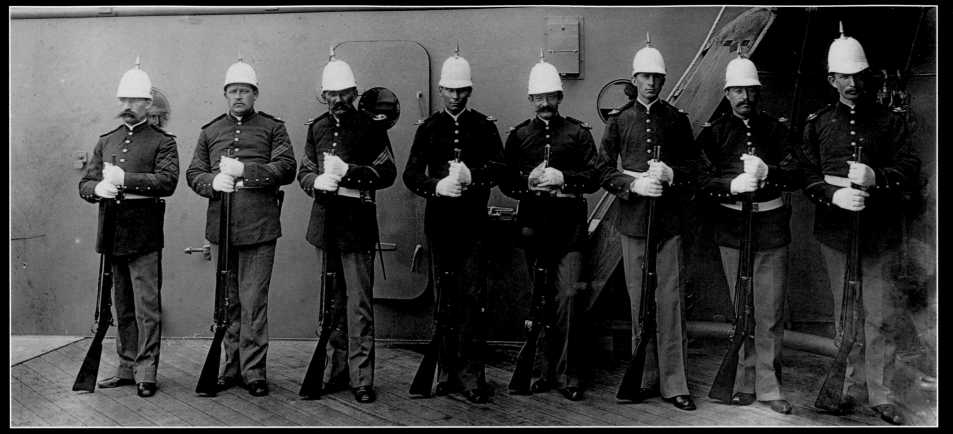

LEFT: The crews of 6-pounder guns practice on the upper deck.
LEFT: The crews of 6-pounder guns practice on the upper deck.
BELOW: Men of the *Massachusetts* gather around for beer call under the awning. Drinking would soon be prohibited on board U.S. Navy ships, a ban that would last until the serving of beer and wine was resumed in the 1980s for official ship-board receptions. Nevertheless, some drinking was done in the intervening years. As these pictures demonstrate, the everyday activities of the crew were crowded in among equipment such as torpedo tubes, ventilation ducts, piping, and rails for moving ammunition. Warship designers of the era paid far less attention to habitability than today's naval architects.

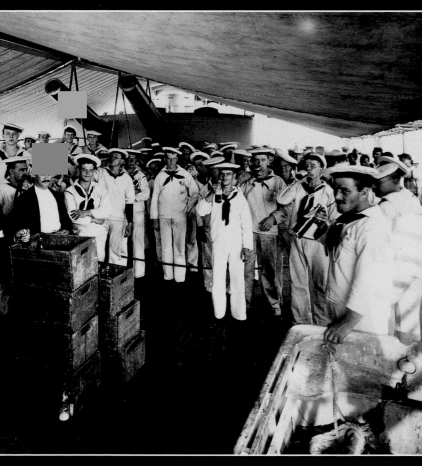

round had subsided. Each ship tried different combinations, but essentially the more rapid fire eliminated the superposed turret as an effective weapon.

During Teddy Roosevelt's eight-year administration, four battleships went into commission after beginning construction in the McKinley era, and keels were laid for sixteen more. A vivid demonstration of this nautical power came on September 2, 1906, when all available ships gathered near Roosevelt's home on Oyster Bay in Long Island Sound. They anchored in two parallel rows. In all, they comprised eleven battleships, four armored cruisers, four protected cruisers, a double-turreted monitor, and several destroyers. Captain Schroeder of the Virginia observed the generally dismal weather that day. At 11:00 A.M. the yacht *Mayflower*, sporting the presidential flag, emerged from Oyster Bay. Just about that time, the sky cleared, the sun emerged, and the wind shifted so that the ships now lined up in two neat columns. The *Mayflower* then steamed majestically between the two rows, and those present commented on "Teddy's luck."

THE GREAT WHITE FLEET

That same year, the *Kearsarge* got a new crewman in the person of Apprentice Harry Morris, who had enlisted in the Navy as an apprentice shortly before his fourteenth birthday in 1903. (Morris did not retire until February 1958, following fifty-five years of active duty. He was the last of the former apprentices to leave the Navy.) He was on board the *Kearsarge* in December 1907 when she was one of sixteen battleships of the Atlantic Fleet, by now rechristened the Battle Fleet, that gathered at Hampton Roads, Virginia. Because the hulls of all the battleships were painted white, the popular term for the collective group was the "Great White Fleet."

The ships were assembled for a cruise to California. As Professor James Reckner describes in his fine book, *Teddy Roosevelt's Great White Fleet*, it was a time of "intensely emotional patriotism and the common belief that the United States was predestined to loom large on the world stage." Even so, the president was coy in the months leading up to the cruise. When press accounts reported the fleet's upcoming voyage from the Atlantic to the Pacific, Roosevelt was evasive, both as to the facts of the cruise itself and its purpose.

The immediate impetus was a brief war scare in 1907 occasioned by anti-Japanese hostility on the West Coast. American workers there were concerned that immigrants from the Far East would take their jobs. Japanese Americans had to go to segregated schools. As had been the case in 1898, newspapers inflamed public opinion against a foreign nation. Diplomatic relations between the United States and Japan were strained, and war loomed as a possibility. In addition to the potential for hostilities, the operations would provide a useful test of American war plans for extended naval deployments. The Navy's infrastructure on the West Coast and in outlying regions of the Pacific was weak; requirements demonstrated by this cruise could help support a buildup. Those were the objectives at the outset. As the Atlantic Fleet battleships embarked on their collective journey, they would also serve as a public relations tool for U.S. naval expansion and as a tool for building international goodwill.

In 1905, the President had announced a plan to build only one new battleship a year as a replacement for older ones. But then came a dramatic development overseas. In 1906, Britain's Royal Navy commissioned HMS *Dreadnought*, a revolutionary

ABOVE: A fireman performs the hellish job of stoking a coal-fired boiler on board the *Massachusetts*. It was physically demanding work, and firemen had to master the art of ensuring the coal was spread evenly over the floor plates of the boiler. Later, crewmen had to remove clinkers and ashes and dump them over the side of the ship.

This view of the *Kearsarge*, circa 1903, depicts the superposed turrets that were a relatively short-lived experiment in the U.S. Navy. A turret of 8-inch (20cm) guns perched atop a turret with 13-inch (33cm) guns gave greater arcs of fire for the 8-inch (20cm) guns than when they were placed along a ship's sides, as they had been in the preceding classes of battleships. Both turrets rotated together, enabling control by a small number of crewmen but preventing the flexibility of independent firing. The *Kearsarge*, named in honor of a victorious Civil War ship, was the only U.S. battleship not named for a state. She was later converted to a crane ship and served until the 1950s.

battleship in that all the guns of her main battery were the same size—12 inches (30cm)—instead of having a variety of different barrel diameters, as was previously the norm. She also carried smaller guns for close-in defense against vessels such as torpedo boats. Essentially, the older battleships were no match for the new type, and thus were rendered instantly obsolete. So effective was this new type that it acquired the generic term "dreadnought" as a shorthand description for the all-big-gun type. In 1906–07, the U.S. Navy commissioned ten new battleships, but all were pre-dreadnoughts. A successful cruise could influence support for a fleet of dreadnoughts.

As the ships of the Great White Fleet prepared to leave Hampton Roads on December 16, bands played such sentimental tunes as "Home, Sweet Home," "The Girl I Left Behind Me," and "Auld Lang Syne." A staff officer on board the departing *Louisiana* used a telescope to spot his wife and family ashore at Fort Monroe on the north shore of Hampton Roads. As he had said he would, he stationed himself on the ship's after bridge, waved a handkerchief at his loved ones, and saw them waving in reply. After he had turned away and returned to duty, one of his shipmates asked, "Did you make out your people, Jones?" With feigned nonchalance, he smiled and replied, "I believe they were over there somewhere in the crowd."

Leading the group of sixteen battleships was the Atlantic Fleet Commander-in-Chief, Rear Admiral Robley "Fighting Bob" Evans. By late 1907, he was the last naval officer on active duty who had served in the Civil War more than forty years earlier. In the Union expedition to capture Fort Fisher in 1864, Evans was wounded in the leg and had to brandish a pistol to keep a surgeon from amputating it. At the outset of the voyage, Evans promised that it would be either "a fight or a frolic." Which one it turned out to be really depended on the reaction from other nations, principally Japan.

On signal from Evans, the ships weighed anchor one by one and got under way in order of divisions. As each ship passed the *Mayflower*, her gunner's mates fired a twenty-one-gun salute to Roosevelt. The battleships formed up in one long column with an interval of only four hundred yards (366m) from masthead to masthead, which meant

TOP LEFT: Work parties have long been a way of life for ships' crews, but in this scene the chore is relatively easy as men are carrying aboard cases of Post Toasties breakfast cereal.

TOP RIGHT: The *Connecticut* sits at anchor in New York for a fleet review by President William Howard Taft. Under Taft's predecessor, Theodore Roosevelt, the *Connecticut* was the flagship of the Great White Fleet. This view shows her painted gray after the cruise.

BOTTOM LEFT: This postcard shows the brand-new *Virginia* and her first commanding officer, Captain Seaton Schroeder.

BOTTOM RIGHT: Lieutenant George Day, navigator of the *Connecticut*, uses a sextant as part of the celestial navigation process.

LEFT: The process of coaling ship was dirty, strenuous work. Here, the crew of the *New Hampshire* takes on coal around 1909. Aboard the barge alongside the ship, men shovel coal into bags. Wires on booms lift the bags, which are dumped into holes in the deck and thence to the bunkers down below. Once the coal has been taken aboard, the men complete the job by cleaning the ship.
OPPOSITE PAGE, TOP: The men of the *Maine* have donned their dress blues for a formal portrait. Construction of the new *Maine* began with the laying of her keel on February 15, 1899, exactly one year after the ship bearing the same name exploded in Cuba's Havana Harbor. She was commissioned in 1902 and subsequently became part of the Great White Fleet. The fleet commander, Rear Admiral Robley Evans, is in the first row in this photo, slightly to the left of the capstan at center. Notice the flat hats enlisted men wore in that era.
OPPOSITE PAGE, BOTTOM: Three thousand officers and men from the Great White Fleet witness a bullfight at Lima, Peru, on February 24, 1908.

that bows and sterns were even closer to each other than that. After the last ship in line, the *Kearsarge*, passed, the *Mayflower* was due to head up the Chesapeake Bay to return to Washington. But Roosevelt's enthusiasm was such that he had the boat chase the fleet some distance to sea.

After two hours, Evans's flagship *Connecticut* signaled for cruising formation, and the battleships maneuvered so that they were in four columns of four, each with a rear admiral's flagship at the head of the column. On board each ship, an officer or midshipman used a mechanical device known as a stadimeter to calculate the distances between ships. Station-keeping then required putting on a few extra revolutions of the propellers or taking off a few to get a comfortable fit. Once the ships were away from land, Admiral Evans announced to the crews that they would return home via the Suez Canal. Since they would first head around South America to the Pacific, that meant their cruise would take them all the way around the world. There was one other important consideration: they had to return home before March 1909, when Roosevelt's presidency was due to end.

TRINIDAD VISIT

The first stop on the cruise was the island of Trinidad, off the north coast of Venezuela, where the men of the fleet celebrated Christmas. Working parties went ashore and collected greenery, with which they draped their ships from the waterline to the top of the mast. A group of officers from the *Vermont* made the rounds of the anchored ships, singing Christmas songs at each stop. The men of the *Minnesota* performed in athletic events, and other ships held parties and distributed gifts. Captain Richard Wainwright, skipper of the *Louisiana*, took childlike delight in pulling out a tin whistle and surprising his junior officers with its shrill tone.

The time off Trinidad was also spent coaling ship, a very difficult, but necessary task. Boatswain's mates covered the wood decks with sand so that the coal dust would mix with it rather than being ground into the deck. A number of the sailors donned unorthodox outfits, including brightly colored handkerchiefs on their heads, civilian hats, old Marine helmets, loud neckties, and socks over shoes. It was a way of having a little fun amid the laborious process. Afterward it was time to clean up and restore conditions to shipshape. The whole process lasted four days in an area near the equator. The *Maine*, commissioned in 1902 and named for the ship sunk at Havana, had the most voracious appetite for coal. She received her load last so she could have as much on board as possible before the next long leg to Rio de Janeiro, Brazil. The other older battleships, *Alabama*, *Illinois*, and *New Jersey*, also had problems with insufficient bunker capacity. Obtaining and loading coal would pose challenges throughout the long voyage. With some exceptions, the bulk of the U.S. fleet had been accustomed to operating fairly close to home shores and the Navy did not have a network of coaling stations set up around the world. Instead, it had to rely on the few colliers it did have and obtain contracts with foreign suppliers for the rest. Much shoveling lay ahead.

SOUTH AMERICA

On January 6, the battleships crossed the equator and the crews celebrated with the traditional high jinks, which included a visit from an old salt dressed as King Neptune. The ceremony was something like a fraternity initiation for those who had not previously crossed the line. The gathered ships carried with them more than fourteen thousand officers and enlisted men, a total that comprised nearly half of all the active-duty personnel in the U.S. Navy at the time. Of that number, about 12,500—nearly ninety percent—had never crossed the equator before, and thus were required to undergo the rites of passage that transformed them from tender "pollywogs" into "shellbacks," the term used to describe veterans of the process.

"Neptunus Rex" took part in the ceremony on board the *Louisiana;* (President Roosevelt had once ridden that ship near the equator). Ensign N.W. Post welcomed the king and his court aboard, and the Neptune character was accompanied by an assortment of oddly dressed characters. Traditional initiation activities included having the shellbacks force pills down the pollywogs' throats, squirting their faces, and letting the royal barber administer his "lather" of coal tar, oil, molasses, and India ink. After the barber inflicted his shaves, he flipped the pollywog victims from ducking chairs into a canvas tank erected on deck and filled with water.

In late January, the fleet visited Rio de Janeiro, Brazil. Besides serving as a coaling stop, it was also an opportunity to collect intelligence on the Brazilian Navy and local ports and defenses. With some self-consciousness, Midshipman Louis Maxfield, signal officer of the *Illinois*, asked his mother not to tell her friends that he was collecting intelligence "because some people might think it wasn't … courteous." The next coaling stop was in Punta Arenas, Chile, about as far south as one could go and still find civilization. The size of the town limited the liberty party to officers and a few enlisted men. As the liberty launches approached the landing pier, those on board saw a big sign on the seawall: "Special Prices for the American Fleet." And, indeed, they were special—about fifty percent higher than those normally charged.

The ships arrived at the port of Callao, Peru, on February 20 and received a rousing welcome. President José Pardo invited the North American Navy-men to see the bullfights. Two trains carried three thousand enlisted men and six hundred officers to Lima for the event. As they alighted, the North Americans were given pamphlets in English that had been prepared by a maker of alcoholic beverages. In addition to information on where drinks could be had, it served as a guide to the sights of the city. Among the advice was a suggestion on how much to pay the sexton of the cathedral for showing them the bones of the sixteenth century conqueror Pizarro: "Don't tip him too much or you'll spoil the market, 'cause this isn't New York." It also contained the Spanish words for bullfighting terms, and was even so helpful as to include some Spanish profanity.

To demonstrate their hospitality, the Peruvians christened the bulls with names that tied in with the fleet visit; included were "The Brave Teddy" and "Yankee Doodle." The bulls, of course, were doomed, which did not sit well with the visiting sailors. They cheered for the bulls and were appalled by the spectacle that the locals considered to be sporting. Many of the visitors left in disgust when the show was only half over.

Once the ships were under way once again, they proceeded up the Pacific Coast to Magdalena Bay in Baja California, Mexico, where they conducted target practice with the many guns of the fleet. Like the journey itself, this was meant as a test of the

OPPOSITE PAGE: As the *Maine* takes aboard coal from barges, 6-inch (15cm) guns of the secondary battery protrude from casemates in the ship's hull. Metal shutters were fitted around them and bolted in place when the guns were not in use. Crewmen lived and worked inside the casemates, so the shutters served to keep seawater out when the ship was under way.

fleet's battle readiness. By this time Admiral Evans had gone ashore for treatment of painful rheumatism in his legs that made it difficult for him to walk or even stand for any length of time. Though he was still officially in command of the fleet, the real duties fell to Rear Admiral Charles Thomas, who shifted his flag to Evans's ship, the *Connecticut*.

CALIFORNIA HOSPITALITY

After Mexico, the ships proceeded northward to California, receiving warm welcomes everywhere they stopped, including Coronado, San Pedro, Long Beach, Santa Monica, Redondo, Santa Barbara, Monterey, and Santa Cruz. This time there were no restrictions on liberty for the sailors. Los Angeles even provided all-day free entertainment for the crews.

The arrival in the Coronado roadstead was a magnificent display of seamanship. As Lieutenant Commander Henry Wiley, executive officer of the *Kentucky*, described the maneuver, the sixteen ships, arranged by division, steamed ahead in column formation at full speed. On signal, the four division flagships turned simultaneously ninety degrees to starboard, and each was followed in the turn by the other three ships of her division. Subsequent flag signals ordered the ships to stop and anchor, which they did, simultaneously and in four parallel rows. As the anchors went down, so did the American flags at their gaffs, and up went union jacks on the jackstaffs forward and national ensigns aft. Thirty-two boat booms swung out simultaneously, thirty-two gangways dropped, and thirty-two boats went into the water.

The most important California stop was San Francisco, which had been announced as the goal of the cruise the year before. The fleet of buff-and-white ships arrived on May 5, 1908, to a tumultuous welcome. Their number had grown temporarily to eighteen with the arrival of the *Nebraska* and *Wisconsin*, which were already on the West Coast. The shorelines were filled with people on both sides of the Golden Gate, which was not yet spanned by the famous bridge. Estimates placed the size of the crowd at a million people. As the ships approached the city of San Francisco, the sun came out and highlighted Telegraph Hill, where fifty-foot-high letters spelled out "Welcome." Once the fleet anchored,

ABOVE: The *Nebraska* and *Wisconsin* sit moored next to each other at the Puget Sound Navy Yard in the summer of 1908. After a cruise from the Atlantic, they are receiving repairs in preparation for the long voyage to the Far East. The newer *Nebraska* has a much higher freeboard (i.e., the distance of the deck above the water). On the *Wisconsin*, an elaborate afterbridge can be seen. She and her two sisters, the *Illinois* and the *Alabama*, were among the oldest battleships in the Great White Fleet. Only the *Kearsarge* and *Kentucky* were commissioned earlier. RIGHT: Crew members of the flagship *Connecticut* display a wide variety of mascots during the fleet's cruise.

Admiral Evans, by now wheelchair-bound because of the rheumatism in his legs, boarded the *Connecticut* one last time to receive visitors. Later, at a reception in the St. Francis Hotel, he was wheeled into the room to deliver a speech praising the fleet's sailors and asking for more ships. The next day, he was officially relieved of duty by Admiral Thomas and headed to Washington, D.C., to retire. Henry Wiley of the *Kentucky* observed, "[Evans] must have endured the tortures of the damned, or he would never have let go of his command, the most powerful that had ever been assembled under the American flag."

Thomas, however, was due to reach the mandatory retirement age in just a few months and would not be able to remain for the rest of the projected cruise. So Rear Admiral Charles S. Sperry, in command of the Fourth Division, fleeted up to take his place. In the game of musical ships, Captain Schroeder of the *Virginia* then received a temporary appointment as a rear admiral and took command of the Fourth Division with the *Wisconsin* as his flagship. Finally, Wainwright of the *Louisiana* became commander of the Fourth Division and moved aboard the new *Georgia*. The addition of the *Nebraska* and *Wisconsin* was intended to increase the size of the fleet to eighteen ships, but because of engineering problems, the older *Maine* and *Alabama* dropped out and the number in the fleet stayed at sixteen.

In the summer of 1908, the ships took a respite from their long journey and spent time in shipyards for maintenance and repairs before crossing the broad Pacific. While the ships were on the West Coast, each received a bear cub (ship mascots were popular in that era). On board the *Wisconsin*, Admiral Schroeder directed his orderly to keep the door to his flag cabin closed when he was out on deck, to make sure Teddy, the ship's mascot, didn't wander in. One day the orderly closed the door without realizing "little Teddy was in there, and that apartment was sadly wrecked, especially the desk." The crew loved the bear, as might be expected, so when he accidentally fell overboard one day, the lifeboat crew rescued him after he had just about exhausted himself. The whole crew cheered when Teddy was lifted safely back onto the deck of his seagoing home.

ON TO WESTWARD

After making several stops along the Pacific Northwest coast, the ships gathered in San Francisco Bay and began the westward journey to Hawaii on July 7. The *Nebraska* was temporarily missing because of an outbreak of scarlet fever on board, and she had to spend a few days in quarantine before steaming west. Built in Seattle, the *Nebraska* was one of the few U.S. battleships constructed on the West Coast. She had gone into commission just a year earlier, on July 1, 1907. Her first navigator was Lieutenant Harris Laning. He marveled at how pervasive the use of electricity was in the new battleship. A decade earlier, he had served in the *Oregon*, which had used electricity only for lights. Now it powered everything except the main engines. One of his initial challenges had been to make sure the *Nebraska*'s magnetic compasses worked correctly given their proximity to the steel superposed turrets. Initially, the compasses always pointed close to south, no matter which way the ship headed, so it took considerable adjustment to get them to point in the right direction. He was grateful some years later when gyroscope-driven compasses entered the fleet.

Another enthusiastic reception greeted the ships in Hawaii. On July 17, crew members marched in a parade in Honolulu. Hawaiian women put leis around the Navy men's necks before the parade and tossed wreaths at the men as they passed. Caswell Saufley had graduated from the Naval Academy in the class of 1908 and reported to the *Kansas* with the rank of passed midshipman (a man was still considered a midshipman after he left Annapolis until two years had passed and he came to what was known as final graduation). Saufley was one of those who marched in the Honolulu parade. He wore a sword with his dress uniform and tilted it as he marched so he could catch flowers with the hilt at the top. The fleet did not visit Pearl Harbor because it was not yet sufficiently developed.

The next leg of the cruise was a long one: to New Zealand, where one hundred thousand people—ten percent of that nation's population—showed up to welcome the visiting Americans. In Sydney, Australia, the crowds on hand totaled more than half a million. Author James Reckner listed some of the entertainment arranged for the visiting

In this magnificent view, a crew of workmen at the New York Navy Yard install a 12-inch (30cm) gun into the forward turret of the *Connecticut* on January 31, 1906. Once both guns were in place, the turret's roof was put on and armor installed. In this depiction, holes have already been drilled for the rivets to come. The ship was commissioned in September 1906, and the following year became Rear Admiral Robley Evans's flagship during the first leg of a world cruise.

sailors: "banquets, balls, teas, luncheons, and tours, plus typically Australian activities such as boomerang throwing, buck jumping, sheep shearing, wood chopping, and sheep dog trials." From Sydney, the ships steamed six hundred miles (965km) to Melbourne. Midshipman H. Kent Hewitt, who was to become a top leader in World War II, quipped, "We have at last escaped the hospitalities of Sydney, only to be swallowed up in those of Melbourne."

Included in the events scheduled for Melbourne was a dinner for three thousand at the Exhibition Building. At the appointed time of 7:00 P.M., just one American sailor had shown up; by 9:00 P.M., there were only seven present. The rest of the men were with Australian girls, whose company they vastly preferred to the men they saw every day. In fact, many of the men had rounded up two young women apiece and had an arm around each. Getting through the swarms of people they encountered en route to their ships was difficult because of the quantity of feminine company. Some sailors didn't even bother: more than two hundred of the visiting American sailors deserted and remained in Australia while their ships steamed off without them. The *Kansas* stayed behind for a while and then brought mail and stragglers to the fleet. Even with the arrival of the latecomers, the absentees still totaled more than one hundred.

In early October, the ships arrived in Manila Bay in the Philippines and took on coal, but men did not go ashore because of an epidemic of cholera. Soon after departure from the Philippines, the ships ran into a problem of another sort: a full-blown typhoon. The ships that fared worst were those of the Kearsarge-and Virginia-classes that had 8-inch (20cm) turrets piled atop the 12-inch (30cm) turrets. All that weight topside made them highly susceptible to rolling. For Lieutenant Commander Wiley of the *Kentucky*, it was nerve-racking to watch the *Virginia* as she rolled over to one side so far that her deck-edge rail dipped under the water for a time. Finally, she would come back upright. Admiral Schroeder of the Fourth Division slowed to eight knots to accommodate the low-freeboard ships, that is, the ones whose decks were not far above the ocean. Even that pace was too fast for the *Kearsarge*. She plunged so heavily into the sea that a shudder

LEFT: A landing party musters with rifles on the stern of the *Alabama* in 1906, a year before she set out with the other ships of the Great White Fleet on a world cruise. Arrayed across the top of the after 13-inch (33cm) turret are three flat cylinders that served as viewing ports so men inside could see the action outside the turret.
BOTTOM: U.S. bluejackets and their officers take part in a parade in Melbourne, Australia, on August 27, 1908. The reception was so welcoming that the parade essentially amounted to a triumphal march.

ran from the keel to the top and snapped off the top of her foremast, taking with it the antenna for that newfangled invention, the wireless radio, which was now useless. Wiley referred to the *Kentucky* and *Kearsarge* as "submarines," because their forecastles were so often underwater in heavy seas. One man fell overboard, but a boat from a later ship pulled him from the drink. A gunner's mate went over the side of the *Rhode Island*, which was, unfortunately, the last ship in line, so no one was behind to recover him. His shipmates looked back and saw him in the water but were helpless to do anything for him.

The big test for the Great White Fleet came on its 1908 visit to Japan, since it was the threat of war with Japan in 1907 that had led to the cruise in the first place. Tensions had calmed down by then, however, and the Japanese welcomed the Americans to Yokohama in mid-October. In order to avoid any unpleasant international incidents, the American officers closely supervised the groups of enlisted men who attended events ashore. The hospitality of the Japanese actually surpassed that of the Americans in one respect: they fed better. American officers were guests at a palace lunch on October 23 and were invited to dinner on board the battleship *Fuji*. There was also a reception on board the battleship *Mikasa*, the flagship of Admiral Heihachiro Togo during Japan's victory in the Battle of Tsushima Strait a few years earlier. The Japanese were liberal in their supply of food and drink, and the Americans tried to reciprocate on board the *Connecticut*. More than three thousand guests were invited, and even more than that showed up. Early arrivals consumed all the available food, so it was gone by the official starting time for the party. The money allocated for entertainment had been far too modest. Despite that gaffe, the visit was a big success. Talk of war had evaporated.

For a variety of reasons, including German efforts to get involved, the fleet's visit to China was tepid by comparison. Apathy was part of the problem. The fleet honored the dowager empress of the country on her birthday, and she reciprocated the kindness. The enlisted men, including the former apprentice Harry Morris, were given cups made from cloisonné china; each officer received a vase made of the same material. The cups were small,

RIGHT: The *Kansas* displays the color scheme of the Great White Fleet. The eagle and other ornamentation on the bow are painted gold.
OPPOSITE PAGE, FAR LEFT: Civilians visit the *New Jersey* during her stop in San Francisco Bay on May 16, 1908. The large ventilation cowls that supplied air below decks could be rotated to face into the wind. Aft of the tall smokestacks is the standard military-type mast used in U.S. battleships prior to the advent of cage masts. At stations on the mast, crew members had various responsibilities, including lookout and searchlight duties. Note the ladders on the stacks.
OPPOSITE PAGE, TOP RIGHT: In this 1902 depiction of the *Illinois'* forecastle, the ship's bridge is seen in the upper left, overlooking the forward 13-inch (33cm) turret.
OPPOSITE PAGE, BOTTOM RIGHT: Crewman load coal aboard the *Illinois* in 1902.

TOP LEFT: The *Kearsarge* takes aboard an 8-inch (20cm) projectile for her secondary battery.

TOP RIGHT: Even though the crews of the early battleships were crammed in among equipment in their berthing compartments, commanding officers lived in style. In this picture of the skipper's cabin aboard the *Kentucky*, the captain is barely visible amidst the overstuffed chairs, rugs on the deck, roll-top desk, and fancy light fixtures. He can be seen just to the right of the flower arrangement on the table. The captain's quarters also included a separate bedroom and head.

BOTTOM: Spewing coal smoke, the ships of the Great White Fleet steam into Puget Sound in 1908.

about the size of a demitasse. The enamel finish was black and gold on the outside; inside was a pattern of flowers on a blue background. Morris brought his home and treasured it for more than sixty years afterward as a memento from an exciting period of his youth.

After China, the fleet headed to Manila and spent most of November there. The ships conducted considerable target practice, and veterans were struck by the fact that turret guns could now shoot comfortably as far as 10,000 feet (3,048m). The *Oregon* had shot nearly that far off Cuba ten years earlier but incurred damage to the turret at that range. As the ships resumed their journey in December, they ventured into the Indian Ocean, where they encountered considerable heat—an unusual phenomenon for the sailors around Christmas time. On board the *Nebraska*, members of a Christmas committee used their ingenuity to create holiday decorations. Men cut up and shredded lumber to make a sort of Christmas tree. Needles were fashioned out of straws and pieces of paper dipped into green paint, and brass rings and balls taken from curtain rods served as ornaments. Santa's whiskers were made from unraveled rope fiber, and his suit was created from a red signal flag cloth adorned with pieces of cotton. His boots were made of black oilcloth, and an empty coffee sack became his bag of goodies.

On their next stop in Colombo, Ceylon, the American Navy men were entertained by Thomas Lipton, a yachtsman and tea magnate. He presented each officer with five pounds (2kg) of his tea; each enlisted man received one pound (0.5kg). By this time, the weary crews were becoming eager to return home. Some enlisted men planned a ball they would hold when they got back to the States, and listened to music on the forecastle of the *Illinois*. As they did so, a number of them paired off and waltzed with each other. Dancing was a popular pastime for many sailors of the era. When women weren't available, men would do—with no raised eyebrows. After Ceylon, it was on to Suez, Egypt. The *Georgia*, commanded by Captain Edward Qualtrough, managed to run aground in the process of going through the canal—a professional no-no. The ships made stops in several Mediterranean ports, including Messina, Sicily, where crewmen aided the local populace in

recovering from an earthquake. Captain Qualtrough's earlier troubles were compounded when he was court-martialed for drunkenness at a reception in Tangier, Morocco. During the remainder of the voyage back to the United States, he was not allowed either on the bridge or the quarterdeck of his own ship, so others had to perform the daily command functions.

HOMEWARD BOUND

In late January 1909, the battleships gathered at Gibraltar to prepare for the last leg of the homeward voyage across the Atlantic. They had to coal to the maximum and even beyond. The *Illinois*, one of the oldest ships in the collection, had so much coal piled topside that her crew could not fall in at quarters. To augment their numbers for the end of the journey, they were joined by a squadron of warships that steamed out from the East Coast. These included the *Maine*; new battleships *New Hampshire*, *Idaho*, and *Mississippi*; two armored cruisers; and three scout cruisers. These were all painted a war-like gray in contrast to the white-hulled ships returning from the world cruise. The new ships had cage masts (to provide a higher vantage point for gunfire spotting), in contrast to the simpler military masts of the older ships.

Meeting its scheduled return date, the combined fleet steamed into Hampton Roads and dropped anchor on February 22, 1909— Washington's Birthday. In total, the ships had covered some 43,000 miles (69,187km). The arriving ships flew large American flags at the masthead, gaff, and on a flagstaff aft. Tens of thousands of well-wishers turned out to see the presidential review. Roosevelt's *Mayflower* followed the seven-mile-long (11km) column of ships into port. Then the president visited each of the division flagships and spoke to crews gathered on board. His message was simple and direct: "Those who perform the feat again can but follow in your footsteps." This was Teddy Roosevelt's moment of glory. He had dispatched his "big stick" to the world, and it had made a momentous and successful cruise; such has never since been achieved by so many battleships.

THE FLEET PROTECTS THE NATION — PRUDENTIAL LIFE INSURANCE PROTECTS THE HOME

ABOVE: Then, as now, advertisers tied-in with popular themes to sell their products. In this contemporary ad, the Prudential Insurance Company used a painting of the fleet steaming past the Rock of Gibraltar as it began its homeward-bound leg across the Atlantic Ocean in early 1909.
LEFT: In February 1909, an exultant President Theodore Roosevelt stands on the *Connecticut's* after turret to address officers and enlisted men following the successful completion of their world cruise. The ships of the fleet sent representatives from their crews to go aboard the flagship and hear the president. The cruise completion date had been set well in advance; Roosevelt left office two weeks later.

Chapter Three

WAR AND DISARMAMENT

ABOVE: Prior to the development of amphibious warfare doctrine in the 1930s, the Navy was accustomed to sending ashore landing parties comprised of both Marines and sailors from the crews of Navy ships. Here at Veracruz, Mexico, in April 1914, the steam launch at right tows a ship's boat filled with a landing force. In the background, a battleship flies the two-star flag of a rear admiral.

OPPOSITE PAGE: The *Arkansas*, left, and *Texas*, right, are shown in the Gatun Locks during a passage through the Panama Canal on July 25, 1919. The perspective is deceiving, because the *Texas*, commissioned in 1914, was slightly larger than the older *Arkansas*, which dated from 1912.

In the years of Theodore Roosevelt's presidency, the outspoken Commander William S. Sims exerted uncommon influence for an officer of his rank. Though Sims had been ordered to command the cruiser *Chester* when she was commissioned in April 1908, Roosevelt asked him to stay in Washington one more year as his naval aide. Roosevelt's payback was to reward Sims with the command of a battleship—a controversial decision, since that was a captain's billet. Sims chose the *Minnesota* and took command on March 1, 1909, just three days before Roosevelt left office. Many in the Navy objected to a battleship command going to a commander, especially because of the obviously political nature of the appointment.

THE GUILDHALL SPEECH

Still more controversy lay ahead. Late that year, the fleet visited England and France. The American ships did not go to Germany, which was then in the midst of a robust arms race with Great Britain. When the ships reached England, there were mutual rounds of visits and hospitality. One important event was a dinner on December 2 held at London's Guildhall and hosted by the Lord Mayor of London. The next day, hundreds of enlisted men from the U.S. ships were entertained at the same Guildhall. There, Commander Sims of the *Minnesota* delivered a luncheon speech that drew wide attention. Most notable was Sims' assertion that, "if the time ever comes when the British Empire is seriously menaced by an external enemy, it is my opinion that you may count upon every man, every dollar, every drop of blood, of your kindred across the sea." The old Guildhall filled with cheers and shouting from the assembled people from both nations.

It came to be known as the "blood is thicker than water" speech, and it drew a mixed response elsewhere. Germans, naturally, were threatened by it and protested. American newspapers were critical of the seemingly off-the-cuff international policymaking by a naval officer, and a relatively junior one at that. Sims' punishment was relatively lenient: a public reprimand in January 1910, and a reminder that the Navy was an instrument of peace. In early 1917, Sims' comments of 1909 seemed prophetic. In the midst of a war with Germany, the British received substantial help from America. The officer in command of U.S. Naval Forces in European waters at that time was Vice Admiral William S. Sims, and he would push repeatedly for U.S. battleships to be sent to reinforce the Royal Navy. That they were delayed in going was in part because Sims was perceived as such an Anglophile that his objectivity on the subject was questioned.

FLEET ROUTINE

In the years following the cruise of the Great White Fleet, U.S. battleships were concentrated on the East Coast and followed an annual routine. In the winter, the fleet headed south to gather at Guantánamo Bay, Cuba. The ships ventured forth from that anchorage for training maneuvers and gunnery practice, and the Caribbean offered off-duty liberty attractions for crews, including athletic competitions among ships. As spring approached, the ships would return to the north and spend some time in their home ports. When they did have maneuvers, they often took place off the Virginia Capes, an area then known to the U.S. Navy as the southern drill grounds. During the course of each year, ships would rotate into navy yards for maintenance and repairs. For the few men who were married, a yard period in the ship's home port was among the few opportunities available to be with their wives and families.

As this routine continued, each year brought a steady modernization of the fleet. From January to April 1910, the United States commissioned its first four dreadnought battleships: *Michigan*, *South Carolina*, *Delaware*, and *North Dakota*. Plans for the first two actually dated from 1904, but their more leisurely construction schedule put them behind

ABOVE: Members of a battleship's landing party are shown with field pieces and small arms as they prepare to go ashore at Veracruz, Mexico, in 1914.
RIGHT: On the occasion of the March 16, 1914 keellaying for the *Arizona* at the New York Navy Yard, threeyear-old Henry Williams, Jr., holds onto the index finger of Assistant Secretary of the Navy Franklin D. Roosevelt. Williams, who inserted the first bolt in the ship's keel, later became a naval officer and was present at Pearl Harbor in 1941, when the *Arizona* was destroyed.

their British counterpart. HMS *Dreadnought* was completed and fully manned in December 1906, the same month the United States laid the keels for the *Michigan* and *South Carolina*. These were the first dreadnought-type battleships in any navy equipped with super-firing main battery gun turrets—the guns of the high turret fired over the top of an adjacent low turret. The arrangement permitted a higher volume of gunfire forward or aft than HMS *Dreadnought*'s turrets, which were mounted at the same level.

During the modernization, the older ships were used for midshipman summer training. In 1912, Midshipman John L. McCrea, who had just completed his first year in Annapolis, joined the rest of his plebe class in going aboard the *Massachusetts*; it was his first time at sea. Fortunately, he was able to find a "sea daddy" in the person of a red-bearded petty officer who spoke with a Norwegian accent. He was the leading boatswain's mate of the ship's fourth division, and his "office" was a sea chest. It also served as his equipment locker; it contained rope yarn, marlinespike, and other tools that were used in working with rope. He also had patterns that sailors would use to make their own uniforms. On Wednesday afternoons, the men were released from their normal duties for a half-day holiday known as "rope-yarn Sunday." It was a day for making clothes A man would buy cloth, then come back to the boatswain's mate, who sized him up with his eyes, reached into his chest, and pulled out a pattern for a uniform that would fit. The men would line the left breast pocket of their jumpers with red silk and the right pocket with green silk. That made the uniforms truly nautical, because then—as now—every ship under way shows a red navigation light to port and green to starboard.

In his developing friendship with the midshipman, the Norwegian petty officer reportedly once said, "Mr. McCrea, the bluejackets today aren't the way they used to be."

"Well," responded McCrea, "that's right I suppose. That's one of the penalties, that as people get older they think that about the young. In what respect are these fellows different now than they were in your time?"

"Well, I'll tell you what. Too many of them can read and write."

Indeed, that was a change, because the Navy was becoming more and more a service composed of men born in the United States and exposed to the American educational system. Moreover, it was taking in recruits from throughout the country and providing specialized training at boot camps. In the nineteenth century, sailors were often foreign-born and illiterate. Beyond that, the line between Navy and merchant marine service was not nearly as distinct as it became in the twentieth century. Men from port areas and foreign countries moved back and forth between the Navy and merchant service as jobs were available. Recruiting and enlistment were also more informal. The *Massachusetts* boatswain's mate, for instance, had served seven years in the Chilean Navy before joining that of the United States. His seamanship skills had been honed during years of shipboard duty. And now, as he lamented to McCrea, along came these young whippersnappers who could learn things out of books.

That same year, 1912, set the precedent for the U.S. Navy and Marine Corps to act as seagoing policemen of a sort in the Caribbean. When a group of Cubans took over a sugar mill near Guantánamo that had been built and operated by Americans, President William Howard Taft dispatched the Navy to deal with the problem, since the Marines were busy in Nicaragua at the time. Charles Pownall was then signal officer on board the *Missouri*, a predreadnought type commissioned in 1903. But on this expedition, he served as battalion adjutant for the landing party sent ashore to deal with the problem. The Navy men dyed their white uniforms with coffee so they would resemble those of the Marines. The group of sailors and their officers drilled at Guantánamo, then went ashore with a band playing and advanced on the disputed sugar mill. The Americans recaptured the mill; the only fatality was one Cuban who was killed by another Cuban.

INTERVENTION IN MEXICO

In October 1913, the United States stationed naval forces off the gulf coast of Mexico to protect American interests during a revolution in that country. For the most part, U.S. battleships just watched and waited; at times they provided temporary hotel services for American citizens who wanted a safe haven until they could be evacuated from the area.

The situation took an ugly turn in April 1914 when a Navy paymaster was detained ashore. Rear Admiral Henry T. Mayo demanded an apology and a gun salute to make amends. President Woodrow Wilson strongly backed Mayo because he was trying to force out Mexican President Victoriano Huerta, a military dictator. The situation was exacerbated when a German ship approached Veracruz with a supply of guns and ammunition for the Mexican government.

The upshot was that a landing force of U.S. Marines and sailors went ashore on April 21 and fought a series of gun battles with the Mexicans. It was a type of urban warfare for which Navy men were not normally trained, though many had practiced marksmanship. Especially proficient was Ensign Willis A. Lee of the USS *New Hampshire*'s landing party. He had been a member of the Navy rifle team and seemed to relish the opportunity to fire at live targets. When the landing party halted in its advance through the city, Lee sat on a curb with a rifle across his knees, essentially baiting a sniper into firing at him. He was effective in returning fire when it came in his direction. And it was hard to see the Mexicans, for they kept themselves well hidden. As Quartermaster Arthur Sweetman of the *New Hampshire* observed, "All you'd see would be a rifle barrel or a hand holding a pistol out a window or over the edge of a roof." Later in the month, Army troops relieved the naval forces ashore. Even so, the warships stayed in the vicinity until the American occupation ended late that year. In the meantime, World War I had started in Europe.

WAR IN EUROPE

In the early years of the century, a naval arms race had been building between Great Britain and Germany. The spark that set off the powder keg in the summer of 1914 was the assassination of Archduke Franz Ferdinand of Austria-Hungary at Sarajevo, the capital of Bosnia-Herzegovina in the Balkans. Within weeks, the continent of Europe had been plunged into what became known at first as the Great War, and later as World War I. In the midst of all this, the Naval Academy had sent its midshipmen abroad that summer for a training cruise. One of the ships was the USS *Idaho*, with Midshipman First Class John McCrea on board.

TOP: The crew of the *Arizona* poses on the forward part of the ship during this shot taken in 1918, at the conclusion of World War I. Because she burned oil rather than coal, the *Arizona* did not get to the European theater until after fighting had concluded "over there." The *Arizona*, like the rest of the new oil-burning battleships, spent much of the war in the Chesapeake Bay and York River training gun crews for other ships.
BOTTOM: Within six months of her commissioning on October 17, 1916, the *Arizona* (at left) joins a group of battleships practicing maneuvers. She is shown with her full original supply of twenty-two 5-inch (13cm)/51-caliber broadside guns. Early in 1917, some of the 5-inch (13cm) guns were removed to arm American merchant ships.

LEFT: This shot was taken from the fantail of the *Florida* in June 1912, about nine months after she was commissioned. The photo demonstrates several of the innovations in the fleet following the advent of dreadnought-type battleships. A group of sailors stands atop a 12-inch (30cm) turret, one of a pair. Farther aft were two more turrets, and forward of the superstructure were two more. Altogether, she mounted ten 12-inch (30cm) guns, compared with four big guns in the standard pre-dreadnought. She also sported cage masts made of interlaced steel tubing; the masts were standard on U.S. battleships commissioned through the early 1920s. The cage masts permitted the use of a fire control station, as shown on top of the mast at left.

OPPOSITE TOP: The *Ohio* passes through the Panama Canal on July 16, 1915. She, the *Missouri*, and the *Wisconsin* made the transit that day—the first U.S. warships to pass through a canal that had been built to facilitate the Navy's ease of operation in both the Atlantic and Pacific Oceans. Like other pre-dreadnoughts in the U.S. fleet, the *Ohio* was modernized by replacing her original pole-type military masts with the cage masts that were standard in the newer dreadnought types.

The *Idaho* got mixed up in a balance of power. In preparing for possible conflict, Turkey had contracted with a British shipyard to build a battleship with seven turrets. To counter this, Greece decided it needed some battleships of its own. The United States decided to make the *Idaho* and *Mississippi* available. Because of a money-saving congressional mandate several years earlier, they were smaller and less capable than their predecessors. Essentially, the two pre-dreadnoughts turned out to be lemons, and the United States was happy to find a buyer for them. They wound up as the *Kilkis* and *Lemnos* in the Greek Navy. (Ironically, when war erupted and Turkey wound up on Germany's side, Britain decided not to let Turkey have its contracted battleship after all. Instead, she became HMS *Agincourt*, widely noted as the only battleship with a turret for each day of the week.)

And so it was that the *Idaho* was decommissioned at the port of Villefranche, in the south of France, on July 30, 1914. The ship would be turned over to a Greek crew, and the U.S. Navy sent the *Maine* to pick up the midshipmen and crew of the *Idaho*. Rather than make a government-to-government transaction, the Navy transferred the ship to the New York Shipbuilding Company, which in turn passed it to Greece. Adding to the mix of events that summer, Secretary of the Navy Josephus Daniels had outlawed officers' wine messes on board naval ships, thus prohibiting the previous practice of drinking on board.

After the *Idaho* was decommissioned, the officers and midshipmen gathered in the captain's cabin. The shipyard representative said, "Well, now you know this is a wonderful occasion as far as I am concerned, and I came on board this ship prepared for it." With that, he opened his briefcase, produced five bottles of whiskey, and invited the Greek and American officers to drink with him. Midshipmen were not supposed to drink, but Lieutenant William Glassford, the navigator, turned to John McCrea and said, "You'd better get a little sip, at any rate." When the drinking was done, the shipyard representative turned the ship over to the Greek Navy, and the Americans left for the *Maine*. On the fourth of August, while they were still in the Mediterranean, war broke out.

In the summer of 1915, the Naval Academy midshipmen embarked in three battleships, *Ohio*,

Missouri, and *Wisconsin*. The ships were not particularly old, having been commissioned when Teddy Roosevelt was president, but they were outmoded in that they were all pre-dreadnoughts. One of the midshipmen on board the Ohio was feisty Dan Tomlinson. He and the other "mids" slept in hammocks and had a powerful inducement to get up when reveille sounded. A tough boatswain's mate would come through the compartment armed with a two-by-four, which he used to whack the bottoms of hammocks that still contained sleeping midshipmen. On July 16, after dredges worked all night to open a channel through a mud slide in Culebra Cut, Rear Admiral William F. Fullam's three-ship squadron became the first American battleships to pass through the Panama Canal, which had opened for traffic less than a year earlier. The cruise of the *Oregon* in 1898 had been a considerable factor in the push for a Central American canal. All were decorated with signal flags and had bands playing to celebrate the occasion. U.S. soldiers lined the banks of the canal and cheered for their countrymen. An effusive officer of the deck recorded in his log, "At 9:00 P.M. emerged on the bosom of the broad Pacific, the first representatives of American sea-power to pass through."

The following year, additional dreadnought-type ships joined the fleet. With the *Nevada* and *Oklahoma*, both commissioned in early 1916, came the all-or-nothing principle of applying armor, in which each ship's vital areas were heavily protected and less important areas were left unarmored, thus concentrating the weight of the armor where it would do the most good. Another important innovation in the Nevada-class was the adoption of oil as fuel. Oil could be pumped instead of shoveled, which meant a lot less back-straining labor for crew members. Later in 1916 came the completion of another pair of sisters: the *Pennsylvania* and *Arizona*.

AMERICA JOINS THE CONFLICT

With the dawning of 1917 came more signs that the United States would be drawn into the European war. In February, Germany adopted a policy of unrestricted submarine warfare around the British Isles. Later that month, the United States intercepted the Zimmermann telegram, in which Germany promised to aid Mexico in regaining territory from the United

States in return for an alliance with Germany. In March, President Wilson gained the authority to arm American merchant ships and then sent Navy crews to man the guns. German U-boats responded by sinking U.S. cargo ships.

War was seemingly in the offing on April 3 when the U.S. battleships headed for an anchorage in the York River, near Yorktown, Virginia, the site of George Washington's victory over the British in 1781. The ships steamed in by divisions and anchored safely behind antisubmarine nets, the newer dreadnoughts in one line and the pre-dreadnoughts, with their distinctive tall smokestacks, in another line, closer to Yorktown. Together, the ships occupied five miles (8km) of the York River. On April 6, Congress declared war on Germany. The immediate contribution from the U.S. Navy was in the form of transports to carry American soldiers "over there," and antisubmarine ships to deal with German U-boats. At the outset, there was little for the American battleships to do, particularly because of political considerations over whether the United States should weaken protection of its own coasts to support its friends overseas. The battleships became training platforms instead of warships. Recruits flooded aboard to be exposed to Navy life and to learn how to operate shipboard guns.

In the autumn of 1917, international negotiations finally led to an agreement that the U.S. Navy would send a division of coal-burning battleships to Europe to beef up the British Grand Fleet, which was entirely committed to maintaining a distant blockade that would keep the German Fleet bottled up in Germany. As it happened, the British did not get the newest and most capable American battleships. Britain's supply of coal was far more plentiful than oil, so older, coal-burning ships were dispatched to the Royal Navy, and the newer ones remained behind for the humdrum chore of training gunners. One of the ships assigned to this role was the newly commissioned *Arizona*. Gunner's Mate Joe Driscoll was among those providing the training. When newcomers arrived, he and some of the more experienced men would explain that the noses of the 5-inch (13cm) projectiles had to be painted with different colors shortly before being fired so that when they hit their canvas target, which was towed by a tugboat, it would be easy to determine which guns had

made which holes. The gullible youngsters were told that it wasn't possible to paint the big 14-inch (36cm) projectiles in advance; instead, the newcomers heard that they were to go up to the ship's bow with a can of paint and a brush. When one of the big guns fired, the rookie was to hold up his brush and paint the projectile as it zoomed by.

During some of the training missions, the battleships fired their guns at an old target ship, the *San Marcos* (formerly called the *Texas*), which was partially sunk in the Chesapeake Bay. It was quite a comedown for one of the nation's first battleships. As the *Texas*, she had fought in the Spanish-American War where she had been on the sending end of naval gunfire. Now she had taken on a different name, and a new battleship was called *Texas*. The more modern *Texas* had the advantage of being both a relatively new ship and a coal-burner, so she was among those designated for duty in Britain. In September 1917, she was to accompany the *New York*, *Arkansas*, *Wyoming*, and *Delaware* to Europe. With a new captain and new navigator on board, she was to steam from the New York Navy Yard to Port Washington on Long Island to rendezvous with the other ships for the voyage across the Atlantic. Instead, she ran aground and had to be refloated, and then spend some time in a shipyard.

BATTLESHIPS TO BRITAIN

On November 25, 1917, Battleship Division Nine, minus the injured *Texas*, set out across the Atlantic. Captain Henry Wiley of the *Wyoming* had sealed orders, as did his counterparts in the other ships, for the geographical points they would pass through. That itinerary would enable them to rejoin in the event they were separated. The destroyer *Manley* accompanied the four dreadnoughts. They steamed in line abreast in the daytime, in column at night. The four ships were painted in camouflage schemes that drew from an overall plan but allowed variations in the individual ships. The camouflage was designed to deceive the enemy as to which direction the ships were traveling. It was deceptive all right, but the victims of the deception were the American Navy men. Captain Wiley observed that when the ships were steaming side by side, the *New York*'s paint scheme always made her seem as if she were converging with his own ship. Later, the Americans

LEFT: As the U.S. Navy's first battleship, the *Texas* was on the delivering end of gunfire in the 1898 Battle of Santiago. When a new ship was constructed with the name *Texas*, the name of this one was changed in 1911 to *San Marcos*, a city thirty miles south of Austin, Texas. In her new role, she became a gunnery target in the Chesapeake Bay and was on the receiving end of fire. She is shown here after taking a pounding from the *New Hampshire* in March 1911.

TOP AND BOTTOM: These two shots provide examples of camouflage schemes used on U.S. battleships during the World War I era. At top, the *Utah* has a sawtooth pattern painted along her deck edge and sheet metal triangles affixed to her masts. The idea was to make it more difficult for enemy range finders (the split-image type used in cameras) to focus and thus determine the range at which to fire. At bottom, the *Nebraska* has a pattern of diagonal stripes; the stripes are designed to make range finding difficult and confuse the enemy about which direction the ship was heading. In practice, such designs produced a hazard for U.S. ships steaming together, as they had trouble determining their fellow countrymen's courses.

found that the British were also confused by the camouflage, so they repainted their ships in all-over dark gray.

The crossing itself was difficult because of stormy weather. The *Delaware* had gotten separated in the storm and rejoined her division mates off Scotland. On December 7, the ships reached the Grand Fleet base at Scapa Flow in the Orkney Islands, north of Scotland. Wiley said of it, "Scapa Flow was the dreariest spot I have ever seen, and I have seen some pretty dreary spots." Battleship Division Nine was absorbed into the Grand Fleet as the Sixth Battle Squadron and followed British procedures. In the early ventures to sea with the British, the Americans—in unknown waters and hyper-alert—reported many false sightings of German submarines, but they eventually settled down into a routine. In one instance, the British destroyer *Valorous* dropped a depth charge on a suspected U-boat. Even though the *Wyoming* was some distance away, the ship was rocked so much by the underwater explosion that those on board were concerned that their ship had been damaged. They also came to realize what a demoralizing effect the depth charges had on U-boat crews.

Captain Wiley of the *Wyoming* was in his glory. As he wrote years later in his memoir, "The command of a great battleship is one of the finest jobs in the world. Nothing I know of compares to it. The responsibility is small compared to the flag command or the command of an army. And yet it is more intimate—greater in the human touch." Wiley ran a taut, disciplined ship, but it seemed that all he heard from the squadron commander, Rear Admiral Hugh Rodman, was about mistakes and shortcomings. There was precious little praise mixed in with the comments. After one incident, in which the *New York*, Rodman's flagship, slowed without signaling, and the *Wyoming* crawled up her stern and got uncomfortably close, Rodman sent uncomplimentary flag signals to Wiley. Once the ships were in port and moored, Wiley went to the flagship to confront the angry admiral. Wiley presented his side of the story and said he should be relieved of duty if the signals Rodman had sent were justified. Rodman then settled down and had a man-to-man talk with the skipper. He explained that he was so committed to making the American ships perform well while in

During World War I, the *New Jersey* was camouflaged in the MacKay low-visibility pattern, which was intended to make the ship difficult to see and to disrupt enemy range finders. This ship was a veteran of the Great White Fleet and the landing at Veracruz in 1914, but she was not exposed to any enemy fire in World War I. Instead, she spent her time in the Chesapeake Bay training gun crews. The mattress-like padding around the bridge and searchlight platforms was standard on U.S. battleships in World War I as protection against splinters produced by shell hits. As with other pre-dreadnoughts, she has been modernized with cage masts. The masts are crowned by the house-like foretop and maintop that contained stations for fire-control crews and elevated viewpoints from which to observe where projectiles fired by the ship fell. (To see the *New Jersey* before the addition of the cage masts, see page 40.)

company with the British that his feedback to the individual ships was harsher than he had realized. After both men had aired their viewpoints, they shook hands and parted as friends.

In the spring of 1918, the fleet base shifted for a time from drab Scapa Flow to Rosyth, on the Firth of Forth on Scotland's east coast. German soldiers in France were making a push to the west and looked as if they might break through. Royal Navy officers were concerned that they might have to cover an evacuation from the continent and so moved the heavy ships to a closer position to do so. At times, the fleet was put on one hour's notice to get under way. The spot at Rosyth, near Edinburgh, afforded opportunities for visits from Britain's royal family, including King George V and his son, the Prince of Wales. During the friendly discussion, the King pointed to a castle and remarked that Mary, Queen of Scots, had spent some time confined in it. Admiral Rodman asked the monarch, "Who was the man this time, Your Majesty?" The King initially expressed mock indignation at this taunt against royalty, then roared with laughter. When the crisis passed, the battleships returned to the far north.

One of the principal objectives of the American and British ships based in the British Isles was to try to bait the Germans into emerging from their protected lairs so the Allied guns could get at them. In May 1916—before the United States was in the war—British and German battleships and battle cruisers had tangled in the monumental Battle of Jutland, an event that would be studied and restudied by naval officers during the period between the world wars. The battle had been inconclusive, leaving many British Navy men feeling that they still had not really done their jobs against the German High Seas Fleet. They wanted another tussle, this time aided by the Americans. The U.S. battleships went to sea a number of times for training, target practice, and the hope of a fleet action, but the Germans refused to take the bait.

As the war continued on into the summer of 1918, the U.S. Navy went beyond the initial division of coal-burning battleships sent to the British Isles several months earlier. In August, Division Seven, comprised of the *Utah* and two modern oil-burners, the *Nevada* and *Oklahoma*, arrived in Bantry Bay, Ireland. The division was commanded by Rear

Admiral Thomas S. Rodgers, and its function was to be on the scene as protection in the event any German battle cruisers attempted to break out and attack convoys arriving from America. The flag secretary on the staff was Lieutenant Commander Olaf Hustvedt. He discovered the Germans weren't the only enemy; 1918 was the year of a worldwide flu epidemic. One day, Hustvedt went out walking with the gunnery officers from the *Oklahoma* and *Nevada*. The *Oklahoma*'s gunnery officer was Commander Gardner Caskey, who had stood number one in the Naval Academy class of 1907 and had a promising career ahead of him. Within a few days of the officers' walk, Caskey was stricken with the flu and died on November 3. For several weeks, the American Navy men were shipping the remains of flu victims out of Bantry Bay on a daily basis. Hustvedt soon found himself filling Caskey's billet on board the *Oklahoma*.

On board Rodman's flagship *New York* during service with the British was Lieutenant John McCrea. When the *New York* was in port, the lieutenant and his shipmates exchanged visits with their British counterparts. McCrea was struck by the openness of the insides of the main battery turrets in the British ships. By comparison, American turrets had a great deal of subdivision inside to prevent damage from spreading. The difference in ship design and construction was brought home to him most vividly when he went aboard the battle cruiser *Lion*, which had been the flagship of Vice Admiral David Beatty in the Battle of Jutland. In the turret that corresponded to his own in the *New York*, McCrea found a sobering plaque, "In this turret on 31 May 1916, Major F. W. Harvey and 58 of His Majesty's Marines gave their lives for King and Country." Harvey's action in flooding the turret's magazines after he himself was mortally wounded had probably saved his ship from destruction. Since the British turrets didn't have as many internal barriers as those in American battleships, the flooding of the powder magazines was most likely the only way to prevent fire from reaching them and blowing up the ship.

In September 1918, Captain Edward L. Beach reported to Scapa Flow to become commanding officer of the *New York*. Upon arrival at the fleet anchorage, he soon discovered why Scapa Flow had been chosen as the base for some fifty capital ships

OPPOSITE TOP: During World War I, the coal-burning *Florida* was dispatched to join the Royal Navy. She and other American battleships comprised the Sixth Battle Squadron of the Grand Fleet, though they never were able to entice the Germans into combat. The *Florida* is shown here steaming past the distinctive Firth of Forth Bridge on Scotland's eastern coast. The firth led to the fleet base and dockyard at Rosyth.

OPPOSITE BOTTOM: The *New York*, Rear Admiral Hugh Rodman's flagship in the Sixth Battle Squadron, is shown here taking aboard 14-inch (36cm) projectiles at what was commonly known as the Brooklyn Navy Yard. Up to 1919, when the fleet's newest ships moved to the Pacific, New York served as a major base for the battleships of the Atlantic Fleet.

LEFT: During the war, the first contingent of U.S. battleships operated out of either Scapa Flow in the Orkney Islands or on the eastern coast of Scotland. The second contingent, which arrived in the summer of 1918, was based in Ireland. This shot, which gives one the feeling of being right on the deck of the *Nevada*, was taken at Queenstown, Ireland, and is from a portfolio produced at the time by photographer Burnell Poole. The *Nevada* was the U.S. Navy's first oil-burning battleship and also the first to mount triple turrets. Her lower turrets had three 14-inch (36cm) guns apiece (one of which is obscured here) and the higher turrets had two.

RIGHT: In the early part of the century, colliers were a vital part of what was known as the "fleet train," that is, the supply ships and repair ships that kept the combatants operating. Here, the collier *Jason* lies alongside the battleship *New Hampshire* during a transfer of coal.
BOTTOM: The bustle of activity in a shipyard served as a subject for one of the posters used by the government to get U.S. citizens to buy bonds and thus finance the nation's effort in World War I. Shipyard trains move about, biplanes hover above, and smoke fills the air. It was a time when smoke was seen as a sign of industrial activity rather than a major pollutant. The ship is either the *South Carolina* or the *Michigan*. Both were commissioned in 1910 and comprised the first American class of dreadnought-type battleships.

JOSEPH PENNELL DEL.

HEYWOOD STRASSER & VOIGT LITHO. CO. N.Y. 1918

PROVIDE THE SINEWS OF WAR
BUY LIBERTY BONDS

of two nations. It was a large area of open water that permitted room for target practice, yet it had only one entrance, which could be shut securely except when ships were passing in or out. After watching the British and American ships practice shooting a target towed at a range of six miles (10km), Captain Beach concluded that the American turrets not only shot faster than the British, but had better marksmanship as well. He ascribed the speed advantage to the U.S. turrets being powered by electricity, while the British ones were moved by hand-cranked hydraulic systems.

The break in the dreary routine of Scapa, where the wind always blew raw and cold, came when combined forces of British and American ships went out for week-long sweeps of the North Sea a couple of times a month. Though German U-boats attacked the American battleships on several occasions, the torpedoes did not hit their marks. The only contact came when one day, as the *New York* was steaming into Pentland Firth, those on the bridge heard a bang and felt the ship shudder. The starboard engine raced wildly ahead and had to be shut down. When the *New York* went into dry dock at Rosyth, the damage was revealed: the starboard propeller was missing all three blades, and the ship's bottom had been indented a foot or two (0.3–0.6m) for a distance of two hundred feet (61m) forward of the propeller. British officers concluded that the ship had struck a submarine, though Captain Beach was not so sure.

Because the American battleships were an ocean away from their normal support bases, they were serviced at shipyards in the British Isles. By mid-October, the heavy steaming with the Grand Fleet had produced leaks in the boiler tubes of the *Texas*, so she went into a dockyard at Newcastle upon Tyne for an overhaul. She also received a bit of modernization. Because winter was approaching, the shipyard enclosed her previously open bridge and installed steam heating to make watch-standers more comfortable in the chill winds of northern Europe. Such comforts, of course, ran counter to the macho image of those who were used to toughing it out in the wind, rain, and salt spray. As one wag put it in describing the new bridge, "Be like going to sea in her aunt's front parlor." (This was in an era when a front parlor was for entertaining

guests, and the back parlor was the equivalent of today's family room.) Also added to the *Texas* was a removable wooden platform and runway atop one of her 14-inch (36cm) turrets. She would now be able to launch a light airplane for scouting and for spotting the fall of shots from her big guns.

END OF THE GREAT WAR
Late that month, when faced with the prospect of going out to fight, German sailors mutinied on board their ships holed up in the ports of Kiel and Wilhelmshaven across the North Sea. It was a turning point in the war, and the end was not long in coming. Hostilities ceased on November 11. When the Germans finally surrendered, a signal went out to the Grand Fleet from Admiral Beatty's flagship, the *Queen Elizabeth*, at Rosyth. Officers and men who had been prepared to steam out and fight now found holiday routine on board their ships. As dusk deepened into darkness, ships turned on their topside lights, no longer forced to be darkened. Ensign Paul Schubert of the *Texas* described the scene: "A searchlight beam penciled out from one of the battle cruisers and swept slender and clean across the sky in a flinging gesture of elation." All over the anchorage, the other ships followed suit, sending up hundreds of shafts of light that crisscrossed in the night sky. Men boarded boats to go around and celebrate. On the British warships, the men received double their traditional rum rations. Officially, the dry American ships couldn't follow suit, so the ingenious bluejackets drained the alcohol fuel from torpedoes and drank that instead.

On November 21, just ten days after the armistice that ended the fighting, the Grand Fleet steamed out in two parallel columns, each ten miles long (16km), to meet the defeated German High Seas Fleet as it approached to surrender. The German crews had removed the breechblocks from their guns and kept them trained on the centerline. But Admiral Beatty was taking no chances; he had the British and American ships keep their batteries manned in the event of anything untoward. Once they came abreast of the arriving Germans, the British and American ships wheeled about and surrounded the newcomers, one column on either side of the defeated ships. The Grand Fleet then escorted the High Seas Fleet into the Firth of Forth. All told, more than half of the world's capital ships were gathered in one place.

The German contingent included nine battle-ships, five battle cruisers, seven light cruisers, and forty-nine destroyers. Since the 1916 Battle of Jutland—the most significant naval engagement of the war—the British had hoped for a rematch in which they could overcome the disappointing results of that encounter. Now that the war was over, that hope was gone. One of the British officers cried because the surrender had deprived them of the opportunity to win on the high seas. As Captain

Beach put it, "This was not the way they had hoped to destroy the German High Seas Fleet."

On December 1, the ships that had comprised the Sixth Battle Squadron got up steam and departed the firth for the last time. As they passed the Grand Fleet, the Americans could hear ringing cheers from the men of the Royal Navy, and they reciprocated. The Marines presented arms, and American bands-men played "God Save the King." On the quarterdeck of the *Queen Elizabeth* stood Admiral Beatty; his band played "The Star-Spangled Banner." An honor guard of dreadnoughts—*Barham*, *Warspite*, *Valiant*,

and *Malaya*—escorted the Americans on their way. At Portland, the ships joined up with countrymen arriving in the *Utah*, *Oklahoma*, and *Arizona*, then sailed to Brest, France. President Wilson arrived from the United States on board the transport *George Washington* (escorted by the *Pennsylvania*) to take part in the postwar peace negotiations. The next day, the nine U.S. battleships departed for New York, where they would pass in review for the Secretary of the Navy. They arrived off Ambrose Light on Christmas Day, entered New York on the 26th, and anchored in the Hudson River off the west side

ABOVE: British and Americans gather on board the *New York*, flagship of the Sixth Battle Squadron. Left to right: Admiral David Beatty, Commander in Chief of the Grand Fleet; Rear Admiral Hugh Rodman, Commander, Sixth Battle Squadron; King George V; Admiral William S. Sims, Commander of U.S. Naval Forces in European Waters; and the Prince of Wales. LEFT: A detachment of Marines is pictured on board the *Nevada* or *Oklahoma*, around the time of World War I. Marine Corps detach-ments were standard crew members on every U.S. bat-tleship—except in 1968–69, when Secretary of Defense Robert McNamara kept Marines off the *New Jersey* as a cost-cutting move.

Sailors' Life Ashore

During the first two decades of the twentieth century, the New York Navy Yard in Brooklyn served as the Atlantic Fleet's major support facility. The area around the shipyard was also a haven for the men who came ashore on liberty. To be sure, they could find their way over to Manhattan or elsewhere in the metropolis (for the citizens that had once shunned sailors now felt a burst of patriotism and welcomed them), but temptation-seekers often had to look no farther than Sands Street, which stretched from the navy yard gate to the Brooklyn Bridge. Often run by ex-Navy men, a variety of businesses, such as a square-knot shop and a number of tattoo parlors, catered to the needs and wishes of the sailors. Whorehouses beckoned, and there, men could encounter women with names such as "Sands Street Sally" and "Dirty Gerty." They could find tailor shops run by characters such as "Battleship" Max Cohen. The bluejacket uniforms of the era were often loose-fitting and dowdy-looking. For a small fee, tailors could take them in or start from scratch and produce uniforms that had a jaunty look. Many ships did not tolerate the tailor-made uniforms, so enlisted men stored them in lockers ashore. Many a sailor had a portion of his pay directed to the Navy Savings Bank in Brooklyn.

Sands Street also had a YMCA which catered to the low budgets of sailors. Seaman George Russell Leymé of the *Arizona* often went there to get a haircut, go for a swim, or participate in other forms of recreation. At times, he even slept there to escape the rigors of shipboard life. However, if he got lucky and found a willing lady friend in Brooklyn's Prospect Park, he was more likely to spend the night in an inexpensive hotel. Because of his love of female companionship, Leymé awarded himself the honorary additional name of Irwin. This allowed him to say that his new initials, G.I.R.L., reflected his favorite interest at that stage in life.

In the summer of 1922, the *Delaware* made her way north to Boston during a midshipman training cruise. Like other ports frequented by the fleet, the city had a supply of sailor-oriented businesses just outside the navy yard. One such place was the Sailor's Haven, which provided inexpensive lodging. Each morning, the proprietor would sound reveille to wake the sailors and send them back to their ships in time for muster. The establishment was not entirely a safe haven, though. When an individual such as Fireman Charles Herget went in wearing a pair of good shoes, he took precautions before retiring. He rested the feet of his cot in the openings of the shoes to keep them from being pilfered as he slept, and he folded his money inside his neckerchief and tied it around his waist like a money belt.

Recreation also came in the form of watching and supporting the ship's sports teams. In 1922, the *Delaware*'s squad played for the Atlantic Fleet football championship in a game at the Polo Grounds, the ballpark in which the New York Giants and Yankees played that year's World Series. Two sailors, clad in peacoats because of the autumn weather, led the ship's mascot onto the field. It was a squealing pig wearing a blanket with the letters "DELA" sewn on the side. Whipping up enthusiasm among the crew was the ship's cheerleader, Tony Augustus, who weighed three hundred and sixty pounds (163kg) and had a waist measurement that was eight inches (20cm) greater than his height.

TOP: After arriving in New York City with a load of American troops from Europe, the *Louisiana* is shepherded by tugboats at the conclusion of World War I. She and other pre-dreadnoughts performed a valuable postwar service as troop transports. Shown here is a type of card that was popular at the end of the nineteenth century and beginning of the twentieth. The photos were mounted in pairs for viewing through a stereo device that gave something of a three-dimensional effect.
BOTTOM: As a band provides music, sailors of the *Arizona* pair off with each other and dance on deck in this scene early in the post-World War I period. At a time long before women became crew members of U.S. warships, this was an acceptable form of recreation.

of Manhattan. The German ships were transferred to Scapa Flow with their crews still on board. When the Paris Peace Conference decreed the following spring that the ships would be parceled out among the victorious Allies, the German sailors opened the seacocks and sent the High Seas Fleet to the floor of Scapa Flow. It was a defiant gesture on the part of the men who had spent most of the war in German ports, then spent still more months imprisoned on board their ships north of Scotland.

NEW PACIFIC FLEET

In the spring of 1919, Lieutenant McCrea had the watch when the *New York* was anchored in Hampton Roads, Virginia. He had just learned that his mentor, Rodman, was to become a four-star admiral and take command of a newly formed U.S. Pacific Fleet. McCrea offered his congratulations, and Rodman told the young officer that he needed him as his aide for personnel in his new job as fleet commander-in-

chief. McCrea said he wanted some time to think about it. Soon he met with the *New York*'s executive officer, Commander Charles Belknap, who said, "Listen, you don't have to take my advice, but let me tell you something. After every war, there is always a period of consolidation in the Navy, and people mark time for the most part. My suggestion to you is that if you can do so, mark time on the staff of the commander-in-chief of the Pacific Fleet."

McCrea took the job and was with Rodman when he hoisted his four-star flag on board the brand-new battleship *New Mexico* at the New York Navy Yard. She was the first American battleship with electric-drive propulsion. Rather than using the steam from her boilers to operate reciprocating engines or turbines, she fed it to generators that produced electricity, which in turn operated her main engines. The *New Mexico* and six other modern battleships—*Idaho*, *Mississippi*, *New York*, *Texas*, *Wyoming*, and *Arkansas*—made their way through the Panama Canal to the Pacific, finally settling into the warm-water port of Long Beach, California, as a new home base. Their immediate mission was to show the flag in West Coast ports; the long-range mission was to be available and ready in the event that the United States became involved in hostilities with Japan.

Secretary Daniels was in Long Beach in August to welcome the arriving fleet, as he had been at New York after the armistice. The battleships were a novelty on the West Coast, and cities up and down California lavished the crews with hospitality, including giving barbecues, providing free transportation, and handing out free tickets to all manner of entertainment. With the secretary along during the visits to coastal cities, frequent gun salutes were the order of the day. Ensign Schubert of the *Texas* wrote that "we burned enough powder in salutes to fight anybody's war." For the visit to San Francisco, the Navy provided a sentimental gesture. Daniels and President Wilson were on board the old *Oregon* to review the fleet.

The ships gradually settled into a routine of operation in and out of San Pedro as they conducted maneuvers and fired gunnery practice. And when they needed to, they went for overhaul and repairs to the Puget Sound Navy Yard in Bremerton, Washington, which would serve as the principal

West Coast battleship yard through World War II and beyond. For the ships home from the war, it was time for more modernization, for a warship is an evolutionary creature, adapting new equipment as it becomes available. In 1920, the *Texas* got new directors for her broadside guns and antiaircraft guns, new torpedo defense stations on her cage masts, a plotting room to improve the tracking of enemy ships and the aiming of the *Texas*' guns, updated radio equipment, and raised searchlight platforms. The Pacific Northwest offered a number of the same amenities as the East Coast, though Prohibition sent men to bootleggers for liquor refreshment. No longer could they take advantage of the tavern that had stood just outside the gate of the Bremerton shipyard before Prohibition. When a man was beginning his liberty, he saw the sign "First Chance" on one side of the building. When he returned hours later, he saw the legend "Last Chance" on the other side.

COAL-FIRED SHIPS

During that summer of 1920, Midshipman Fred Edwards took a summer training cruise on board the *Michigan*, traveling from Annapolis to Panama, where the ship took on coal, and then on to the West Coast. The business of coaling ship acquainted Edwards with a much-hated function that was a way of life in the Navy from the time steam replaced sail in the nineteenth century until the early twentieth, when oil became the preferred fuel. The fatiguing, all-hands job of taking on coal could last twenty-four hours or more. The only breaks were for sandwiches, coffee, and an occasional trip to the head. After the chore was finally completed, it was time for the men to clean themselves and their ship, for the coal dust permeated the whole ship, even invading closed lockers and putting black streaks on uniforms. Coal dust settled in ears, eyelashes, and various bodily crevices. Edwards once sent his mother some pictures. She didn't recognize her own son— he was entirely black, from shoes to hat. As Edwards joked many years later, "They always said that after you coaled ship, you had to watch it; you might be shaving somebody else's face by mistake."

Duty inside a turret was a revelation for many. In the early 1920s, Midshipman Ed Walker was on board the *Delaware* for a summer training cruise.

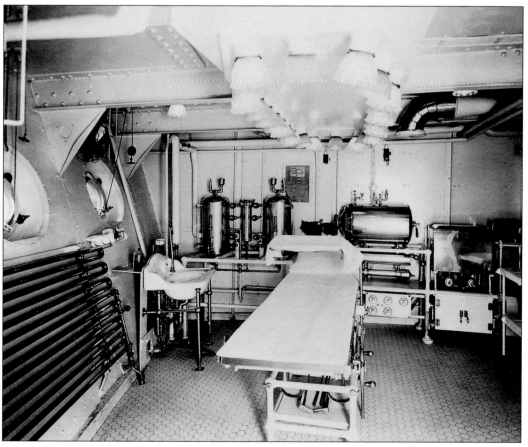

These pictures are from the then-recently commissioned *New Mexico*, which went into service in May 1918 as the first ship in her class. She was also the first equipped with electric drive, meaning her boilers drove generators that supplied power for the motors turning the propellers.
TOP: The wardroom, where the officers ate their meals and relaxed while off duty.
BOTTOM: The operating room in sickbay is pictured. The cluster of lights over the operating table enhances the surgeon's view of the patient. Surgical implements are sterilized with the apparatuses against the bulkhead behind the table.

The *Idaho*, commissioned March 24, 1919, at the New York Navy Yard, is shown here entering Dry Dock Two of Bremerton, Washington's Puget Sound Navy Yard on September 23 of the same year. In the six-month interim, the Navy's newest battleships had migrated from the Atlantic to constitute a new Pacific Fleet. Because of a switch in strategic interests, Japan was considered a potential enemy, so the most modern ships went to the West Coast. The shipyard at Bremerton would become a vital part of the logistic support infrastructure that provided maintenance and repair for West Coast battleships. The yard functioned in that capacity for the next eighty years, whether the battleships were in active service or mothballs. The last battleship to leave Bremerton was the *New Jersey*, which was towed away in 1999 to become a memorial in the state for which she was named.

As a loader, it was his job to push powder bags into the breech of a 12-inch (30cm) gun after the projectile had been rammed into place. Once four bags were in place, the gun captain closed the breech-block, forming an airtight seal at the rear end of the gun. Walker then moved aside and grabbed hold of a couple of handles to steady himself. When the turret fired, the projectile went spinning on its way at hundreds of feet per second. The breech of the gun recoiled to take up the shock, moving past Walker only a foot or so from his stomach. It provided a vivid demonstration of the force involved in sending a naval projectile on its way toward a target.

In January 1922, Charles Herget, fresh out of trade school, reported to the *Delaware*, in Hampton Roads. He was a fireman and as such qualified for a rate (pay grade) as petty officer because of his schooling. But the ship had a shortage of coal passers and an excess of men striking for ratings. (A rating was an occupational specialty for enlisted petty officers.) So he became a coal passer. Though the day was cold, the fireroom was steaming. Herget surveyed the situation, which included four boilers, each with four firebox doors. Piled on floor plates between the boilers, the black fuel was being steadily fed into the roaring fires by bare-chested men. Herget's assignment was to enter a storage bunker and shovel the coal out onto the floor plates so

others could feed it into the fiery furnaces. When he saw what duty would be like on board his first ship, he concluded that "hell can't be any worse than this."

Time passed and Herget got into the ship's routine. On a slow watch, when the need for shoveling wasn't constant, the men in the firerooms enjoyed night rations. That included the pleasures of mulligan stew, made by putting the ingredients (including pilfered potatoes and onions) on a coal scoop and sticking it into one of the boiler fireboxes to cook. Coffee was brewed in a sixteen-quart bucket, and the galley provided a few loaves of fresh bread. The camaraderie of the firemen was heightened by eating food that came from somewhere other than the routine division mess; such chow often seemed to taste a little bit better.

WORLD NAVAL DISARMAMENT

By the time Herget reached his ship, deliberations were already under way in Washington, D.C., to seal her fate. President Warren Harding took office in 1921 with a pledge to restore "normalcy" after the disruption caused by "the war to end all wars." As a result, Secretary of State Charles Evans Hughes convened an international naval disarmament conference in late 1921. Already, criticism of battleships had risen in other quarters. Brigadier General Billy

LEFT: Late in World War I and in the following few years, U.S. battleships were fitted with take-off platforms on their turrets. They could thus launch airplanes that could go higher and fly farther than the tethered balloons. Shown here is a light plane being hoisted aboard the *Oklahoma*. Launched from the wooden platform atop the turret and 14-inch (36cm) guns at the right, it will fly a spotting mission and then land at Guantánamo, Cuba. A tugboat will then deliver it back to the ship so the process can be repeated. By the mid-1920s, battleships were equipped with catapults to launch the planes, and the planes themselves had pontoons so they could land on water.

RIGHT: Another of the Burnell Poole shots of the *Nevada* at Queenstown, Ireland, this was taken from a kite balloon tethered to the ship by a cable that can be seen angling upward from near turret three. The balloons provided a higher vantage point for spotting the fall of shot; without them, spotters used the foretop and maintop on the ship's masts. There were drawbacks to the balloons, though, as they were susceptible to lightning.

LEFT: No longer useful as a battleship, the *Illinois* was loaned to the New York Naval Militia in 1921 for training purposes. Following the Washington Naval Treaty, she was fitted out at the New York Navy Yard as a floating armory, which is how she is depicted here. The name "Illinois" is still visible on the stern portion of her hull. In January 1941, she was renamed *Prairie State* so a new battleship, BB-66, could become *Illinois*. As it happened, shifting priorities in World War II precluded the completion of the new ship, but the *Prairie State* continued on as a Naval Reserve training ship until 1955. She was scrapped the following year.
BELOW: A shower of white phosphorus covers the *Alabama*, one of the *Illinois'* sister ships, after a direct hit by a 100-pound bomb from the Army Air Service plane flying above. The bombing took place on September 23, 1921, in the Chesapeake Bay, with Brigadier General Billy Mitchell demonstrating that warships were vulnerable to aerial bombing.

Mitchell of the Army Air Service had bombed old battleships to demonstrate their vulnerability to aerial attack. The diplomats added their own form of attack on capital ships.

The Washington Naval Treaty of 1922 had a severe impact on the U.S. Navy's warship plans. Along with the older ships that were scrapped, including Herget's *Delaware*, other victims of the treaty were ships that were partially completed. Of the projected class of battle cruisers, the *Lexington* and *Saratoga* were converted to the Navy's first large aircraft carriers. The rest were broken up, though parts of them were recycled.

Though the treaty required scrapping a number of ships, it did permit the United States to complete two battleships then under construction, *Colorado* and *West Virginia*. Ensign Fred Edwards was assigned to the latter. He joined her at the New York Navy Yard, where workmen installed fire control equipment and the associated cables. While his new ship was being beefed up, he saw the old *Illinois* going in the other direction. She had been commissioned in 1901, but the new treaty specified that she be demilitarized. As Edwards watched, men removed her armor and put it onto the nearby dock. The superstructure was replaced with a barn-like wooden house built atop the steel hull. She then became a barracks ship and training vessel, and served in that capacity for many years for the New York state naval militia. On the pier next to the *Illinois* were armor and turret sections intended for two ships of the South Dakota class whose construction had

been stopped in the early stages. Though the objective was peace, Edwards was saddened to watch workmen with cutting torches as they dismembered the recently built hulls before they could be turned into battleships.

The scrapping process played out to a most curious end. By the terms of the treaty, the Navy was obligated to dispose of the last of the incomplete battleships by February 17, 1925. Though the treaty permitted completion of two of her sisters, the *Washington* could not be finished. She had been started in 1919 and launched in September 1921, shortly before the disarmament conference. Work on the ship, which was then more than three-quarters completed, stopped on February 8, two days after the signing of the Washington Treaty. She was scheduled to serve as a target for gunfire to test the strength of her armor and the protection it afforded. All this did not sit well with William B. Shearer, a civilian who had previously worked for the Navy. He argued that destroying the *Washington* rather than building her to completion would weaken the U.S. Navy in relation to the British and the Japanese. In November 1924, Shearer, acting as a citizen and taxpayer, filed suit in court in Washington, D.C., to save the unfinished battleship. The court pointed out that it had no jurisdiction over the subject, and dismissed Shearer's case. A subsequent appeal upheld that decision.

The efforts of a patriotic citizen, William Shearer, had failed to overturn the results of an international tribunal that had agreed to its own vision of how best to preserve world peace. And so the *Washington* was towed to a spot off the Virginia Capes. For a time, she was a test ship to see the effects of torpedoes and aerial bombs. On November 25, it was time for 14-inch (36cm) gunfire from the battleship *Texas* to finish the job. She unleashed a ten-gun salvo, then a boat took a party aboard to measure the damage and take photos. An hour later another salvo found the mark, and the *Texas* steamed to a spot a mile away to watch the end. The collection of metal, once intended to become a battleship, now listed and took on water through holes punched into her hull. Slowly she settled, then the bow lurched and made a roar as it pointed downward. The slender tail of the *Washington* pointed upward and then descended out of sight. On board the *Texas,* a bugler played "Taps" in salute.

RIGHT: Designated BB-47, this ship was to have been the USS *Washington,* a sister ship of the *Colorado, Maryland,* and *West Virginia.* Instead, her construction was halted in February 1922 after completion of the Washington Treaty on naval disarmament. With battleship construction incomplete, she was converted to a target ship. The unfinished hull is shown here being towed to sea.
BOTTOM, LEFT AND RIGHT: Once safely offshore, the partially constructed vessel was subjected to a barrage of bombs, torpedoes, and naval gunfire, before finally being sunk. The *Texas* steams nearby in the background.

Chapter Four
PEACETIME INTERLUDE

The 1920s brought the nation a yearning for peace and domestic order. In addition, a newly ratified constitutional amendment and its enabling legislation prevented the manufacture, transportation, and sale of alcoholic beverages. Prohibition was generally unpopular and widely flouted. On board the *Utah*, for instance, was a boatswain's mate who did his job well and professionally, but who had a weakness for drink. Several times he

ABOVE: On Easter morning 1937, aboard the fleet flagship *Pennsylvania*, these four salty-looking sailors pose with their boatswain's calls, preparing to pass the word to the ship's crew over the general announcing system. At a time when warships operated many boats, these men were rated as coxswains. The progression went from seaman first class to coxswain to boatswain's mate second class. Following World War II, the coxswain rate was replaced by boatswain's mate third class.
OPPOSITE PAGE: The USS *New York*, stripped of her old cage-mast superstructure, is shown on April 10, 1927 while undergoing modernization at the Norfolk Navy Yard. The U.S. Navy commissioned no new battleships between 1923 and 1941, so rebuilding the older ships was the only way to upgrade the fleet. The Navy's main Battle Force operated on the West Coast during the 1920s and 1930s. The modernization work, including conversion from coal to oil for some of the ships, was done on the East Coast to distribute the workload among the various navy yards.

had been a chief petty officer, and several times he had been demoted. One especially flagrant case of drunkenness took him all the way down to seaman. He was an older man by then, and looked particularly out of place in a sailor suit.

Generally, such punishment was dealt out to individuals who caused injury or property damage. If a sailor could get back to the ship and get up to do his job, drinking was tolerated. And when the *Utah* was in the Caribbean, prohibition didn't apply, so the men could drink legally. Some creative individuals decided to take full advantage of this fact. One night, the ship was in Guantánamo Bay, Cuba, while a local dealer was loading his boat with some three hundred gallons (1,136L) of rum and perhaps two hundred quarts (189L) of various whiskeys and liqueurs. The dealer brought his boat under the bow of the battleship at a time when he knew that a sympathetic lieutenant was on watch. Through a port-

hole descended a line with a hook attached; the liquid cargo was reeled in and hidden on board ship. The contraband was then sneaked ashore once the ship reached the States. One story, perhaps apocryphal, illustrates the rather cavalier attitude many had toward Prohibition. Upon arriving in Norfolk one day in the late 1920s, an executive officer warned the crew of the *New York*: "We're going to have an inspection tomorrow. The boats will run all night tonight. I don't want any liquor found on this ship tomorrow." The crew did what they had to do to avoid detection.

FEMALE STOWAWAY

In March 1924, the *Arizona* stopped at New York City and opened the ship to the public for general visiting. At some point during the ship's stay in the metropolis, an attractive nineteen-year-old brunette named Madeline Blair stowed away. She either

remained on board during a visiting day or sneaked aboard disguised as a sailor. She apparently planned to ride the ship all the way to southern California when the *Arizona* returned to her homeport of San Pedro. She hid out in a gun turret for a time and later in the ship's engineering spaces. Several crewmen smuggled food to her, and someone stole Seaman Melvin Foulds's seabag to provide uniforms for the young woman. Blair rewarded the men with regular sexual favors.

After a time, the stowaway became more brazen and went out at night to sit on a turret top and watch silent movies that were projected on the ship's fantail. One evening, a sailor was sitting next to her and wanted a match to light a cigarette. Keeping his eyes on the screen, he reached over to the breast pocket of the uniform worn by the person sitting next to him. He quickly jerked his hand back and later reported, "What I grabbed hold of didn't belong to no man." A while afterward, when the ship was anchored in the Panama Canal Zone, one of the *Arizona's* radiomen told shipmates that he had just seen a girl with whom he had danced when the ship was in New York. Chief Radioman Schuyler Ford overheard the remark and reported it to the officer of the deck. At 3:45 A.M., the ship's master-at-arms found Blair in her hiding place. Incredibly, she had been on board for nearly a month. She was ejected from the ship and taken ashore by boat, swearing almost constantly during the forty-five-minute boat ride. She was then sent back to New York by commercial ship.

Retribution was harsh for the sailors who had conspired to hide her and provide her food and clothing. Pictures found in Blair's purse gave away

some of them. All told, twenty-three crewmen were tried by court-martial, found guilty, and sent to prison; the longest sentence was ten years. Chief Ford retired soon afterward. Disgruntled former shipmates threatened his life, and for years he carried a pistol to protect himself.

GUNNERY PRACTICE

During gunnery practice in that era, crewmen were often sent to other ships as independent observers to watch and measure the competitions between ships. On June 12, 1924, Ensign George Bauernschmidt of the *New Mexico* was an observer on board sister ship *Mississippi*. As he took measurements on the roll and pitch of the ship, an unusual cloud of smoke rose from the *Mississippi*'s turret two, the high turret forward. The turret, which was trained around to starboard, suddenly swung to port and stopped; greenish-yellow gas, produced by burning powder, escaped from its openings. Then Bauernschmidt heard the ship's bugler sound fire call with "an inspired bit of bugle-blowing." When the turret crew had pushed powder bags into the open breech of a 14-inch (36cm) gun, there was, unfortunately, a still-burning remnant of a silk powder bag from the previous firing of the gun inside. The ember set off the new powder in a thunderous explosion that killed four dozen men. It was the single worst battleship tragedy of the inter-war period. Typically, compressed air was blown into the gun to eject such embers, but in this case, it didn't work. Some theorized that wind coming down the barrel had prevented the gun from being completely cleared. Others suspected that the gun captain had felt pressure to fire rapidly in that day's target practice and hadn't been careful enough in checking for a clear bore. In his final moments of life, Lieutenant Junior Grade Thomas Zellars pulled the lever that activated the sprinkler system in the turret. The water wet down the powder that was in the hoist, preventing the flare-back from spreading downward. Bodies in the turret jammed the hatch at the bottom rear, so a crew member used an acetylene torch to burn off the hatch cover. Inside were the suffocated crew members, a few of whom were burned. Shipmates went in to pull out the bodies. As they did so, the hand of one dead man brushed against the firing switch for a gun that was still loaded at the

THIS PAGE: One of the effects of the 1922 Washington Treaty on naval disarmament was the scrapping of a number of battleships, both those already existing and those that had been planned. The painting (ABOVE) depicts what the ships of the South Dakota (BB-49) class would have looked like. The ships were slated to become the *South Dakota, Indiana, Montana, North Carolina, Iowa,* and *Massachusetts,* though all were scrapped prior to completion. Several older ships were also scrapped because of the treaty, including the U.S. Navy's first two dreadnought-type battleships, little more than a dozen years old. Shown at the Philadelphia Navy Yard are the *Michigan* (TOP RIGHT) on October 26, 1923, and the *South Carolina* (RIGHT) on October 2, 1924.

time of the explosion. Since the firing circuit was still energized, that movement closed the circuit and sent a 14-inch (36cm) projectile on its way, just as if it had been fired on purpose. Fortunately, the turret was on a safe bearing, and the projectile fell harmlessly at sea. The disaster hit the fleet hard. The men of the *Mississippi* were mourned in a mass funeral in Long Beach, and the fleet was once again reminded that living and working on board a warship, surrounded by thousands of tons of explosives, was an inherently dangerous business.

Getting battleship projectiles on target improved over the years as fire control systems became more and more sophisticated. In the spring of 1924, Ensign Fred Edwards reported to the *Nevada* in the Pacific. By later standards, the equipment on board the *Nevada* was crude, but it was state-of-the-art for the time. Battleships were now equipped with plotting rooms, which were reached by climbing down a ladder that was vertical rather than slanted. The ladder also afforded the only means of escape from the compartment if the ship took on water down below. Fire control men still

made their readings from optical range finders in the superstructure, that is, the portion of the ship above the main deck. The range finder consisted of a horizontal tube with an arrangement of lenses and prisms at the end. Using the same principle used to focus a camera, the operator determined the range to the target, a figure that constantly changed as the target moved. The plotting room crew used the figures to plot the course of the target and to calculate where next to shoot. They then transmitted an electrical signal to the ship's turrets as to the range and bearing of the target. This signal was backed up by the same message delivered over the internal telephone system.

The idea was that the first salvo sent toward the target should straddle it, some projectiles being long, some short. Then spotters, either in the tops of the masts or aloft in airplanes, would call down corrections in terms of both range and azimuth to redirect the guns. Once the guns had been coached onto the target, the turrets could pump out the rounds. Depending on how far away the target was and how fast the loading crews were, it was possible for a tur-

LEFT: In their intended use, U.S. battleships were expected to steam forth in a great battle line and engage in long-range gunnery duels with the enemy; during the period between the wars, they often held exercises doing just that. Here, ships steam in column during maneuvers near Panama in 1923.
BOTTOM: This photograph of battle practice in the early 1920s features, from left to right, the *West Virginia*, *Maryland*, *Colorado*, and *Tennessee*. These ships, plus the *California*, comprised the "Big Five," so called because they were similar in appearance and were the last five completed before the disarmament treaty embargo took effect. Since they were the newest, they did not undergo the extensive modernization work in the 1920s and 1930s that was the norm for older battleships.

ret to have more than one salvo in the air at a time. When ships were steaming in column, their view of the target was sometimes fouled by their own gun smoke. To get around this, when one ship spotted the target, it displayed the range and bearing on a range clock, positioned high in the superstructure, to signal to those ahead and astern of her.

FUTURE CODE BREAKER

That same spring, Ensign Thomas H. Dyer graduated from the Naval Academy in the class of 1924. He and several friends had worked together on the academy's yearbook and decided to stay together as shipmates. They applied for duty in the *New Mexico* and received it. That choice was the first in a chain of events that would have far-reaching effects for Dyer—and for the nation—nearly twenty years later. Once he reported to the ship, an ensign who was a year senior to Dyer asked for volunteers to serve in the ship's communications department. Dyer had been leaning toward a gunnery post, but instead decided to get in with the radio gang so he could learn something about vacuum tubes, which were at the heart of radio in those days.

In faraway Washington, D.C., Lieutenant Laurence Safford in the research division of the Navy Department created encrypted crossword puzzles for the communication bulletin that was circulated in the fleet. Those who solved the puzzles were encouraged to send their answers to Washington. Tommy Dyer did so for a couple of years and was so good at solving the puzzles that in 1927 he was ordered to Washington for training in code breaking. Subsequently, he became a specialist in that discipline and was assigned to Pearl Harbor to work with the fleet intelligence unit there. In 1942, the Pearl Harbor code breakers, with Dyer foremost among them, decoded Japanese radio messages that led to a standoff in the Battle of the Coral Sea and a tide-turning victory in the Battle of Midway. Dyer's path toward that monumental success began with his decision to join the radio gang of the *New Mexico* in 1924.

CRUISE TO AUSTRALASIA

For the most part, the U.S. Fleet was concentrated in West Coast ports in the 1920s and 1930s. The battleships and aircraft carriers were based in the home

port of Long Beach, California. Their repair schedules took them to the navy yard at Bremerton, Washington, and they made occasional forays to Hawaii and the East Coast. On the West Coast, they continued the sort of port visits—"flower shows," as they were called—that Admiral Rodman had inaugurated when he established the Pacific Fleet in 1919. A huge exception to the fleet routine came in 1925 when the bulk of the ships followed up a war game around Hawaii by making a voyage to Samoa, Australia, and New Zealand. It would be the American fleet's longest deployment in the more than twenty years between the world wars. It was a test of the ships' ability to operate on a sustained basis away from normal facilities, and in that sense resembled the cruise of the Great White Fleet. The major difference was that the ships' fuel had switched from coal to oil. As a nice added touch, Admiral Rodman, by now retired, made the cruise as a passenger.

Before the ships set out from San Francisco, the Australian Commissioner was in that city to tell the American naval officers what to expect in terms of friendly hospitality when they reached his country: "When your young men encounter Australia's young ladies in Sydney or Melbourne, they will be taken right to their bosoms, and I mean that literally as well as figuratively. Permit me to suggest, gentlemen, that you advise your men accordingly."

Ensign Tommy Dyer of the *New Mexico* observed a different kind of hospitality when his ship arrived in Sydney. One day, he and a couple of other junior officers went to a local cricket ground to watch a demonstration put on by schoolchildren. They figured they would have a nice, quiet afternoon. The officers, who had come from a nation where Prohibition was the law of the land, happened across an Australian man who was handing out tickets for free drinks. He had a roll of tickets big enough to choke a horse and asked, "Do you think you can keep one down?" They allowed as how they thought they could and were shown to the longest bar Dyer ever saw, before or after. After they'd had a drink and returned to watch the children's program, the man offered each another ticket. The pattern of drinking and watching went on for quite a while, to the point that Dyer concluded, "That quiet afternoon was about the roughest afternoon any of us had

had." For the grand finale of the program, the ten thousand children aligned themselves in giant patterns on the cricket ground, but the effort was wasted on Dyer, whose head was whirling with alcohol-altered images.

Captain Harris Laning was skipper of the *Pennsylvania* during the long voyage. As a lieutenant, he had been to the Far East in 1908 during the cruise of the Great White Fleet. During the 1925 trip, Laning was reminded of an advantage of shipboard living that he had taken for granted—central heating. The "Pennsy" was in Australia in July—the Southern Hemisphere winter—and many of the local homes were heated by fireplaces. He gave a lunch in his shipboard cabin for the local hospitality committee. The guests arrived at 11:00 A.M., enjoyed lunch, and were still around at 7:00 P.M. When he politely excused himself to dress for dinner, one of the guests said, "You know, Captain, we realize as well as you do that we should have left this ship hours ago, but we were all warm for the first time this winter and decided to make the most of it."

In the same year as the cruise, Ensign Ed Walker reported to the *Utah*, a ship commissioned in 1911 as a coal burner, now serving on the East Coast. As a midshipman, he'd had to load coal and particularly disliked the powdery Welsh coal. Even with a gauze mask over his face, he felt nearly smothered. In the *Utah*, he witnessed the end of an era. After his one-year tour of duty, she went into a shipyard for conversion to oil. Out came twelve coal-burning boilers, and in went four that burned oil. The boilers were available because of the 1922 naval disarmament agreement. They had been intended for one of the planned battle cruisers whose construction was cancelled by the treaty. The old coal bunkers were replaced by storage tanks for oil, which was pumped aboard through hoses and then piped automatically into boilers. No longer was it necessary for men to handle coal; to pitch it into bunkers, then take it out again and pitch it into the fiery furnaces of the boilers. The *Utah*, which was subsequently converted to a target ship for bombing practice, capsized during the Japanese attack on Pearl Harbor and remains there to this day as a memorial to her crew members. Still on board are those old battle cruiser boilers.

OPPOSITE TOP: Mindful of the gas warfare that had been part of World War I, members of the crew of this 5-inch (13cm) gun wear gas masks during a loading drill on board the *California*. The men at left are holding projectiles and those at right have the powder charges. The man at right is preparing to take a powder bag out of its storage can.

OPPOSITE BOTTOM: Crewmen of the *Oklahoma* pose with containers of small arms ammunition, which was useful in a period when sailors still trained as potential members of landing parties. Barely seen in the background is part of one of the *Oklahoma's* cage masts.

RIGHT: The *Oklahoma* is pictured here in August 1929, just after her rebuilding was completed at the Philadelphia Navy Yard. In place of the former cage masts are much sturdier tripod masts, crowned by the three-story foretop and maintop. The ship has been widened by the addition of metal "blisters" outside the skin of the ship to provide waterline protection against torpedoes. Japanese torpedoes overwhelmed the blisters at Pearl Harbor, however, and the ship capsized there in 1941. In this photo, a spare conning tower can be seen on the dock, near the automobiles.

AIRCRAFT CARRIERS

Though battleships were still the undisputed queens of the fleet, the Navy was experimenting in the 1920s with a new type of ship, the aircraft carrier. The USS *Jupiter*, which had been built as a collier before World War I, became an aircraft carrier when a flight deck replaced her coal derricks. In March 1922, she was recommissioned as a carrier and now carried the name *Langley* in honor of aviation pioneer Samuel P. Langley. The 1922 disarmament treaty permitted the U.S. Navy to convert two of its battle cruisers—then under construction—into aircraft carriers. These were the *Lexington* and *Saratoga*, which were commissioned in 1927 and were much larger and more capable than the *Langley*.

Those two ships did much to develop the carrier doctrine that proved so effective in the next war. Even so, many in the battleship Navy believed that aircraft carriers had only a subordinate role of scouting and spotting the fall of shot for the big-gun ships. Ensign Herb Riley served in the *New Mexico* following graduation from the Naval Academy in 1927. While on board, he ran the range keeper, an analog computer in the plotting room, and became an effective member of the fire control team. Still, he yearned to become an aviator, so he put in an application for flight training. His department head, Lieutenant Commander William H.P. "Spike" Blandy, did his best to put obstacles in his way, but Riley persisted and finally got orders to commence pilot training. When he left, Blandy told him that aviation would never go anywhere, adding, "You're just a natural to go into the Gun Club, and that's the guts of the Navy anyhow. I just hate to see you throwing your career down the drain that way. But if you've got to go, you've got to go."

The sequel came nearly twenty years later, when Blandy, then a vice admiral, was in command of Joint Task Force One, which was to conduct atomic bomb tests at Bikini Atoll to determine warships' ability to withstand the explosions. Riley, who by then had commanded an escort aircraft carrier at the end of World War II, was surprised to learn that he had been chosen by Blandy to be on his staff. When he went to talk to the admiral, who greeted him cordially, he asked why he had been chosen,

especially since Blandy had told him years before that he was throwing his career away by leaving the battleship fleet. The admiral replied, "I sent over to the aviation side of personnel and told them I wanted them to give me ten names of the top captains they could pick in naval aviation. I got ten names, and yours was the only damned one on the list that I recognized." Riley eventually retired as a vice admiral himself.

SHIPBOARD LIVING CONDITIONS

As a result of the London Naval Disarmament Conference of 1930, the United States agreed to demilitarize two more of its battleships, the *Utah* and *Wyoming*. Both remained on the Navy register, serving primarily as training ships. In the years to come, they would provide summer training for midshipmen and gunnery training for a variety of individuals. But they would no longer be battleships. That left the *Arkansas*, a sister ship of the Wyoming, as the oldest active battleship. Though nearly twenty years old by that point, the "Arky" still had a good deal of life left in her, and went on to serve through the end of World War II. Because no new battleships had been commissioned since the early 1920s, the living conditions on board the *Arkansas* were fairly typical of those in other battleships of the U.S. Fleet. They were still a long way from the "habitability" that is so emphasized in today's Navy.

Midshipman Ed Batcheller found out just what living conditions were like when he reported to the *Arkansas* for a Naval Academy training cruise in the summer of 1931. During the training, the midshipmen, who were future officers, were taught to appreciate the hardships endured by junior enlisted men by living like them. Each sailor and midshipman was assigned a hammock and a pair of hooks from which to hang it. The hooks were attached to the overhead, or ceiling, in various locations scattered throughout the ship. The hammocks were suspended quite a distance above the deck. It was something of an acquired skill to be able to climb up into the hammock and then maintain one's balance. In the process of gaining that skill, one was likely to find himself falling to the hard steel deck several times before mastering it. When reveille sounded in the morning, each man had to take down his hammock, roll it up with the bedding inside, and stow it in a bin known as a hammock netting. In the evening, he reversed the process.

Often the same compartment served for both eating and sleeping. U-shaped brackets in the overhead were used to store the ten-man mess tables and their accompanying benches when they were not in use. The tables and benches had fold-up legs to facilitate their overhead storage. Unlike today's warships, which have cafeteria-style serving lines, the battleships in the pre–World War II period had central galleys in which the food was cooked; it was then carried to the living compartment in stacked tureens.

Sailors washed and went to the toilet in rooms known as heads, a holdover from sailing ship days when sanitary facilities were in the bow of a ship. In the case of the *Arkansas*, the head for midshipmen was on a lower deck, all the way at the stern. Toilets consisted of inclined troughs divided into stalls by sheet metal partitions. Privacy was not a consideration. The flushing system pumped seawater in at the high end of the trough and then pumped it overboard from the lower end. Sailors had used that arrangement from time immemorial to play a trick on their shipmates. They would wad up some toilet paper, put it into the trough at the high end, and set it on fire. As it made its passage, sailors literally got hot seats and rose involuntarily, one at a time—like pistons in an engine.

Produced by distilling seawater in evaporators, fresh water was a precious commodity. Each sailor and midshipman had his own two-and-a-half-gallon (9.5L) bucket, and he was issued one bucketful of fresh water a day. It had to serve his needs, except for drinking water, for the entire day. He used it for brushing teeth, shaving, and washing his body. Saltwater showers were available, but were less desirable than washing with fresh water. If all those functions didn't use up the water, what was left over could be used to wash his clothes. He could heat the water by using a nozzle from an auxiliary steam drain line. The living was far from luxurious by today's standards, but in many cases the security of a bed, running water, and three meals a day provided a better lifestyle than many Navy men had known while living on farms in an America wracked by the Depression.

OPPOSITE TOP: In the mid-1920s, chief petty officers on board the *Colorado* study an assignment from a Navy training course in personnel management. Some appear genuinely interested; others less so.
OPPOSITE BOTTOM: These crew members of the *California* are in a much more carefree atmosphere during swim call. To the left of the crane near the foremast, a man is in the midst of a high dive. Some shipmates watch from vantage points on deck, while others stand atop the waterline armor belt. Lines suspended down the side of the ship are an aid to men coming out of the water. Barely visible near the smokestacks is a pontoon plane bearing the legend "Battle Fleet," of which the *California* was flagship. Her nickname in the fleet was "Prune Barge."

TOP LEFT: The New Mexico–class ships underwent the most radical reconstruction between the wars. Here, the *Mississippi* sits in New York's Hudson River in 1918, the year after she was commissioned.
TOP RIGHT: The *Mississippi* is shown here on May 12, 1933, during her rebuilding at the Norfolk Navy Yard.
LEFT: "Missy" emerges at Norfolk on September 1, 1933, upon completion of her "makeover." She does not have the high spotting tops of the older ships, as it was expected that all gunfire spotting would be done by aircraft. She sports airplane catapults on the fantail and atop turret three.

FLEET FLAGSHIP

When Radioman Al Pelletier served on board the fleet flagship *Pennsylvania* in the early 1930s, he was impressed by the majesty of the great battleships as they steamed together in battle formation. The sense of battleships' majesty was magnified by the pomp and circumstance on board these great warships on the occasion of a special ceremony. For Pelletier, the ultimate in this regard came on June 10, 1933, when Admiral David Sellers relieved Admiral Richard H. Leigh as Commander-in-Chief of the entire U.S. Fleet on board the flagship *Pennsylvania*. Officers and enlisted men were outfitted in their dress blue uniforms. For the officers, this meant cocked hats, long frock coats, epaulettes, and swords. These impressive uniforms, throwbacks to an earlier age, were abandoned when war arrived several years later.

A bugler called the crew to quarters and sailors assumed their positions in straight rows on the polished teakwood decks. (The wooden planks, which were laid atop steel decks, were also a throwback to the age of sail, but this anachronism remained until the very end of the battleship era in 1992.) Ships in the harbor fired multi-gun salutes to the admirals, and the *Pennsylvania* answered, gun for gun, with her own saluting battery. Admiral Leigh made a short speech, and his voice broke as he asked God to bless the men of the fleet that he would no longer command. His personal flag, four white stars on a blue background, was hauled down, and a signalman hoisted the four-star flag of his successor. As the ceremony unfolded, the aft turret and an airplane catapult were crammed with newsreel cameramen and sound technicians, who recorded the event for later viewing in movie theaters worldwide. A radioman first class stood next to Al Pelletier and exclaimed, "After fourteen years in the Navy, I finally had the chance to see this event. It was worth waiting for." The petty officer's sense of awe is difficult to imagine in today's more cynical world.

The following year, the fleet made a trip to the East Coast. On the way, it passed through the Panama Canal, one ship after another, to test the canal's readiness to transfer many ships from one ocean to the other in a short period of time. Once in the Atlantic, the warships proceeded to New York City to be reviewed by the Navy-minded President Franklin D. Roosevelt, who had taken office in 1933. The crews went to even greater effort than usual to make sure their ships sparkled for the event. Roosevelt was on board the heavy cruiser *Indianapolis* to review the ships as they passed by him one by one; the cruiser *Louisville* was nearby. At the head of the parade was the *Pennsylvania*. As she came abreast of Roosevelt, the fleet flagship roared out a twenty-one gun salute, one round at a time, and the band played the national anthem. Then the *Pennsylvania* hauled out smartly and took up position alongside the *Louisville*. The parade filed past, led by the aircraft carriers *Lexington* and *Saratoga*, with the rest of the battleships coming along soon behind. On board the great dreadnoughts, crews manned the rails topside to honor the president. They were covered by smoke as their saluting batteries barked out the rounds. The fleet then moved in to anchor in the Hudson River, and the men of the fleet set off to enjoy the great city of New York.

Radioman Al Pelletier called New York City "a sailor's dream." He and a friend went to the top of the Empire State Building, walked around Times Square, and attended baseball games. First, they saw the New York Giants host their rivals, the Brooklyn Dodgers, at the Polo Grounds in Harlem. When the Yankees returned from a road trip, the visitors went to Yankee Stadium for a game where they saw Babe Ruth strike out, eliciting a great roar from the crowd; next time up, he hit a home run, and the response was even louder. As a special treat, Navy men in uniform were admitted to the ballparks without having to pay admission; all it cost was ten cents for city tax. In fact, the city was so hospitable that the sailors had a hard time paying anywhere. Free theater tickets were readily available, and the girls who took tours of the ship returned the favor by going on dates with the men afterward. It was a most enjoyable compensation for the long days and nights at sea.

In the autumn of 1934, the *Pennsylvania* was involved in short-range battle practice with her 14-inch (36cm) guns. Lieutenant Thomas Dyer was turret officer during the firing and was manning his station in the turret booth, aft of the gun room. As one of the guns was being loaded in number-three turret, a powder bag broke open, spilling some of its contents onto the deck. (In a sense, "powder" is a mis-

nomer, because it was not actually powdery, but in the form of cylindrical pellets.) In the rigid safety regulations of the period, such an accident was to be followed by the command, "Silence." Everyone was then supposed to freeze until the powder was picked up and properly disposed of. In this case, a turret captain, who was an enlisted man, just picked up a pillow case, put the pellets into it, put the pillow case into the breech of the gun, closed the breech, and fired. Though this was a fairly common practice, it was incautious, since a cotton pillow case would not necessarily disintegrate completely, as the silk powder bags were designed to do. A burning ember might be left behind and ignite the powder charges when they were inserted for the next round. In the investigation that followed, Dyer was deemed not culpable, but he was relieved of his turret duty and reassigned to the post of ship's secretary. Safety was not to be trifled with when handling high explosives.

ON BOARD THE NEVADA

In the mid-1930s, Lieutenant George Bauernschmidt was the electrical officer on board the *Nevada*. His predecessor told him the loudspeaker system in the officers' wardroom was inoperative, and he had been unable to find the problem. Bauernschmidt, too, was unable to fix the system when he took over. He happened to have the shipboard duty on New Year's Eve. At the stroke of midnight, as he sat in the wardroom, he heard a click in the loudspeaker. Then, coming through clearly, he heard, "Happy New Year, you sons of bitches." He heard another click, and the system never worked again. Some clever fellow knew what was wrong with the system, but wouldn't tell. The ship had to put in a whole new wiring system at the next overhaul.

During a shipyard period that same year, the *Nevada* acquired a machine gun platform, known as a "birdbath" because of its shape, on the maintop. The maintop, which sat on the tripod mainmast, was a three-story house-like structure whose occupants observed and controlled shipboard gunnery. The new machine gun platform provided a slight advance in antiaircraft capability, though the ships of the fleet were woefully inadequate in that regard. As the *Nevada* proceeded through the Panama Canal to return to her home port, she encountered a merchant ship of Japanese registry. Bauernschmidt

LEFT: A noonday band concert is held around 1930 on board what was then the newest battleship in the fleet, the *West Virginia*. As part of that era's predilection to assign the battleships nicknames, she was known as "Weevee" because of her initials. A 5-inch (13cm)/51-caliber broadside gun is prominent in the photo. Designed for horizontal fire against enemy surface targets, it had no shield to protect the gun crew. When the *West Virginia* received an extensive reconstruction following damage at Pearl Harbor (see pages 92–93), she was equipped with enclosed dual-purpose 5-inch (13cm)/38-caliber gun mounts that could fire at both air and surface targets.
BOTTOM: Men of the *Pennsylvania* scrub the ship's wooden deck during field day in the late 1920s. The ships in the background still sport cage masts.

71

watched as an officer came out on deck and, observing the changed appearance of the maintop, went to get a camera so he could take pictures of it. It struck Bauernschmidt that a merchant marine officer was apparently sufficiently navy-wise to recognize a change in the *Nevada*'s military characteristics and was dedicated enough to take pictures for intelligence purposes.

A NEWCOMER'S EXPERIENCES

Reporting aboard a battleship was often a daunting experience for a young sailor, who became a junior citizen in a floating city. So it was for seventeen-year-old Herb O'Quin when he reported to the *Maryland* in 1936. Initially, he reported to the X division, which was an indoctrination outfit. While learning the ways of their seagoing home, new sailors spent a few days each in various parts of the ship, often performing menial chores such as swabbing decks, cleaning bilges, and shining the brass "bright work" that was often the mark of a smart ship.

O'Quin had a slight relationship with one of the *Maryland*'s pilots and so decided he'd like to get into the ship's aviation division. But when it came time for assignments, the assistant navigator pointed to O'Quin after inspection one Saturday and said,

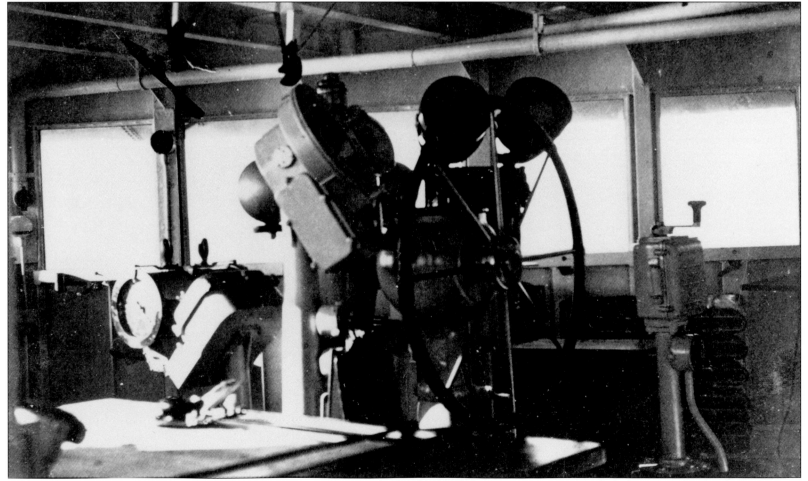

"You, get your gear and move it down to the N division compartment." O'Quin protested the assignment, whereupon the officer curled his lip, repeated what he had said, and walked away. The chief petty officer who was in charge of the X division turned to the unhappy sailor and said, "Do as you are told and keep your mouth shut." So it was that O'Quin became a member of the navigation gang and went into training for the rating of quartermaster, which he found he enjoyed. Years later, he retired after a successful career in which he had become a chief quartermaster. His career path had been chosen for him that Saturday morning on board the *Maryland*.

His time on board the battleship also produced another long-lasting consequence, though it was not as happy. One of O'Quin's chores was to chip old paint off metal surfaces and then put on new paint. The chipping in particular was hard, tedious work, so O'Quin liked to take a break once in a while. As soon as he laid down the scraping tool, a boatswain's mate gave him hell for not working. But he noticed that those who quit chipping and lit up cigarettes had no problem. So he began smoking to get his breaks and, got hooked; it took a number of years afterward before he was able to kick the habit.

NAVY FAMILES

The Navy between the wars was composed mostly of single men. The old saw was, "If the Navy wanted you to have a wife, you would have been issued one with your seabag." The ship was a sailor's home and his workplace, and he spent much of his time on board when he was not ashore on liberty. Because a junior enlisted man couldn't afford a wife on the meager pay he received, a ship's captain had to evaluate an individual's financial circumstances and give permission for the marriage of anyone under the grade of petty officer second class. Despite the obstacles, some did marry. Married enlisted men were referred to as "brown baggers," because they often left the ship carrying a brown satchel of dirty laundry. Some sailors used the laundry bags to smuggle food ashore for the family table. Officers of the deck were aware of the situation and generally chose to ignore the petty thievery when inspecting the liberty party before it shoved off. On board the *Maryland*, however, one mean-spirited officer took pleasure in whacking the brown bags with his telescope in order to break any eggs that were being smuggled. He accompanied the gesture by chortling, "Your laundry is leaking, sailor."

Many junior officers were unmarried as well. The Navy prohibited marriages for the first two years after graduation from the Naval Academy, preferring the officers to concentrate first on learning their profession; a wife and family could come later. One who defied the ban was Ensign Slade Cutter of the *Idaho*. He and his fiancée, Frances Leffler, were married in Tijuana, Mexico, in April 1936, less than a year after his commissioning. Their marriage was an open secret. Cutter's father-in-law was uneasy with the Mexican marriage, so as soon as the Navy officially permitted, the Cutters went through another wedding ceremony in June 1937. To symbolize the Navy's blessing of the previously prohibited union, the *Idaho*'s commanding officer, Captain Arthur Stott, and his wife made a courtesy call on the Cutters the day after the second wedding.

The Navy's medical system provided care only for the sailors, not for their families. On April 17, 1936, Rose Herget, the wife of Chief Carpenter's Mate Charles Herget of the *New Mexico*, gave birth to their first child, a daughter, at Seaside Hospital in the ship's home port of Long Beach. When the *New Mexico* shoved off for fleet exercises around Hawaii, the wife of one of Herget's shipmates kindly took mother and baby home with her, since Chief Herget's absence prevented him from caring for the baby. Rose had a kidney infection that forced her to stay in bed for a while, so the friend's help was essential. The following January, the ship traveled to Bremerton, Washington, for overhaul. Friends in Seattle made room in their home for Herget and his family until he could get them into an apartment. A shipmate's wife accompanied Rose and the baby during the train trip north from California. Soon after they moved in, Mrs. Herget's kidney infection flared up again, her temperature rose to 104 degrees Fahrenheit (40°C), and she was admitted to Seattle General Hospital. Again, friends cared for the baby during the illness. Chief Herget was on board ship during the day and in the evenings was shuttled to shore, where he did laundry and spent time with his daughter, catching what little sleep he could in the remaining time available.

Finally, his wife was released to go home to the apartment they had rented in Bremerton. Rose was still frail, so the bulk of the domestic chores fell on her husband. The stay in the hospital had used up the family's savings. Herget went to settle up with the physician, Park Willis, a physically imposing man whom he had found through the local doctors' service bureau. The chief petty officer explained that his resources had been drained and promised to work out a payment schedule on an installment plan. Dr. Willis responded, "Son, I know how much you make, and I know you don't have the money to pay me. So, as one sailor to another, we will call it squared away. Just you take care of that lovely wife and baby." Dr. Willis had been a coal passer in the Navy during World War I before going to medical school. Though the Navy's medical system had not taken care of Herget's family, his Navy connections helped him nevertheless.

This view of sailors exercising on the port quarter of the *Arizona* was shot while the Warner Brothers crew was on board to film *Here Comes the Navy*. The plot of the comedy was fairly preposterous, typical of the Hollywood approach to depicting the Navy. James Cagney's girlfriend in the film was played by actress Gloria Stuart, then in her early twenties. She was later nominated for an Academy Award as best supporting actress for her role in another seagoing film, the 1997 epic *Titanic*.

The deck force of the *Pennsylvania* rigs an awning on the forecastle, forward of turrets one and two. During the Depression years of the 1930s, fuel budgets were often scarce, so the battleships spent considerable time at anchor in the Battle Force homeport of San Pedro–Long Beach California. Awnings provided shade during the in-port periods. Many of the men on liberty gravitated to a waterfront amusement park known as the Pike. In addition to the rides and games, females were a major attraction. One seaman from the *Arizona* summed it up by saying there were three types of women to be encountered at the Pike: professionals, semi-professionals, and "gifted amateurs."

dramatically for the better: now he rode a passenger train and ate in the dining car with meal coupons supplied by the Navy.

He was among seven hundred young midshipmen who made a cruise to the Caribbean. He was supposed to sleep in a hammock, but couldn't master the position necessary to remain in it. Instead, he spent his nights sleeping on the steel deck. The breakfast menu was baked beans, bread, and coffee. That wasn't exactly what he would have chosen, but he had no choice, so he went along with the program. It was better than some of the thin or nonexistent meals he'd had during his hobo days in the 1930s. And he found that others were even worse off. The poverty he saw when he went ashore in Panama was worse than anything he had encountered in the United States, even during the darkest days of the Depression. On the cruise's return leg, which went to Norfolk, the *Arkansas* made a stop at Guantánamo Bay, Cuba. One Sunday, Merritt heard an announcement that a Protestant worship service would be held on board the battleship and a Catholic service on board a nearby aircraft carrier. Merritt had never been to a carrier, so he went along on the boat ride, even though he was not a Catholic. He didn't attend the service, but instead used his time to explore the carrier. As he walked along a catwalk adjacent to the flight deck, he wasn't paying attention and tumbled to a platform below. In the brief time of falling, a thought flashed through his mind: "God knows you are not a Catholic." After he landed, he realized he was safe and not in the water, as he had feared. He returned to the *Arkansas*, later took his midshipman training at Annapolis, and became a wartime submarine officer. Doug Merritt was one of many for whom the enlistment opportunities in a growing Navy provided an alternative to the hardscrabble life they had known.

FLEET MOVES TO HAWAII

From 1923 onward, the U.S. Navy held a fleet problem, or war game, each year. Generally, the format called for the fleet to be divided into segments designated by color, and they operated against each other under simulated combat conditions. The war games were a means of training officers and enlisted men, building teamwork within and among ships, finding weak spots in existing procedures, and advancing

ENGINEERING COMPETITION

In the mid-1930s, officers and men in the *New Mexico* were exposed to a man who already demonstrated many of the characteristics that would make him a legend throughout the Navy when he was in charge of the nuclear power program. As a lieutenant, Hyman Rickover was the assistant engineer officer of the *New Mexico*. Since the chief engineer took a hands-off approach to the job, Rickover essentially ran the department. When junior officers such as Ensign Ed Batcheller were on board, he ran them through an extremely thorough training program that got them dirty as they crawled through bilges, tanks, boilers, and other parts of the propulsion plant. When they stood watches, they had to make thorough inspection rounds. And Rickover wouldn't just take their word for it. They had to punch a time clock, similar to those carried by night watchmen, to demonstrate that they had carried out their duties. This involved a great deal of climbing up and down ladders to reach the keys that were used to punch the clock. Years later, Batcheller praised the Rickover regimen and philosophy: "We learned there was no substitute for hard work or for coming to grips with the sometimes oil-soaked realities of hardware. Above all we learned not to assume because it was decreed something be done that it would therefore automatically happen."

Rickover's approach included a fanatic devotion to fuel conservation. Along with the gunnery and athletic competitions among the battleships, engineering crews also vied with each other. Using the least amount of fuel and having the fewest equipment malfunctions were the primary criteria for the competition. The crew of the winning ship was entitled to paint a red E on the smokestack, an indicator for all to see and an incentive for those that didn't have it. The *New Mexico* won the red E on Rickover's watch because of a combination of sound engineering practices and gamesmanship.

Heating radiators in officers' staterooms, for instance, were rendered inoperative so they wouldn't use up steam. (The captain's wife complained that he came home sick from underway periods because his cabin was so cold.) Fresh water in showers slowed, and the ship even issued instructions on how to take showers using the least amount of water.

Ships rode better and had fewer waves break on deck if the bow rode higher, but the *New Mexico* shifted ballast water in her tanks so that the stern rode higher. This used less fuel because the propellers faced less resistance closer to the surface. Even when refueling accompanying destroyers, the *New Mexico* crew would recover the last bit of oil from the fueling hose once the pump had stopped. Since all the fuel had already been charged to the receiving ship, the recovered bit was like a gift sent back to the battleship's own tanks.

In addition to chilly staterooms and meager showers, the men of the *New Mexico* experienced another downside from the Rickover regime—a climate of fear had been instilled in the men who worked for him. Lieutenant Fred Edwards reported as the ship's assistant engineer officer in the summer of 1937, a few days after Rickover was transferred to other duty. He discovered that when somebody opened or closed the wrong valve or committed some other mistake, he wouldn't admit knowing anything about it. It took Edwards the better part of a year to get men to acknowledge their mistakes. It wasn't that he wanted to punish them, which Rickover did when he discovered errors. Rather, Edwards sought to use the mistakes as training devices so they wouldn't be repeated. In addition, Edwards sought to make the ship more livable than it had been. In place of the buckets that had been the standard for washing, Edwards had his men install nickel-plated wash basins with both hot and cold water. The change provided a huge boost in morale.

Like Rickover, Edwards sought to conserve fuel and thus do well in the engineering competition, but he didn't go to the same extremes. He also had an advantage because of earlier renovation in the ship's engineering plant. Just as some of the old coal-burners had been outfitted with battle cruiser boilers in the mid-1920s, the *New Mexico* had received some of the unused boilers herself when she was modernized in the early 1930s. She had gotten four of the battle cruiser boilers, whereas her sisters, *Mississippi* and *Idaho*, had six each of older type boilers. *New Mexico* had also been fitted with steam turbines in place of her original electric-drive propulsion system, and the new boilers were able to produce even more steam than the turbines could take. As a result, the *New Mexico* needed only two boilers to make the usual operating speed of eighteen knots and only three for full power, approximately twenty-one knots. More than fifty years later, Edwards recalled with pride that his ship had been "maybe half a knot" faster than her sisters.

ROYAL CORONATION

In the spring of 1937, following the abdication of King Edward VIII of Britain, his younger brother was crowned as King George VI. In connection with the coronation, Britain hosted an impressive naval review. One of the American naval officers on duty at the time was Lieutenant Elliott B. Strauss, who was an assistant naval attaché. His father, Rear Admiral Joseph Strauss, had been in command of the laying of the North Sea mine barrage that had bottled up German U-boats in World War I. Now the younger man saw a reminder of World War I. Most nations sent their newest and most impressive warships to the naval review. For example, Germany was represented by the armored ship *Admiral Graf Spee*, which became notorious as a commerce raider at the outset of World War II. The United States chose a sentimental touch. It sent the old *New York*, which had been Rear Admiral Hugh Rodman's flagship in the Sixth Battle Squadron nearly twenty years earlier. To make the symbolism complete, Rodman was the nation's top-ranking representative at the gathering, and the *New York* honored him by flying the four-star flag of his retired rank.

The event marked the last great international convocation of warships prior to the next global conflict, which was to begin two years later. Lieutenant Strauss was particularly impressed by the display at night when the gathered ships were festooned with strings of electric lights and showered with fireworks. That display also caught the attention of an inebriated British radio announcer named Tom Woodrooffe. In his excitement, he told his audience, "The whole fleet is lit up." He then proceeded to tell about the various types of ships that were "lit up." Soon the mocking statement, "The fleet is all lit up" was seen and heard throughout the country, for the listeners had concluded that Woodrooffe had been pretty well lit up himself.

OPPOSITE TOP: Ships of the battle force put on a searchlight display at the fleet anchorage in San Pedro, California. The occasion is Navy Day 1935. For many years, the nation celebrated Navy Day on November 27, the birthday of President Theodore Roosevelt, who had done so much during his administration to give the country a powerful fleet. The searchlights' more pragmatic function was illuminating targets during night battle practice.
OPPOSITE BOTTOM: Whaleboat racing competitions between crews were popular until World War II, when overseas enemies provided even stronger competition. Here, the boat from the *Maryland* is ahead of one from the *West Virginia*. In this picture from the mid-1930s, the *Texas* is in the background, with three biplanes perched on her amidships catapult.
RIGHT: Aircraft and battleships maneuver during a fleet exercise off the coast of Southern California in October 1939. The ship in the foreground is the *New Mexico*. The aircraft are among the first monoplanes in the U.S. fleet.

Chapter Five

BUILDUP TO WAR

ABOVE: In the years leading up to World War II, the Navy trained tens of thousands of men who would later form the nucleus of the fleet's wartime manpower. Here, a fireman, in training to become a machinist's mate, takes readings from an engine revolution counter on board the fleet flagship *Pennsylvania*.
OPPOSITE: To augment the old twenty-one-knot ships that had been in the fleet for years, a brand-new type began emerging on the eve of war. These were the fast battleships, capable of twenty-seven knots of speed and thus able to operate with aircraft carriers. Here, the *Washington* sits next to the giant hammerhead crane at the Philadelphia Navy Yard in 1941. Her superstructure tower is not yet complete; it needs to be capped with a range finder. The ship also does not have her fire-control radar yet.

For many years, Yale University had been a bastion of the sons of the privileged. In the late 1930s, the school cast a wider net and pulled in Jerome King, a young student from Ohio. His family was far from rich, so he helped pay his way by waiting tables. Soon after his arrival in New Haven, Connecticut, he went to the post office to arrange a campus mailbox and to send his parents a postcard. While he was waiting in a long line, recruiters for the Naval ROTC program gave him a sales pitch. He liked what he heard and signed up. The naval coursework during the academic year was mostly elementary. His real education as a future naval officer came during summer cruises. In 1939, while many of his fellow Americans were enjoying the New York World's Fair, Jerry King made his way to that city to go aboard the *Wyoming*, a former battleship now relegated to training duty.

As with Naval Academy midshipmen, the first cruise for their NROTC counterparts put them in living arrangements like those of the ship's enlisted crew. And those enlisted men weren't above having some sport with these Ivy Leaguers who would someday outrank them. Because the young lads would be operating in a watery environment, they had to undergo a mandatory swimming drill. King was apprehensive to begin with because of a near-drowning experience as a small boy. When the

Wyoming was at Guantánamo Bay in Cuba, he had to jump off the port side, swim around the stern of the ship, then climb up the starboard accommodation ladder. He made out all right around the port side, going with the current. But then it was tougher swimming against the current to starboard, and made even more unpleasant when the ship's crew—probably deliberately—failed to close up the overboard discharges from the heads. Nothing like raw sewage to make swim call more exciting.

The wise university students learned from men who had been doing things the Navy way for years. In particular, Midshipman King was impressed by a huge chief boatswain's mate, the sort of gentle giant who spoke softly but whose muscles suggested he was not to be trifled with or ignored. He commanded the respect of the newcomers, and imparted valuable lessons, such as the importance of being observant of weather conditions and taking precautions against

possible hazards. He also passed along the idea that the Navy was not the place for experimentation. King observed that if some smart-ass midshipman from Yale or Harvard suggested using a different method from the standard procedure, the chief would patiently explain, "Well, because after years and years and years of doing this, it's been refined down to where this is the way we do it." His counsel made a deep impression upon King, who eventually became a vice admiral and developed a firm reputation as a stickler for following rules. He finally retired from the Navy thirty-seven years after he signed up for NROTC in the New Haven post office.

A CHANGE OF LIFESTYLE

Along with the new ships it was building, the Navy had to increase its manpower greatly as well. During the Depression, it had been quite selective, since jobs were scarce, and the Navy offered opportunities. Now those opportunities were growing. Doug Merritt had just turned nineteen when war broke out in Europe in September 1939. The 1930s had been difficult for him. His father had been imprisoned as a bank robber, and his mother was unable to support him, so he had to find whatever means of support he could. Often that meant riding freight trains from city to city in search of work. In 1940, Merritt heard that the Navy was offering a new officer training program known as V-7. Having managed to gain just enough college credits to be eligible, he enlisted in late August after riding one last freight train from California to Missouri. From Kansas City, he had orders to report to New York City to board the USS *Arkansas* for a training cruise. His life had changed

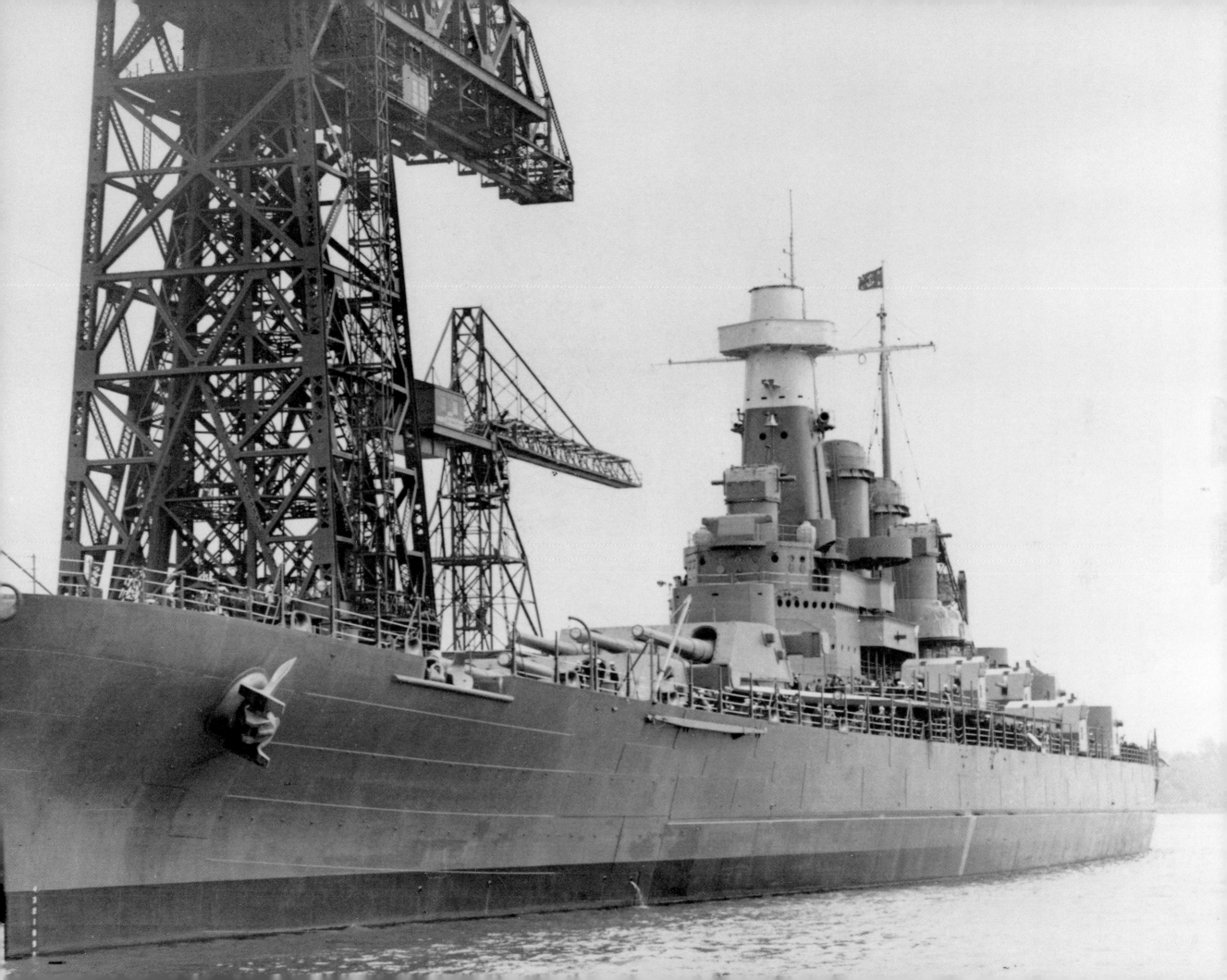

tactical doctrine by developing new methods as new equipment became available. In the late 1920s and early 1930s, for example, war games had demonstrated the growing potential of aircraft carriers and their planes to constitute an offensive strike force, rather than just serving as auxiliaries to the battle line. The second half of Fleet Problem XXI, which was conducted in the spring of 1940, was held in the Hawaiian Islands. Real war was already raging in Europe, and the Allied cause was growing increasingly desperate.

The bulk of the U.S. Fleet left the West Coast on April 2, 1940, for Hawaii, where the ships were scheduled to remain until May 9, then return to their West Coast bases around May 17. But the international situation intervened, much to the consternation of Admiral James O. Richardson, the fleet commander-in-chief on board the *Pennsylvania*. He at first received orders to keep the fleet in the Hawaii area for an additional two weeks; later, he was instructed to hold the warships there indefinitely. Meanwhile, German blitzkrieg forces were rampaging through Western Europe; France was falling; and Italy was poised to enter the war as a combatant on the Axis side. President Roosevelt believed that as the situation in Europe worsened for the Allies (the United States was still officially neutral), Japan would be more inclined to seize territory in the Dutch East Indies to support the war it was waging against China. Moving the fleet's base westward, he felt, could serve as an effective deterrent against the Japanese. Admiral Richardson, by contrast, held that the fleet could best prepare for war by returning to the West Coast, where there were more plentiful supplies of ammunition, fuel, and training facilities. Richardson protested the decision forcefully and, in early 1941, lost his job as a result. The President installed Admiral Husband Kimmel as the new Commander-in-Chief Pacific Fleet.

Richardson was not the only officer unhappy with the decision, in part because it interfered with the personal plans of many who had expected to return soon to California. The executive officer of the *Pennsylvania*, Commander John McCrea, overheard two members of Richardson's staff complaining about the order. He was concerned that members of his own ship's wardroom might also harbor such feelings and might not be taking seriously the threat

Prior to World War II, the most exalted U.S. seagoing officer was the Commander in Chief of the U.S. Fleet. In 1940, that was Admiral James O. Richardson, seen here with his aide, Lieutenant Tom Eddy, in the admiral's office aboard the *Pennsylvania*. Because Richardson objected strenuously to basing the fleet at Pearl Harbor, President Roosevelt directed that he be relieved in 1941. Admiral Husband E. Kimmel took his place and subsequently received a great deal more blame than he deserved when the fleet was caught by surprise in December 1941. By that time, Kimmel had moved the fleet headquarters ashore to a building at the Pearl Harbor submarine base. The shift was made to give him more flexibility in communications: When aboard a ship at sea, it was sometimes necessary to operate under radio silence to avoid giving away her location. Shore-based headquarters also allowed him a larger staff than could be accommodated on board ship.

of war. McCrea, who had been through World War I on board the *New York*, was from the old school that followed orders without complaining. He gathered his officers together and announced: "More than ever, it behooves us to get this ship ready for war. Every time you go through the ship now, in addition to looking out for little odds and ends and cleanliness, is there something you see that should be done in the event of hostilities?" Word of McCrea's message—and its forewarning of a pending war—soon reached the ears of Captain Elwin F. Cutts, the *Pennsylvania*'s commanding officer. He talked to his exec and said, "John, I think you are taking too serious a view of this; we will be home by the first of June." Long afterward, by which time he was a retired vice admiral, McCrea summed up the situation by saying, "The first of June came and went six times before we got home."

Gradually, the base at Pearl Harbor became capable of supporting the fleet as the navy yard there increased its facilities, but accommodating the large influx of sailors in Honolulu proved to be problematic. On the one hand, enlisted men had access to an island paradise that, at the time, was available only to the richest in society. On the other, the sailors held a lowly position in the island society and thus had very few opportunities, for instance, to date respectable girls. The result was that many, many of them turned to bars and brothels for their entertainment. There was a connection between the bars and brothels, because the young men often needed strong drink to work up their courage for the sexual initiation they would receive from prostitutes. The latter were, in many cases, experienced professionals imported from the mainland. At the going rate of three dollars, they were able to turn tricks on essen-

tially an assembly-line basis, moving from room to room and providing an experience that often lasted less than five minutes.

The Navy tolerated the setup, though never encouraged it. Alternative activities were available at the Army-Navy YMCA in downtown Honolulu, and the Navy set up a fleet recreation center at a place called Nanakuli on the western side of Oahu, the island where Pearl Harbor is located. Radioman Ted Mason and shipmates from the *California* went to Nanakuli on a narrow-gauge railroad nicknamed the "Toonerville Trolley," after a comic strip railway of the time. At the recreation center, they discovered a white sand beach where they could swim and body surf. They also played touch football on the sand and availed themselves of galvanized laundry tubs full of ice and "limitless quantities of beer." And the Navy provided hot dogs, cold cuts, beans, and slaw to

accompany the beer. On at least one occasion, the combination of sun, sand, sailors, and beer led to a wild and reckless brawl. Mason captured the time, place, and atmosphere masterfully in a memoir titled *Battleship Sailor*, which was published by the Naval Institute Press in 1982 and remains the best book written about that final prewar era from the perspective of a fleet sailor.

ATLANTIC OPERATIONS

In 1941, the old *New York* operated in the North Atlantic on what was officially known as a Neutrality Patrol but, in fact, had a pro-British inclination. The patrols provided opportunities for liberty in various ports, so the ship's supply officer, Lieutenant Commander George Bauernschmidt, tried an experiment to try to keep crew members from getting into trouble ashore. His theory was that a number of men got into scrapes when they were on their way back to the ship. They'd stop to have a meal or snack and would wind up having drinks as well and

perhaps being distracted by a woman. Then they would get back to the ship too late and be put on report. Bauernschmidt's idea was to keep the galley open and available for men coming back to the ship and thus encourage them to return early to eat. He had soup, eggs, and sandwich fixings available. The food bill went up for a while as people took advantage of the offer, then tapered off. The biggest payoff was in the reduced number of men coming up for punishment at captain's mast. In the summer, however, the supply officer had to suspend his program while the midshipmen were on board for a training cruise. As he later put it, the experiment "fell flat on its face when the midshipmen came on board, because there is no limit to the midshipmen's capacity to eat."

The ship also was part of an expedition to deliver Marines to Iceland to provide a garrison. While the *New York* was there, a German plane flew over. Until then, the ship's crew had had trouble getting battle stations manned in a timely fashion when

the call for general quarters was sounded. This time, with a genuine threat visible to all, the response was much faster. The plane flew over without attacking because the United States was still officially neutral, but the ship's crew demonstrated it was ready for the real thing.

The ship later operated out of Argentia, Newfoundland, which had become a U.S. base for support of convoy operations. During one of the *New York*'s stays in that port, an enlisted man in the supply department went to Commander Bauernschmidt's stateroom and requested three days' leave to go to the ship's homeport of Norfolk. The supply officer pointed out to the sailor that the journey would take a day and a half each way, so he wouldn't be able to do anything more than arrive home, then turn right around for the return trip to Newfoundland. "That's plenty of time," said the man. "I just want to go home and shoot my wife." He had learned from letters written to him by his neighbors that his wife was having affairs with various men and

leaving their young child alone and neglected in their apartment for long periods. He wanted to use a direct approach to deal with his offending spouse. Bauernschmidt persuaded him that it would be better to take ten days of leave, work with authorities to get the child cared for, and take action to divorce his wife. The man followed the supply officer's suggestion and returned to the ship with his wife still among the living.

Another of the old battleships, *Arkansas*, was also operating in the Atlantic, though in August of 1941, she received a most unusual assignment. She steamed from Newport to Argentia and was present when the cruiser *Augusta* arrived with the commander-in-chief, President Roosevelt, on board. He had managed to elude members of the press, who had no idea that he had come to Newfoundland for a secret meeting with Britain's Prime Minister, Winston Churchill. They had been in frequent communication for months, as Churchill pleaded with Roosevelt for help in fighting off the Nazis. Roosevelt had done as much as he could, given the constraint imposed by a great deal of isolationist sentiment in the United States. Many Americans, particularly in the Midwest, felt it best to leave the European fighting to the Europeans. Now the two leaders would meet face-to-face for the first time since World War I. Ensign Ed Forrest, a reserve officer who had been a newspaperman in civilian life, felt a great sense of frustration. He had firsthand knowledge about a meeting that would be a sensation if it were made public, but security restrictions absolutely prevented him from saying anything about it. From the meeting came the formulation of the Atlantic Charter, a statement of war aims for the two prospective allies. In a way, it was reminiscent of Commander Sims's Guildhall speech in 1910, when he spoke of American aid to a beleaguered Britain. But FDR was in a much more powerful position to make commitments than the battleship skipper had been a generation earlier.

While his ship was in Newfoundland, young Forrest had an opportunity to visit HMS *Prince of Wales*, the new battleship that had brought Churchill from England to Canada. He talked with a British midshipman who showed him where projectiles from the cruiser *Prinz Eugen*—while accompanying the battleship *Bismarck*—had damaged the ship in

May of that year. The gunnery of the *Bismarck* had mortally wounded the British battle cruiser *Hood*, and the *Prince of Wales* had to maneuver gingerly to avoid the dying *Hood* before she sank. It was a sobering lesson for the American officer on the realities of warfare at sea. And then he heard the order "Attention!" on the British battleship's announcing system, so he quickly followed suit. When he did so, he saw Churchill, who was standing nearby on the ship's deck, take a quick look at him. The prime minister was wearing his famous one-piece siren suit and carrying a rod and tackle box. Soon, Churchill descended the gangway ladder into a boat, and eight sailors rowed him away to a spot where he could fish for a while as a respite from the affairs of state.

HUSH-HUSH RADAR

Radar was a magical new invention that gave a battleship's crew the means of seeing other ships electronically, even in low-visibility conditions. A few battleships began receiving radar shortly before the war; the equipment was linked to antennas resembling bedsprings that were mounted high in the superstructure. The new device was kept highly classified. During fleet exercises off Hawaii in early 1941, the submarine *Pompano* made an approach on the surface one night. To the great surprise of Lieutenant (junior grade) Slade Cutter and others on board the submarine, the *California* spotted the *Pompano* on radar at a range of about 2,000 yards (2km) and illuminated her with a 36-inch (91cm) searchlight to simulate gunfire. To the submariners, accustomed to being able to make stealthy approaches on their targets, it was a new and unnerving experience.

In the summer of that year, Ensign Fred Michaelis, who had reported to the *Pennsylvania* a year earlier, was summoned to talk with the ship's executive officer. The exec informed him that he had received a letter directing him to select a radar officer for the ship. Michaelis, he said, had been chosen for the job. The ensign responded by saying, "I'm flattered. Commander, could you tell me what a radar is?" The exec responded, "I was afraid you were going to ask that." "It wouldn't happen to be that rack that I saw on the Prune Barge," he asked, using the fleet nickname for the *California*. "Yes, I

think so," said the executive officer. Indeed, the *California* was one of the few ships equipped with radar at the time. Michaelis soon began learning about this exotic new device.

A few weeks later, new equipment began arriving aboard the fleet flagship and Michaelis was expected to operate it. The man who saved Michaelis's bacon with his understanding of radar was Chief Radioman Charles Klouck. Radar transmits radio waves that bounce off a target and return a signal, or echo, to the original ship, where an image on a radar scope reveals the position of the target. Klouck understood the guts of the new equipment and demonstrated how to use a small dial to swing the radar face around to read the azimuth—that is, the compass bearing—of the returning signal. By reading the angle and distance off the radar tube, one could locate approximately where a target ship or aircraft was located. Even so, it was a primitive device, but one that developed rapidly in capability over the course of the next few years. And, in the beginning, radar technology was truly hush-hush within the U.S. Navy.

NEW FAST BATTLESHIPS

During most of the 1930s, the newest American battleships, commissioned in 1923, had a maximum design speed of about twenty-one knots. In the middle of the decade, the Japanese, refusing to remain bound by previous disarmament agreements, began constructing new battleships. The United States and other powers responded by preparing designs for new ships, and these were a new type as well—fast battleships. These new ships, beginning with the North Carolina class, were designed for twenty-seven knots, which would enable them to run with aircraft carriers. After a period of some indecision, the Navy opted to arm them with 16-inch (41cm) guns. They would be arrayed in three triple turrets, two forward of the superstructure and one aft. In addition, the ships would have 5-inch (13cm) guns capable of shooting at both air and surface targets, an advancement over the older battleships that had to have two different types of 5-inch (13cm) guns.

In September 1939, when the *North Carolina* was under construction at the New York Navy Yard, World War II broke out in Europe. There was now a new sense of urgency about her completion. In the

This is a dramatic bow-on view of the *Indiana* under construction at Newport News Shipbuilding and Dry Dock Company in Newport News, Virginia. She and her sister ships *South Dakota*, built at New York Shipbuilding Corporation in Camden, New Jersey, and *Massachusetts*, built at the Bethlehem Steel yard in Quincy, Massachusetts, were the only fast battleships constructed in private shipyards. The other seven came from the Navy Yards in New York, Philadelphia, and Norfolk. In this view, the *Indiana* is nearing the end of her time on the shipbuilding ways. She was launched in November 1941 and commissioned in April 1942.

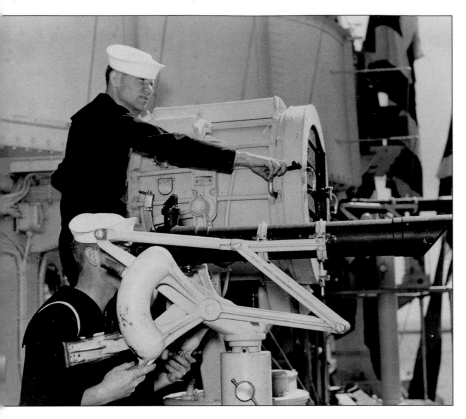

ABOVE: Two signalmen on board the Battle Force flagship *California* participate in flashing light communications in the late 1930s. One man operates a shutter that sends the dots and dashes to another ship. His partner is equipped with a high-power telescope to read signals from another ship.

TOP RIGHT: The *North Carolina*, the first of the fast battleships, still has scaffolding around her foremast as she nears completion at the New York Navy Yard in 1941. She is painted in the light gray color that was standard for ships of the U.S. Fleet in the years between the world wars.

BOTTOM RIGHT: The crew of the *North Carolina* gathers on the ship's fantail shortly after her commissioning in the spring of 1941. The men are framed by the port and starboard catapults used for launching floatplanes. In the oval at top is the ship's first commanding officer, Captain Olaf M. Hustvedt.

spring of 1941, installation and testing of equipment went on around the clock, six and seven days a week. The ship's prospective engineering crew, led by Lieutenant Commander Fred Edwards, had to be ready day and night to observe the tests of various pieces of machinery. Edwards, who had turned black from head to foot while coaling ship as a midshipman, noted with pleasure the superb fueling system in the ship. She could take on oil rapidly because of a series of tanks that were fed from a central tank. The fuel went down a trunk into each master tank, then the other tanks filled automatically as they were opened. With two or three such master tanks receiving oil at the same time, the process was faster than in older battleships. When the *North Carolina* went out for her engineering trials, she and her sister, *Washington*, developed severe vibration problems as they reached higher speeds. To deal with the difficulty, the Bureau of Ships had to change propellers and try various combinations with different numbers of blades. The fix was eventually successful in eliminating the problem.

Edwards encountered still another change on board the *North Carolina*. Earlier battleships had junior officer messes for the ensigns in the crew. These messes often developed a sort of informal, fraternity-house atmosphere because the ensigns were newly freed from the restrictive confines of the Naval Academy, and because they were away from the watchful eyes of the more senior officers. Now all of the officers ate in a single, large wardroom. The challenge for Edwards, as the mess treasurer, was to try to feed the differing tastes of the two groups. To do so, he had to develop two different menus. As he put it: "The young studs wanted meat and potatoes, and the old fuds wanted salads and lighter food."

The *North Carolina* was the first U.S. battleship equipped from the outset with radar. Security precautions were still tight, so officers and crew had to be careful in discussing the miraculous new device. Somehow, a report of the equipment appeared in a New York newspaper, leading the ship's first gunnery officer, Lieutenant Commander Tom Hill, to pose a devilish question to the executive officer: "Is it all right now to say that dirty word?" It was certainly all right to use the equipment that went with the word, and it provided a spectacular advance in antiaircraft gunnery—an area in which the fleet had been woefully primitive. Previously, gunners had to try to take visual ranges on moving airplanes and send them to a director—an electro-mechanical device high in the ship that used target range and bearing to direct aiming. The director calculated settings for projectile fuzes, and then gun crews inserted the projectiles into the guns and fired them. Radar and modern directors automated a good deal of the work and enabled much faster solutions for the 5-inch (13cm) guns. In addition, when the *North Carolina* went out for gunnery trials off Cape May, New Jersey, her new 5-inch (13cm)/38-caliber guns could shoot down drone aircraft at 12,000 to 13,000 feet (3.7km to 4km)—about double the range of the 5-inch (13cm)/25-caliber guns on previous battleships. (A naval gun's caliber is calculated by dividing the barrel length in inches by the gun's diameter in inches. The larger the caliber, the longer the gun.)

"THE SHOWBOAT"

Because she had been commissioned in New York City, the media capital of the country, the *North Carolina* received a great deal of attention as the year 1941 progressed. Reporters accompanied her as she conducted trials at sea and fired her guns.

In the spring of 1938, sailors sunbathe on the forecastle of the *Pennsylvania* during a break in war games. On occasions such as this, the wooden deck of a battleship was known as "splinter beach." To the right of turret one, a band provides entertainment. The *Pennsylvania* was a young ship in World War I but an old one in World War II. Like other older battleships in the second war, she was relegated mostly to shore bombardment. She was present for one fleet action during the October 1944 Battle of Surigao Strait and then was torpedoed off Okinawa near war's end. Her final service was as a target for atomic bomb tests in 1946, and she was sunk off Kwajalein in the Marshall Islands two years later.

FAR LEFT: Inside the circle, an experimental radar antenna is seen mounted on the superstructure of the *New York*. This remarkable new electronic device enabled ships to "see" through fog and darkness, and to ascertain the ranges and bearings of distant ships and aircraft. Fire control radar, mounted in directors, made the aiming of guns, both large and small, more accurate than it had been when depending on visual range finding. LEFT, TOP AND BOTTOM: These two views show the mainmast of the *Arizona*. The round device is a concentration dial, much more commonly known as a range clock. When battleships were steaming in column, gun smoke might interfere with some crews' abilities to ascertain the range to a target at sea. On board ships in which men were able to see, the range of the target was transmitted to other ships in the column by the range clock. One hand indicated thousands of yards of distance, and the other indicated hundreds. With the advent of radar, range clocks became obsolete.

Her commissioning ceremony was broadcast on the radio to a wide audience. She was especially news-worthy because it had been so long since a new battleship had joined the fleet. The *Washington* was commissioned in Philadelphia shortly afterward, but did not receive nearly as much publicity as her slightly older sister.

When it came time for shakedown training, the pair operated together for the first time. In September, the two ships anchored in Hampton Roads, at the mouth of Chesapeake Bay. Captain Olaf Hustvedt of the *North Carolina* was the senior skipper. He called a meeting with the top officers of the *Washington* so they could collaborate on plans and procedures for the upcoming training cruise to Guantánamo Bay. Near the end of the meeting, the *Washington*'s executive officer joked that the men in their ship were referring to the *North Carolina* as "The Showboat" because she was so much in the public eye. The men of the *Washington* had just as fine a ship, but weren't getting nearly as much public validation, so the nickname they bestowed was in the nature of a friendly jibe. Hustvedt decided to turn the dig into a positive thing for his ship. When the ships were to leave the harbor, the *North Carolina* would get under way first because of seniority and then steam past her sister on the way to the channel and the open sea. It was customary that the junior ship render passing honors, comparable to a junior man saluting a senior if they passed on the street. Hustvedt told his executive officer, Commander Andy Shepard, to have the crew stand at quarters on deck as the *North Carolina* got under way. After the exchange of formal honors, the *North Carolina*'s band played the national anthem and then launched into a rousing version of the tune "Here Comes the Showboat" from the popular stage musical, *Showboat*. So what had been, up to then, a teasing name was adopted with pride, and the *North Carolina* was widely known as "The Showboat" from then on.

ANTIQUATED ENGINEERING PLANT

As the *North Carolina* was strutting her stuff as the new kid on the block, the three old battleships in the Atlantic Fleet were becoming real relics. Ed Logue, who had grown up in the dust bowl of Kansas during the Depression, had been drawn to the Navy by the example of his older brother, who had been a machinist's mate in the 1930s on board the heavy cruiser *Pensacola*. Ed went through boot camp and was then fortunate enough to take the machinist's mate training provided to Navy men by the Ford Motor Company in Dearborn, Michigan. The company patriarch, Henry Ford, took a personal interest in the welfare of the sailors who underwent the training. Once, he approached a group of sailors, shook their hands, and said to them, "Now, boys, if you ever see me anywhere, I don't care if I'm talking to the president of the United States, I want you to come up and interrupt me. Tell me who you are, where we met, and shake hands with me. I want you to promise you'll do that. Will you?" Naturally, all of them did. After Ford had left, Ed Logue turned to one of his fellow trainees and said, "I don't think I'll interrupt the president. You can suit yourself."

Once his time at Dearborn was complete, Logue had temporary duty in a few different battleships before ending up on board the *New York*. Because of his training, he was assigned to an engine room, and was surprised to discover that her propulsion plant was a triple-expansion steam engine, the sort that dated from the earliest American battleships in the Spanish-American War. The *New York* had been converted in the 1920s from coal to oil, but she still had those old sewing-machine engines rather than the steam turbines that became the norm soon after she was built. The triple-expansion type was like a giant version of a car's internal-combustion engine, though the impetus in this case came from steam produced in boilers rather than from spark plugs igniting gasoline. The steam moved through a series of cylinders, from high pressure to low. At each stage, some of the energy was drained off as the big pistons turned crankshafts that led through reduction gears to the ship's propellers. The low-pressure cylinders had the biggest pistons. Logue observed that each was so large that four or five men would be able to stand on top of one of them. After the steam had done its work, it traveled to a hot well, passing through a condenser that turned it into water and through oil extractors that removed the oil and grease. Then it returned to the fireroom so the boilers could make steam from it once more. The system was old, but it was reliable, just as it had been when the *New York*

operated as part of Britain's Grand Fleet in World War I. On the other hand, the *New York* still had about the same puny antiaircraft capability it did in World War I—3-inch (8cm) guns and .50-caliber machine guns. Enemy aircraft had become far more potent since then.

OPERATIONS FROM PEARL HARBOR

Seaman Oree Weller discovered, upon reporting to the *Arizona* at Pearl Harbor in the summer of 1941, that the standard uniform was different from the one he'd worn at boot camp. In tropical Hawaii, he realized that he'd have to adapt to the local uniform to avoid being recognized quite so quickly as the newcomer he certainly was. That meant low-cut black oxfords instead of high-tops, along with black socks, white T-shirt, white shorts, and a white hat. He also soon learned that on board the ships of the fleet, particularly the battleships, the officers seemed intent on enforcing the idea that cleanliness was next to godliness. Indeed, it was a real obsession, and was one way that ships were measured at the time. The next year, battle action would bring the true measure.

After a required indoctrination period, Weller began working as a yeoman in the navigator's office. To prepare for captain's inspection, he removed the file drawers from the desk and file cabinet, scrubbed the resulting cavities, and gave them a coat of fresh paint. He polished the dogs—that is, the bolts that held the battle ports closed—and used steel wool to shine the grooves. He cleaned and waxed the linoleum on the desktop and the deck, and coaxed a mirror shine on the faceplate for the light switch. He wiped clean the steam line that ran through the office and even painted the battle port with new gray paint. He was more than ready when the ship's skipper, Captain Franklin Van Valkenburgh, came through for weekly inspection. As the captain observed the results of the seaman's careful preparation, Weller's chest swelled with smug satisfaction. As he was ready to depart, the captain spotted a small rotating fan over the door and switched it off. Each brass blade had greasy dirt and corrosion on it. Weller would get no liberty that day.

On the evening of October 22, the battleships were at sea for maneuvers and had their lights turned off to simulate battle conditions. The

Oklahoma moved in to take station on the *Arizona*. Instead of taking the correct position in formation, however, the *Oklahoma* ran her old-fashioned ram-type bow into the *Arizona*'s port side. Ensign Paul Backus of the *Oklahoma* observed that it was skillful seamanship on the part of Captain Edward Foy that kept the damage from being much worse. He reacted quickly and ordered the *Oklahoma*'s engines into reverse. Because she had the reciprocating type rather than turbines, she had as much power backing as going forward. The blow was a glancing one, but it still meant a trip to dry dock to repair the hole punched in the side of the *Arizona*. Her crew members hoped the damage would mean a trip back to Bremerton, Washington, for repairs, but by now the shipyard in Pearl Harbor had sufficient facilities to accommodate her.

As Musician Second Class Clyde Williams, a cornet player, wrote to his sister Molly in Oklahoma,

the *Arizona*'s crew did get some entertainment in Hawaii, including Armistice Day festivities that included a steak fry, beer bash, and football game. The ship left dry dock the next day and resumed training maneuvers. When the ship was in port, Williams and other members of the band took part in a Battle of Music, a competition held at the Pearl Harbor recreation center, Bloch Arena. Men from the various ships played big-band music, then in its heyday, as well as other numbers. In a semifinal contest on the night of November 22, the *Arizona*'s band finished second in the dance band competition and won a loving cup. That night, Tai Sing Loo, official photographer for the navy yard, took a group shot of the ship's band. It was the last picture of them ever made, for they died to just over two weeks later in the attack that destroyed their ship. Williams's sister, now Molly Kent, has written a collective biography titled *USS Arizona's Last Band*. It

This picture of the *Arizona*'s band was taken during a musical competition at Bloch Arena at Pearl Harbor, a few weeks before all these men were killed on board their ship on December 7, 1941. Molly Kent, the sister of musician Clyde Williams, has written a book about the band that is both a collective biography of the band members and a description of shipboard life in the last few months of peacetime.

Tom Freeman's magnificent painting *The Last Mooring* shows the doomed *Arizona* coming alongside quays on December 5, 1941, two days before her destruction. Sailors on board the concrete quays pull in mooring lines to attach them to bollards and secure the ship snugly into place. Beyond the *Arizona*, the *Nevada* is on the left side of the painting. She is preparing to swing around and moor to the quays next astern. The intent was for the ships to point their bows toward the harbor entrance so they would be ready to get under way for sea. The *Nevada* did indeed make a dash for that channel on the morning of December 7. To this day, the *Arizona* remains at the berth where she moored on December 5; a white memorial marks her watery grave.

spells out, in saddening detail, the impact of the deaths of these young men on their families back in the States. In early December, many other relatives would also be grieving.

JAPANESE SURPRISE ATTACK

A year earlier, in the spring of 1940, President Roosevelt had ordered the fleet to remain in Pearl Harbor to serve as a deterrent to Japanese designs on territory and resources in Southeast Asia. Admiral Isoruko Yamamoto, Commander-in-Chief of the Japanese Combined Fleet, recognized the U.S. Fleet's power to inhibit his forces, so he planned an attack on Pearl Harbor that would knock out the American warships, rendering them unable to respond to forays to the Dutch East Indies, the Philippines, and Singapore. Thus, instead of serving as a deterrent, the fleet's presence at Pearl Harbor made it a magnet for attack. The Japanese arrived in force on the morning of December 7, sending six aircraft carriers and more than three hundred aircraft on a strike that caught the American forces by surprise and stunned the citizens back on the mainland.

The Japanese carrier strike included fighters, torpedo planes, high-level bombers, and dive-bombers. They struck with deadly efficiency. The American carriers were not in port that Sunday morning, so it was the battleships, most lined up neatly alongside Ford Island, that bore the heavy brunt of the attack. All were damaged, two fatally. The *Oklahoma* capsized at her berth. An armor-piercing bomb dropped from an aircraft at 10,000 feet (3,048m) went into the bowels of the *Arizona*, exploded, and started a fire that burned for three days. All told, 1,177 men died on board the *Arizona*, more than three-quarters of her crew.

One of those who survived was Seaman Oree Weller. When the call to general quarters sounded, he began climbing one of the tripod legs of the mainmast in order to reach his battle station in secondary battery control. Located in the enclosed three-story maintop atop the mainmast, it was the control station for the ship's 5-inch (13cm) broadside guns, which were to be used against enemy ships. Though the guns could have no real purpose in this sort of engagement, duty, habit, and instinct carried him to his assigned place. He put on his sound-powered telephones and tried to contact the

forward part of the ship. Then, at about 8:10 A.M., the entire forward part of the *Arizona* erupted in a massive geyser of flame as powder magazines exploded. A plume of black smoke came out through the smokestack as it was vented upward. The concussion hurled Weller and several Marines to the deck in the lofty battle station. The whole mainmast vibrated as if shaken by an earthquake. Weller and the Marines realized that they could serve no purpose where they were, so they decided to leave. Again following habit, he disconnected the phone wire, carefully coiled it up, and stowed the phone in the proper box. Only then did he begin climbing down the mast.

When he got down to the main deck, the seaman found a mass of flames. For a time, he and his shipmates took cover under the overhang of a 14-inch (36cm) turret to escape strafing bullets from a Japanese plane. He spotted one of his shipmates, Charles Brittan, whom he had known since boot camp. Brittan was so badly burned that he couldn't see or speak. Weller knew who he was only because he recognized a small tattoo on the man's shoulder;

it showed a bird in flight. Brittan, who was only seventeen, died of his burns.

The ship's turret three officer, Ensign Jim Dick Miller, ordered a number of men to abandon ship because they could serve no further purpose on board. Weller took off his shoes and socks, placed his white hat neatly atop the pile, and shoved it under an ammunition locker. Then he abandoned ship on the starboard side, going into harbor water covered by a layer of oil released from ships' tanks. He began swimming toward shore, at times ducking under water where the oil was on fire. Because of the oil, he was having trouble, so he was most grateful when a motor launch from the hospital ship *Solace* came by and strong arms pulled him out of the water and into the boat. Scared, numb, and covered with black oil, Weller felt relieved that he had been rescued and would live to see tomorrow.

When the Japanese struck, Radioman Henry Long of the *Oklahoma* was polishing his shoes in preparation for going on liberty. Over the ship's announcing system he heard a call to man battle stations. It seemed incongruous with the ship in port

ABOVE: This overhead photo, taken from a Japanese aircraft on the morning of December 7, shows the devastating effects of the hit-and-run air raid. In the lower part of the photo is Ford Island, in the center of Pearl Harbor. From left to right are the *Nevada*; the *Arizona*, with the repair ship *Vestal* alongside to port; the *Tennessee*, with the *West Virginia* to port; and the *Maryland*, with the *Oklahoma* to port. Fuel oil rings the water beside the *West Virginia* and *Oklahoma*, both of which received massive torpedo damage.

Floatplanes

In the twenty years following World War I, the fleet's battleships and cruisers utilized airplanes equipped with floats for the purpose of spotting the fall of gunfire and, secondarily, for scouting. The staple craft from 1934 onward was the Curtiss SOC Seagull, a sturdy aircraft that survived into the early part of World War II and was the Navy's last combat biplane to serve in the fleet. Generally, a squadron of floatplanes would serve a division of battleships, with detachments being parceled out to individual ships. When Ensign Lionel McQuiston joined the *Nevada*'s detachment in March 1941, the OS2U Kingfisher, a high-wing monoplane, had replaced the SOC. He quickly discovered that taking off from a battleship was a good deal different from making a rolling takeoff from a runway ashore. He and the enlisted man who served as his radioman and gunner were sent aloft from a catapult that fired a powder charge akin to that used in a 5-inch (13cm) gun. The catapult was supposed to fire when the *Nevada* was on an up roll, thus providing some additional lift to the plane and its occupants. On one occasion, an inexperienced ensign was the catapult officer. He fired the catapult on a down roll before McQuiston had settled into his cockpit. Jolted by the launch, McQuiston was lucky he had full throttle on. The pontoon float at the bottom of the plane touched the sea, but the plane was able to climb to get altitude.

When flying, McQuiston found he had a variety of missions to practice, though not all were realistic for the combat that lay ahead. He and his crew practiced dive-bombing, machine-gunning air targets, and strafing land. The Kingfisher towed targets for the ship's antiair gunnery practice and spotted for the firing of the *Nevada*'s 14-inch (36cm) guns. The radioman sent back fire control corrections to the ship by Morse code. There was some inconvenience to the ship's operations because of the need to launch the plane before gunnery practice and then pick it up afterward. The recovery procedure called for the ship to make a hard turn that created a temporary slick on the water. The plane would set down on the slick, hook onto a mat towed by the ship, and be hoisted aboard by a crane at the stern. Despite the inconvenience, the aviators generally had good relations with the ship's other officers, and they bantered back and forth about individual capabilities. The gunnery people believed they could keep enemy dive-bombers far enough away to prevent them from dropping their bombs; the pilots disagreed. As McQuiston observed years later, "Regrettably, the question was effectively settled by the Japanese on 7 December."

RIGHT: In this 1941 picture of an OS2U Kingfisher floatplane taken from the *Arizona*, Ensign Laurence A. Williams is the pilot in the cockpit. Radioman Third Class Glenn Lane stands by, preparing to hook the plane to the ship's crane so it can be lifted aboard. Williams was killed on December 7; Lane survived.
TOP RIGHT: In the left foreground, the *Maryland* is relatively undamaged; at right is the bottom of the capsized *Oklahoma*'s hull. In the background, boats attempt to put out the raging shipboard fires. The *Arizona* burned for three days.

and on a Sunday, so no one moved. Then came a second announcement, spoken with much more urgency, "All hands man your battle stations! This is the real thing! No shit!" That sent people scrambling. He went to the ship's main radio room and felt several jolts as torpedoes slammed into the *Oklahoma*'s exposed port side. Because the ship had been opened up internally in anticipation of an inspection to be held Monday morning, she began flooding even faster than if she'd been buttoned up. Long and his shipmates sought to leave the ship. When they arrived topside, the officer of the deck wouldn't allow them to go out on deck, but Long did so as soon as the officer left. He could see that the ship was rolling over to port, and he made it into the water. His efforts to swim didn't get him too far, but then he saw a boat approaching. In it was the same officer who had impeded the departure of his shipmates earlier. Though he objected, because of the distaste he felt for the officer, Long was pulled into the boat. As soon as he got ashore, he found another

boat and returned to the water, picking up as many men as he could from the oil-covered harbor.

In the course of his rescue efforts, Radioman Long felt a thrill at seeing the one battleship that was able to get under way that terrible morning. She was the *Nevada*, sister ship of the *Oklahoma*. The *Nevada*'s captain was not on board, so she was under the direction of Chief Quartermaster Robert Sedberry, who was at the steering wheel. He pulled the ship away from her berth at Ford Island and headed toward the channel that led out of the harbor to the open sea. The movement of the battleship drew the Japanese bombers toward her, and she took a terrible pounding. Because of a concern that she might be sunk in the entrance channel and plug it up, the crew beached the *Nevada* near the entrance. She provided a rare bright spot in an otherwise most gloomy day.

Back on board the *Oklahoma*, nineteen-year-old Seaman Steve Young had responded to the urgent summons of the loudspeaker and reported to his battle station inside the cylindrical barbette of turret four. After the torpedoes hit and the ship was obviously wounded, he and others tried to get up to the interior of the turret itself. They were prevented from doing so by an officer who ordered them below so they would be protected by the armored deck. When he went down the ladder to the powder-handling room, Young encountered a chief petty officer who had shown little mercy in dealing with his subordinates. Now Young observed that the chief was crying.

As the *Oklahoma* steadily listed farther and farther to port, she rolled through one hundred and fifty degrees of arc, eventually coming to rest nearly upside down. Steve Young and his compatriots from the crew of turret four were trapped underwater. They found a compartment that had air in it, but water was coming in. The young sailors observed the bodies of shipmates floating in the water, and Young said a silent prayer as he pleaded for salvation. But he held little hope. In a bit of grim humor, he turned to Seaman Wilbur Hinsperger and said, "Wimpy, I'll bet you a dollar we'll suffocate before we drown." Hinsperger bet they would drown first, and each produced a soggy dollar bill. As the hours passed, Young prayed some more, and then on the following day, Monday, he heard the faint sounds of tapping. The men down below hammered out SOS with a wrench. Workmen atop the *Oklahoma*'s overturned hull had cut through the bottom and eventually made their way to the sounds produced by Young and his mates. One drilled a hole into the compartment, and water rushed in as air escaped. The workers cut through and made an opening big enough for the men to escape. Altogether, thirty-two members of the *Oklahoma*'s crew made it out through the bottom of the ship into the welcoming daylight above. As a boat took them away toward a hospital ship, Steve Young turned to Hinsperger. He said, "Put the buck away for a souvenir, Wimp. Neither of us won that bet, thank God."

LEFT: The *Nevada*, the only battleship able to get under way on the morning of December 7, is shown here after being beached deliberately to avoid having her sunk in the harbor's entrance channel, where she would have blocked traffic. During her brief sortie that morning, she became a magnet for attacking Japanese planes. In this shot, she is much deeper in the water than normal, an indication of the punishment she has absorbed.

BOTTOM: The heavily damaged *California* lists to port. Eventually sinking at her berth, she required considerable patching and salvage work before being refloated on March 25, 1942, so she could be dry-docked and made seaworthy again. In the background are the buildings of Ford Island, next to which the battleships moored.

Chapter Six

GLOBAL CONFLICT

ABOVE: The gun captain of a 16-inch gun (41cm) peers into the breech to make sure there is no burning residue from the previous round. Simultaneously, he uses his rag-encased forearm to wipe clean the "mushroom" that is part of the hinged breech mechanism. After the projectile and powder bags have been rammed into position in the barrel, the portion under his elbow swings upward and rotates a quarter of a turn as the interrupted screw threads engage each other. That forms a gas-tight seal so that the ignition of the powder will send the explosion in only one direction—out through the muzzle of the gun.
OPPOSITE PAGE: On August 20, 1945, a few days after the end of hostilities, the *Missouri*, left, transfers landing party members to the *Iowa* in preparation for the American occupation of Japan.

After the Japanese attack, the situation for the battleships would never be the same again. On December 20, Ensign Fred Michaelis of the *Pennsylvania* went out to his car and found that someone had deflated all four tires with an ice pick. To remedy the damage, he began the laborious process of removing the tires one at a time and taking them to a garage to have the inner tubes patched. As he was doing so, the ship's chaplain came to tell

him the *Pennsylvania* was going to shift to another berth. So Michaelis, leaving the car up on jacks and his tools lying on the seat, returned to the battleship. Once aboard, he found that the preparations for getting under way went beyond those for merely moving to another berth in the navy yard. The flagship was headed for repairs in San Francisco, and only a few of those in the crew had been told she was leaving. Such was the state of security in the weeks shortly after the attack. The ship proceeded to Hunters Point, where she was repaired and her antiaircraft ability was beefed up. For the first time, she received fire control radar for her 5-inch (13cm)/25-caliber guns. It was an improvement, but she was still no match for new ships such as the *North Carolina* and *Washington*. Michaelis remained on board for a few more months, then left the ship for flight training. Naval aviation loomed large in the Navy of the future. The *Pennsylvania* symbolized the fleet's past.

AID TO THE BRITISH

Though the British had sunk the *Bismarck* in May of 1941, her sister, *Tirpitz*, still posed a considerable threat, as did a number of other large German surface combatants. The Royal Navy needed help. As a result, on March 25, 1942, Task Force 39, built around the *Washington*, carrier *Wasp*, and two heavy cruisers, departed Casco Bay, Maine, for the British Isles. Two days later, the *Washington* lost a man overboard at sea. The ship's officers and petty officers conducted a muster to determine who the missing man was so they could report to the embarked task force commander, Rear Admiral John Wilcox. All the ship's officers and men were present and accounted for—it turned out that the missing man was Wilcox himself. No clear-cut explanation ever emerged to explain the mysterious event—whether he was washed overboard, jumped, or was pushed.

On April 4, after running through a spate of heavy weather, the task force reached Scapa Flow, the British fleet base in the Orkneys. The situation was somewhat reminiscent of the arrival of American battleships there in December 1917. Ensign John "Bud" Gore, one of the *Washington*'s junior supply officers, was on deck as the ship made her approach to the anchorage with officers and men doing calisthenics. He concluded that the British probably thought the arriving Americans were crazy. For entering port, the crew got into dress uniforms, ready for a formal arrival ceremony. It wasn't as impressive as in 1917. The American battleship fired a twenty-one-gun salute and heard an answer from a distant gun. The Americans had everything in readiness to render honors, including a saluting gun crew, band, Marine guard, and bugler. The first ship they passed was a destroyer whose appearance showed the effects of war. From her bridge came the welcoming salute, the skirl of a bagpipe.

Gore's assessment of the local recreational opportunities echoed those of American visitors in World War I. Gore wrote later that "Scapa Flow itself was the most uninviting liberty port most of us had seen." He and his shipmates managed to board Royal Navy ships to drink, and in turn invited their new friends aboard their ship, where the food was better and more plentiful. Another nostalgic touch was a visit to the *Washington* by King George VI; his father, George V, had visited the flagship *New York* a war earlier. The crew of the *Washington* had been mustered early for the visit—far too early, it turned out—and had to stand in the rain for a considerable time. When the king arrived and saw the condition of the crew, he doffed his own rain cape as a gesture

Commissioned in 1923, the *West Virginia* was the U.S. Navy's newest battleship through the rest of the 1920s [ ] of the 1930s. While the pre-1920s battleships had undergone substantial rebuilding to upgrade them, the *West Virginia* and her sisters had not. The heavy damage she suffered during the attack on Pearl Harbor necessitated a major reconstruction of the ship.

TOP LEFT: The *West Virginia*, in the foreground, is wreathed in smoke on December 7 as the crew of a nearby boat rescues a sailor from the water. She suffered heavy torpedo damage to her port side. Alert counter-flooding measures, however, brought water into the starboard side and thus enabled her to settle on a relatively even keel and avoid capsizing as the *Oklahoma* did. Both the *West Virginia* and the *Tennessee*, seen beyond her, sport their original cage masts with the foretop structures above.

TOP RIGHT: *West Virginia* is in dry dock at Pearl Harbor after salvage work brought her afloat again on Memorial Day 1942. The many compartments open on her port side reveal the heavy damage she sustained in the attack. She received sufficient repairs in Hawaii to make her seaworthy for the voyage to Bremerton, Washington, where she underwent extensive reconstruction.

BOTTOM: The *West Virginia* under way for the West Coast on April 25, 1943. Gone are the towering cage masts and the fire control tops that went with them. She is capable of steaming from one place to another but is no longer a fighting ship. She retains few guns except the 16-inch (41cm) ones in her four turrets.

LEFT: The *West Virginia*, at the Puget Sound Navy Yard, has lost what little superstructure she retained for the trans-Pacific voyage. Only the turrets remain above the deck level. In the foreground, hundreds of people listen to speeches and band music during a war bond rally.

BELOW: The ship is near the Puget Sound yard on July 2, 1944, after receiving a completely new superstructure; it is compact enough to permit wide arcs of fire for her new antiaircraft guns. She is now a far more capable warship. The *West Virginia* was in Tokyo Bay during the September 1945 signing of the Japanese surrender papers, the only battleship present for both that event and the attack that had brought the United States into the conflict.

of shared suffering and proceeded to inspect the men of the American battleship.

"MARKET STREET COMMANDOS"

In the early months of the war, older battleships such as the *Pennsylvania* were not of much use and so spent a good deal of time in San Francisco. The *Tennessee* and *Maryland*, lightly damaged at Pearl Harbor, had been repaired and restored to duty. They were joined by four ships that had not been at Pearl Harbor: the *Colorado* in the Pacific, and the *Mississippi*, *New Mexico*, and *Idaho*, which had been recalled from the Atlantic. The old ships were too slow to steam with the aircraft carriers and were poorly armed against aerial attack. Moreover, the Navy was short on oilers, so fuel would be a problem as well. While in San Francisco, Radioman Ted Mason of the *Pennsylvania* and many other battleship sailors enjoyed the delights of liberty in that city to the degree that their meager pay and a midnight curfew would allow. For the most part, the only action Mason and the other battleship sailors experienced in those early months of the war was recreational. They dubbed themselves the "Market Street Commandos."

In April came a flicker of activity. On the 14th, the *Pennsylvania*, six other battleships, and a squadron of destroyers got under way as Task Force One. They steamed out under the Golden Gate Bridge and headed southwest with no air cover. To Mason, the ship's overloaded condition made her movements sluggish and uncomfortable, even in moderate seas. The ships performed maneuvers, launched their floatplanes to perform reconnaissance flights, and practiced firing all their guns. Scuttlebutt concerning the task force's mission was rampant during the time at sea, but nothing came of it. In late April, the ships headed back to the West Coast, engaging in war games as they steamed. Far to the west, off Australia, American and Japanese forces were engaging in the Battle of the Coral Sea, an aircraft carrier engagement and the first naval battle in which the opposing ships did not come within sight of each other. The old ships of Task Force One would have only been an impediment in that environment, requiring antiair protection themselves, and unable to use their big guns against an enemy far out of range.

TOP RIGHT: As the new year of 1942 dawned, the *South Dakota,* first in a new class of fast battleships, was being rushed to completion at the New York Shipbuilding Corporation in Camden, New Jersey, across the Delaware River from Philadelphia. This is the view looking down from the superstructure toward the fantail and shows turret three with its 16-inch (41cm) guns installed, the roof not yet in place over them. The scene is reminiscent of the picture on page 38 showing the installation of a 12-inch (30cm) gun in a turret of the *Connecticut.* BOTTOM: The forward part of the superstructure is taking shape. Forward of it, the framework for turret two is in place, with the guns not yet installed. Remarkably, the *South Dakota* was commissioned on March 20, 1942, less than three months after this picture was taken.

On May 31, Vice Admiral William Pye, Commander of Task Force One, dispatched the *Maryland, Colorado,* and a screen of three destroyers northwestward from San Francisco following a report that a small Japanese aircraft carrier might be approaching as a threat to that West Coast city. In command of the task group was Rear Admiral Walter Stratton Anderson, type commander for the battleships. Once again, the *Maryland* was his flagship, as she had been on December 7. On June 5, Pye, his other five battleships, three destroyers, and the escort carrier *Long Island* also steamed west after hearing reports of the momentous Battle of Midway far to the west. The Japanese Combined Fleet had gone to sea in force, sending its attack probes toward both Midway Island and the Aleutians. American carrier-based dive-bombers scored a great victory at Midway by sinking four aircraft carriers. The small carriers that might have threatened San Francisco went to the Aleutians instead. As it was, the two groups of old battleships rendezvoused at sea, then returned to port. Their crews saw only empty ocean, which was just as well. With scant air cover, they would have been easy targets for carrier planes.

FIRST COMBAT FOR FAST BATTLESHIPS

In July 1942, after months in which the first fast battleships had operated in the Atlantic as a support to the Royal Navy, the *North Carolina* arrived in Pearl Harbor. The wrecks of some of the old battleships were evident in the fleet port, which was still licking its wounds several months after the devastation of the Japanese attack. Now came a new ship, bristling topside with dozens of antiaircraft guns: without question, it was the most modern battleship that had ever reached Hawaii. Lieutenant (junior grade) Julian Burke, who before the war had been on board the *West Virginia,* was now taken aback by a roaring ovation from the crews of the older ships that ringed the harbor. His first reaction was one of wonder, for these other ships had been in combat, and "The Showboat" had not. But she was more than just a warship in that moment. She was a new symbol of hope, a commodity that the men of the other warships had hungered for in the last few months. Even beyond that, she was a promise of

more to come. Years afterward, when he had settled into retirement as a rear admiral, Julian Burke's eyes glistened once again as his mind replayed that scene at Pearl Harbor in the summer of 1942.

The *North Carolina* became the first of the new ships into combat when she provided antiaircraft support for the carrier *Enterprise* during the Battle of the Eastern Solomons in late August. U.S. Marines had invaded the island of Guadalcanal on August 7, and the Japanese had subsequently interjected numerous naval forces in an effort to recapture the island, particularly its airstrip, Henderson Field. Despite the help, the *Enterprise* caught three bombs on August 24. On September 15, "The Showboat" once again served as a protector, this time steaming with a convoy that included the aircraft carrier *Wasp.* That afternoon, Radioman Alan Campbell was on watch in the flag radio space on the bridge. He witnessed explosions on the *Wasp,* heard a call to general quarters, and then a radio report from the destroyer *O'Brien:* "Torpedo under our ship headed for you." Captain George Fort ordered the battleship's rudder hard to starboard, and Radioman Campbell got a good grip on a nearby railing. The torpedo smacked home on the port bow and threw up a geyser of water higher than the ship's mast. The torpedo, launched by the submarine *I-19,* tore a 32-foot (9.8m) by 18-foot (5.5m) hole in the hull. The *North Carolina* kept steaming and speeded up to twenty-five knots, but then she had to retire for repairs.

That November, the *Massachusetts* became the first of the new fast battleships to fire her 16-inch (41cm) guns in anger. The Allies were not yet ready for a full-scale invasion of the European continent, but they did establish a toehold in North Africa with Operation Torch. The *Massachusetts* was among the bombardment ships during the November 8, 1942, assault on Casablanca, Morocco—then under the control of Vichy France. The incomplete French battleship *Jean Bart,* moored at a Casablanca pier, began flinging salvos seaward, which was the signal for the American ships to retaliate. The *Massachusetts* found the range on the *Jean Bart* and landed a projectile on a barbette, putting the turret out of action for hours. Maneuvering frequently, in part to avoid torpedoes, the *Massachusetts* continued shooting, sinking two destroyers, damaging

shore batteries, and generally making a mess of the port. She was hit twice during the engagement and fired about sixty percent of her main battery rounds that day. It was a tiring workout for the ammunition passers who spent hours manhandling powder and projectiles up to the turrets.

It was also an interesting experience for the crews of the ship's OS2U spotter planes. One crew, Lieutenant C. R. Dorflinger and Aviation Radioman Dale Moudy, was in the air for about five hours and finally ran short of fuel. They landed on the water, a few miles away from the action, and watched the rest of the battle while sitting on the wing of their floatplane. The other plane, manned by Ensign Tom Dougherty and Radioman Robert Ethridge, landed in a marshy area near the shore after being shot down by French fighter planes. Frenchmen on the ground captured the two *Massachusetts* aviators and imprisoned them. The ship's crew presumed the two had been killed in action and held a memorial service for them. After the two men had been in captivity for a week, Army Rangers rescued them, and they eventually returned to the United States separately before being reunited in the Norfolk Naval Hospital, where Ethridge was recovering from gunshot and shrapnel wounds sustained when he was captured. Dougherty returned to the *Massachusetts*, and Ethridge, after his recovery, became a member of a bomber crew.

MORE GUADALCANAL SUPPORT

Back in the Pacific, the *Maryland* and *Colorado* headed west from Pearl Harbor in early November to provide possible backup support for the Guadalcanal operation. Their crews were a mix of young and old. The ships had on board newly trained reserve officers and enlisted men not long from recruit training. Those men sought guidance from the veterans who had grown up in the prewar Navy, when a ship might be a man's home for years at a time. Such was the case for Boatswain's Mate First Class Dutch Hoderlein of the *Maryland*. He had advanced slowly through the years since reporting aboard the ship as a plank owner at the time of her commissioning in July 1921. His seniority and experience gained him the respect of the crew.

As they steamed down the channel toward the sea, the ships and their escorts passed a housing development. Ensign Howard Sauer of the *Maryland*

was intrigued when he saw that the 5-inch (13cm) guns of the secondary battery—along with their telescopic gunsights—were pointing together toward a house ashore. He got his own telescope and spotted the attraction, a pretty young woman wearing a white dress with a flower in her hair. She had stepped out of her kitchen and was waving a friendly goodbye to the men on board the departing ships. As Sauer put it, "She was the last girl we saw for many months. For [some] she was the last girl they ever saw."

In August 1942, about the time Marines were invading Guadalcanal, the new *South Dakota* left Philadelphia and headed for the Pacific so she could team up with the *North Carolina* to form the first division of 35,000-ton (31,745t) fast battleships in the South Pacific. Rear Admiral Willis A. Lee, Jr., was in command as Commander, Battleship Division Six; he had taken the empty billet created when Admiral Wilcox was lost overboard from the *Washington* a few months earlier. Soon afterward, the *South Dakota* was damaged when she struck a submerged coral pinnacle at Tongatabu; Lee shifted to the *Washington*. On October 26, after being repaired and taking aboard additional guns, the *South Dakota* steamed with the carrier *Enterprise* in the Battle of Santa Cruz Islands. There she put on an impressive display of firepower with her forest of antiaircraft guns, including 5-inch (13cm), 40-millimeter, and 20-millimeter. As there were no surface targets, antiaircraft guns were the weapons of necessity in that action. Someone began making chalk marks to indicate Japanese planes that the ship's guns had shot down, or perhaps noting the number of planes that guns of any ship knocked down. The *South Dakota*'s crew eventually claimed to have shot down thirty-two planes, although others believed the number to be either a bit lower or substantially lower. In any event, the *Enterprise* was well protected that day, while the carrier *Hornet*, which was not protected by a battleship, was sunk.

By mid-November, the plight of U.S. forces was desperate as they sought to prevent the Japanese from retaking Guadalcanal. Marines battled the enemy ashore, while Navy ships sought to provide protection and support. The ships fought off air raids and nocturnal runs made by the "Tokyo Express," the name for the heavy ships that bombarded the island, making life miserable for those

LEFT: The *South Dakota* ran aground at Tongatabu in September 1942, a fortuitous accident, because it necessitated a trip to the Pearl Harbor Navy Yard for repairs. During the repair period, the ship received a complement of light antiaircraft guns that proved remarkably useful at the Battle of the Santa Cruz Islands on October 26. In combat artist Dwight Shepler's action-filled watercolor, the ship is shooting furiously to protect the aircraft carrier *Enterprise* at right. Men on other ships thought the *South Dakota* herself was on fire because of all the flashes from her antiaircraft guns.

BOTTOM: Captain Thomas Gatch, commanding officer of the *South Dakota*, speaks during a memorial service on the ship's fantail to honor the men killed in the night battle of November 15, 1942. Gatch can be seen just to the left of the American flag at the base of the aircraft crane. After suffering damage during the battle off Guadalcanal, the ship returned to the New York Navy Yard for repairs. There, she received a good deal of publicity, although her name was not revealed. She thus acquired a number of interesting nicknames: "Old Nameless," "Battleship X," and "The Big Bastard."

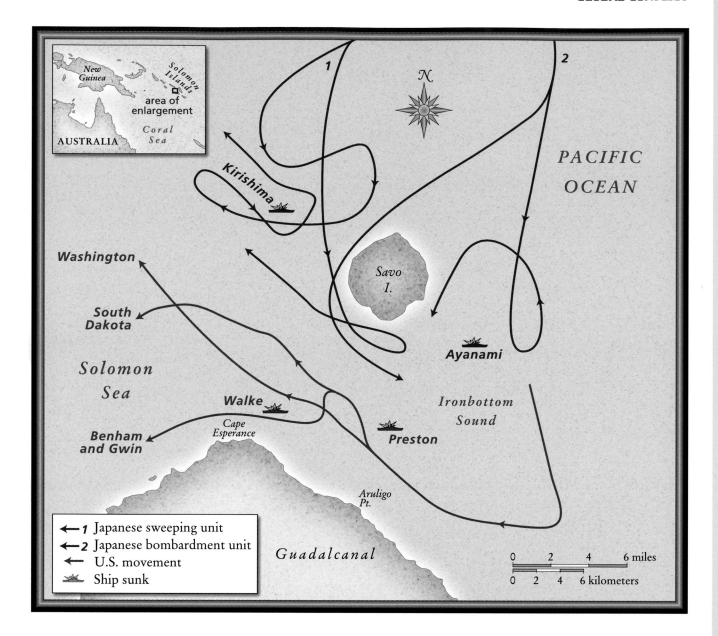

NAVAL BATTLE OF GUADALCANAL, NOVEMBER 1942

On the night of November 14, a formation of four U.S. destroyers (the *Benham, Gwin, Preston,* and *Walke*) and two U.S. battleships (the *Washington* and *South Dakota*) steamed in the narrow waters between Guadalcanal and nearby Savo Island to intercept a force of Japanese bombardment ships. What ensued was a confusing melee at close quarters. Following their customary tactics, the Japanese split their forces, capitalizing on their superior night-fighting abilities. They slaughtered the U.S. destroyers; only two survived the action, and one of those two sank the next day. Benefiting from their radar-controlled gunnery, the U.S. battleships fared better. The *Washington*'s fire was particularly effective, and of the six U.S. ships, she was the only one to escape unscathed. The Japanese lost the battleship *Kirishima* and destroyer *Ayanami* as a result of the battle. The *Kirishima* was the second Japanese battleship sunk in action during the war (the first had been the *Hiei*, sunk on November 13).

Battleship Admiral

Up to the attack on Pearl Harbor, the Navy was run by the "Gun Club," officers who believed that the big gun was—and would remain—the predominant naval weapon. For years, the path to the top for naval officers had been to specialize in ordnance and to command battleships. That changed quickly, however. As World War II proceeded and aircraft carriers and submarines were obviously the U.S. Navy's main offensive weapons, the terms "Battleship Admiral" and "Gun Club" came to seem old-fashioned—even pejorative. For some, though, the terms still carried a note of pride. In particular, the most noteworthy battleship admiral of World War II was Vice Admiral Willis Augustus Lee, Jr., an officer who sought constantly to improve the Navy's gunfire and its tactical use of the great dreadnoughts. To the end of his life, Lee was a card-carrying member of the Gun Club.

The future admiral was born in the hamlet of Natlee, Kentucky, in May 1888, and was a mischievous lad from the beginning. He was raised in the town of Owenton, Kentucky, where he often showed up in school with snakes and other forest creatures in his pocket. He shot at weather vanes, at least one bedroom window, wildlife, and anything else that struck his fancy as a potential target.

Though he was quite clever and had a real talent for both mechanical devices and mathematics, Lee had the habit of applying himself only when things interested him. Thus, he stood slightly below the middle of his class when he graduated from the Naval Academy in 1908. One of the things that did capture his fancy was the Far East. He had a number of tours of duty on the Navy's old China Station early in his career and was widely known in the Navy by the nicknames "Ching" and "Chink"—obviously in the days well before political correctness.

During the 1920 Olympic Games in Antwerp, Belgium, the young naval officer demonstrated the marksmanship that he had fine-tuned during his youth in Kentucky. He had been a member of the Navy Rifle Team at various times in his career, and now he was a member of the team that represented the entire nation. He and a teammate, fellow naval officer Carl Osburn, each earned five gold medals, one silver, and one bronze.

In the early 1930s, after a decade alternating shore duty with destroyer commands, Lee became navigator and then executive officer of the battleship *Pennsylvania*, the spit-and-polish fleet flagship. He also served tours of duty ashore in the Fleet Training Division in Washington. As part of the staff of the Chief of Naval Operations, Fleet Training was in charge of the tactical preparation of the fleet for war at sea. That included supervising tactical exercises and annual competitions in such areas as gunnery and communications. In the late 1930s, Lee commanded the obsolete light cruiser *Concord*; ironically, the officer who commanded all of the Pacific Fleet battleships in World War II had not commanded an individual battleship when he was a captain. When Admiral Harold Stark became CNO in 1939, Lee, who was a member of his staff, accompanied Stark to Washington, once again to Fleet Training. In the months that followed, the U.S. Navy was preparing for combat in earnest

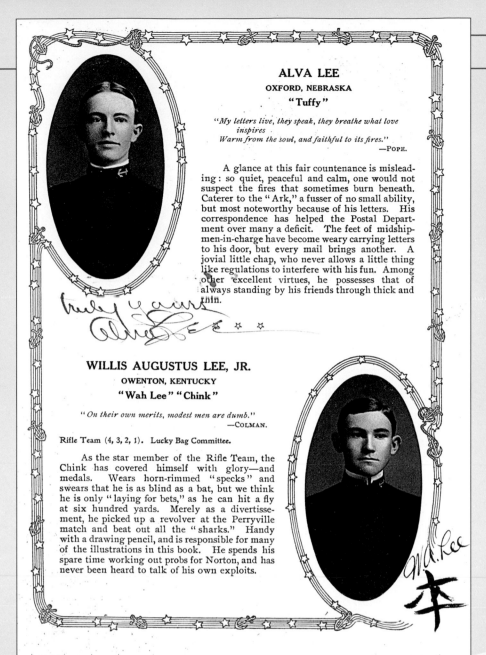

ALVA LEE
OXFORD, NEBRASKA
"Tuffy"

"My letters live, they speak, they breathe what love inspires
Warm from the soul, and faithful to its fires."
—POPE.

A glance at this fair countenance is misleading: so quiet, peaceful and calm, one would not suspect the fires that sometimes burn beneath. Caterer to the "Ark," a fusser of no small ability, but most noteworthy because of his letters. His correspondence has helped the Postal Department over many a deficit. The feet of midshipmen-in-charge have become weary carrying letters to his door, but every mail brings another. A jovial little chap, who never allows a little thing like regulations to interfere with his fun. Among other excellent virtues, he possesses that of always standing by his friends through thick and thin.

WILLIS AUGUSTUS LEE, JR.
OWENTON, KENTUCKY
"Wah Lee" "Chink"

"On their own merits, modest men are dumb."
—COLMAN.

Rifle Team (4, 3, 2, 1). Lucky Bag Committee.

As the star member of the Rifle Team, the Chink has covered himself with glory—and medals. Wears horn-rimmed "specks" and swears that he is as blind as a bat, but we think he is only "laying for bets," as he can hit a fly at six hundred yards. Merely as a divertissement, he picked up a revolver at the Perryville match and beat out all the "sharks." Handy with a drawing pencil, and is responsible for many of the illustrations in this book. He spends his spare time working out probs for Norton, and has never been heard to talk of his own exploits.

ABOVE: Throughout his life, Willis Lee was known for his clever, wry sense of humor. During a training cruise while a Naval Academy midshipman, Lee saw a Chinese laundry operated by a man named Wah Lee. The midshipman's first two initials, W.A., could be pronounced as "Wah," so he copied down the Chinese characters for the man's name. In this page from the 1908 *Lucky Bag*, the Naval Academy yearbook, Lee has signed in both English and Chinese.

because war was already under way in Europe. In particular, Lee was concerned with getting as many ships as possible equipped with radar and antiaircraft guns, because older systems were ineffective against modern dive-bombers.

In November 1942, he was the tactical commander of the task force that sank the battleship *Kirishima* off Guadalcanal, largely ending Japanese attempts to retake the island. In the many months that followed, the general expectation was that the U.S. and Japanese battle lines would eventually duke it out—the sort of climactic gunnery duel that had been anticipated by both sides throughout the years between the world wars. Because of his tactical skill and his knowledge of radar and gunnery, Willis Lee was the man chosen to command the battle line when the titans finally did go at each other. In the meantime, though, the duty was a good deal less glamorous. Because the battleships had become so effective in providing antiair protection for the carriers, they became tied to them. During the Central Pacific amphibious campaign, the carriers provided the striking power, while the battleships served as part of their screen. Lee was essentially relegated to a role as a passenger.

On two separate occasions, he and his battleships might have gotten into action but didn't: during the invasion of the Mariana Islands in June 1944 and in the Battle of Leyte Gulf in October of that year. In June, Lee elected not to engage in a melee at night; in October he wasn't permitted to get his ships into the fight.

That was the last opportunity, because after that, the Japanese heavy ships emerged only sporadically and never in force. Lee himself was called back to the United States in the spring of 1945 to command an experimental task force that sought a remedy to a serious threat that plagued the U.S. fleet—Japanese suicide planes. He was chosen because of his analytical ability and knowledge of gunnery, but he was greatly disappointed to be pulled out of the fleet just as it was closing in on Japan. He and his staff ran experiments in Casco Bay, Maine. In early August, his wife Mabelle wrote in a letter to her sisters back in Illinois, "Lee will be here all this month but doesn't know how much longer. He is anxious to get back to his battleships—you'd think they were his toys and afraid someone will damage them while he's away."

But he never did get back to them. After the Americans dropped two atomic bombs, Japan surrendered, and Lee was far away in Maine. He felt a sense of letdown because the war to which he had contributed a great deal had ended without him. And in the new era of the aircraft carrier, the influence of the old Gun Club was waning. Ten days after hostilities ended, Lee got into his boat one morning for a ride to work. After long months of wartime pressure, short sleep, chain smoking, and little exercise, the fifty-seven-year-old battleship admiral suffered a fatal heart attack. An era ended with him.

ABOVE: This picture of Lee was taken in early 1942, shortly after his promotion to rear admiral. It was one of the last formal portraits made of him, as he was on board ships in the Pacific—and not in photo studios—during much of the rest of the war. At left, a membership card for Lieutenant Oscar Gray of the battleship *New Jersey* is countersigned by the ship's commanding officer, Captain Carl Holden, and Admiral Lee as Commander, Battleships, Pacific Fleet. The Acme Gun Club was essentially an inside joke for officers serving on battleships. They were proud of their skills in naval gunnery but didn't take themselves too seriously—as is evidenced by the fact that the turret's "gun" is a beer bottle firing a bottle cap.

Often an artist can offer viewers an image no camera was able to capture. So it was with the battle off Guadalcanal in the early morning of November 15, 1942. Here, artist Dwight Shepler has used descriptions provided by participants in the battle to depict the night action. In the foreground, Rear Admiral Willis Lee's flagship *Washington* sends off salvos of 16-inch (41cm) gunfire. In column astern of her is the *South Dakota*, which Shepler had depicted in close-up on page 95. Savo Island looms in the background; the American task force had steamed around it that November night before unleashing a barrage against the Japanese.

ashore. In a desperate melee on the night of November 12–13, U.S. cruisers fought the Japanese at close range. Two American admirals were killed, in part because they did not know how to make the best use of radar.

DREADNOUGHT SLUGGING MATCH

Two nights later, the "Tokyo Express" again threatened the island, this time bolstered by the battleship *Kirishima*. The narrow waters between Guadalcanal and Savo, the tiny island to the north, were a less than ideal location for a gunnery duel between battleships. This type of ship was intended to fight on the high seas, where each could begin engaging the enemy at long range, and where the absence of shallow water gave them plenty of maneuvering room. But the circumstances were such that Vice Admiral William F. Halsey, Jr., Commander, South Pacific Force, had few other options but to use his big ships here and now against the Japanese.

To defend against the Japanese, Admiral Lee commanded a task force that comprised his flagship *Washington*, *South Dakota*, and four destroyers. As

they made their approach, American PT boats challenged them by radio. Lee responded by using his nickname to let the boats know his forces were friendly, so they wouldn't attack by mistake. He said, "Refer your big boss about Ching Lee. Chinese, catchee? Call off your boys."

Once the Japanese and American ships neared each other, the Japanese split their ships and pounced upon the destroyers, inflicting serious damage. As Ivan Musicant described in *Battleship at War*, a book about the *Washington*, ships on both sides were soon engaged in a slugging match at ranges far shorter than those for which the big-gun ships were designed. Down in the main battery plot of the flagship, Lieutenant Ed Hooper, the *Washington*'s fire control officer was keeping track of the Japanese through the excellent fire control radar. When the okay came to him through the gunnery officer, Lieutenant Commander Harvey Walsh, Hooper directed his people to start shooting 16-inch (41cm) rounds. When the *Washington* opened up with her big guns—the first use of a battleship main battery in anger in the Pacific War—the concussion knocked Lee's glasses to the deck of the ship's

bridge. Lee and Lieutenant Al Church then had to grope in the dark to find them.

As the American ships pumped out rounds, Church thought it looked like a "red snow-ball fight." Ensign Bob Reed, in the destroyer *Preston*, saw the 16-inch (41cm) rounds trace parabolic arcs, glowing cherry red, as they left the guns. They disappeared for a time into low clouds, then reappeared as they descended on or near the Japanese ships. Captain Jonas Platt of the *Washington*'s Marine detachment was directing the starboard battery of 5-inch (13cm) guns and attempting to shoot out enemy searchlights. Commander Arthur Ayrault, the executive officer, went out on deck to order that life rafts be thrown overboard for the men who'd gone into the water after the destroyers were badly chewed up. Throughout the flagship, some men could clearly see what was happening, but many others could see nothing. Down in the main pump room, Fireman John Brown heard the concussions as the big guns fired and wondered, "What the hell is happening up there?" He had a lot of company on board both battleships.

The *Washington*'s gunnery was excellent that night, and effective. Though the *Washington* was unhurt during the battle, a great deal of Japanese response was drawn to the *South Dakota* as she was silhouetted by the fires from the burning destroyers. Lieutenant (junior grade) Paul Backus was turret officer of turret two, and his assistant was Lieutenant (junior grade) Charlie Francis. Francis's job was to watch through the turret's periscope and report what was happening. At one point, he came away from it with eyes as big as saucers and proclaimed, "It's right out there; I can touch it." And he described in detail the battleship *Kirishima*, which was much closer than he had expected.

Near the end of the battle, Lieutenant Hank Seely, who was manning a main battery director topside on the *Washington*, had a firing solution on the enemy battleship *Kirishima*, which had already been the target of considerable punishment. He was in communication with Lieutenant Hooper in the plotting room, and he sent a solution to the guns. Just before he was due to shoot, the order came down to hold fire. Because of the way the surface search radar was mounted on the *Washington*'s mast, the sector astern was blanked out. In the darkness,

Admiral Lee could not be sure whether the target on the fire control radar was the *South Dakota* or the *Kirishima*—and he didn't want to make a fatal mistake. Hooper, confident that the guns were trained on the enemy battleship, was frustrated by the delay. Later, though, he conceded that it was better to be safe than sorry.

Even without any further incoming projectiles, the *Kirishima* was doomed. She and the destroyer *Ayanami* sank as a result of the battle. The night's action derailed the "Tokyo Express" and essentially broke the back of Japanese efforts to recapture Guadalcanal. The *South Dakota* received considerable topside damage and personnel casualties. When Paul Backus went to his stateroom after the battle he found a dead Marine's body in his bunk. When he went out on deck the following morning, he found, near turret three, a damaged hatch coaming, which was a metal lip that extended perhaps a foot above the deck to keep water from pouring through the hatch into the deck below. Backus noticed that there were half-moon-shaped holes on each side where a projectile had passed through the previous night. When he measured the holes, he found they were 14 inches (36cm) in diameter, the size of the *Kirishima*'s big guns. The flat trajectory indicated that the enemy ship had been shooting at essentially point-blank range. Years later, while serving in a cruiser, one of Backus's shipmates was a chief boatswain's mate who suffered from recurring nightmares. Backus got him to a hypnotist, who discovered that the chief had been in a working party on board the *South Dakota* during the night battle and had had to go up into the superstructure—with no flashlight—to clear away bodies and parts of bodies. The horror of this experience continued to haunt his subconscious, and was removed only through the hypnosis.

NORTH PACIFIC VENTURE

In May 1943, several of the old battleships ventured north to the Aleutians for the seizure of the islands of Attu and Kiska. The Japanese had limited air power in this area, so the ships were safer than they would have been in a place such as the Solomons; and they were also cooler in the northern climes than they had been near the equator. They were accompanied by some small escort carriers that provided a modicum of air support. Submarines were still a concern, and both lookouts and sonarmen reported submarine contacts that proved to be whales. The cool, foggy weather was enlivened at times by an Aleutian phenomenon known as the williwaw, a sudden gust of wind that could reach speeds as high as one hundred knots. The wind churned the seas, sending up waves and spray onto the decks of the battleships and their escorts. In the cool weather, many crewmen grew beards. Ensign Paul Barnes of the *Mississippi* concluded that the beard greatly improved his appearance and was disappointed when the captain ordered the men to be clean shaven once they left the area.

Because the fog was so thick, the ships had to rely heavily on radar to navigate and to maintain position within formation. One day, the fog lifted and the *Mississippi* launched her OS2U Kingfisher floatplane for antisubmarine patrol. The fog soon closed in again and the ship lost radar and radio contact with the plane. There was no way to get back in touch to recover the plane. The aircraft and crew were lost. The men probably perished quickly in the cold waters of the north. The radar and radio situation was complicated by unusual atmospheric effects that sometimes made it possible to pick up signals at a far greater range than usual. This phenomenon led to the most unusual "Battle of the Pips" in the early morning hours of July 26. The *Mississippi* reported surface contacts at a range of fifteen miles (24 km), and radar operators on board the *Idaho* and the cruisers *Wichita* and *Portland* spotted them as well. Soon, the ships were banging away merrily at the phantom targets. But return fire never came from any Japanese ships, for the Americans were shooting into empty ocean. The *Mississippi*'s combat information center officer, Lieutenant Ed Svendsen told the ship's executive officer, Commander John Ocker, that there were no real targets. Ocker replied, "Keep your mouth shut. We're having too much fun; don't spoil it." Eventually, the radar operators concluded that the phosphorescent images on their scopes were actually islands a hundred miles away.

ATLANTIC CONVOYS

In the Atlantic, the old battleships accompanied the convoys that ferried fuel, equipment, weapons, ammunition, and soldiers to the European theater.

Though they could provide little protection against aircraft and no protection against submarines, their 12-inch (30cm) and 14-inch (36cm) guns would be valuable if a surface raider such as a cruiser lurked on the convoy's path. Ed Logue, who had started as a machinist's mate striker on board the *New York*, had opted to become an electrician's mate instead. Among his many duties, he had to ensure that the ship's 36-inch (91cm) searchlights were operating properly. As a convoy slogged its way through fog, the *New York* would sometimes shine her lights on cargo ships to provide a point of reference. Ships also blew their steam whistles as a way of warning others against steering too close.

The end of a convoy run brought a sense of relief at having made it through the danger zone, if only for the amount of time in port in Scotland, before turning around to make the return voyage to the United States. Sometimes the Scots invited them into their homes to share their meager rations of food. To reciprocate the kindness, Logue took the man of one family a bunch of cigars he'd bought from the ship's store. The man derived much pleasure from his smoke, once remarking, "Hmph, hmph, Churchill ain't got nothing on me." When he had smoked it down to the bitter end, he put it into his pipe and finished what little was left of it.

On another occasion, as Logue and shipmate John Diamond were strolling through a park, they came upon some gray-haired Scottish ladies sitting on benches doing their knitting. To the surprise and chagrin of the American sailors, the women stood and bowed as they passed. After the suffering they had endured, they were grateful to the American Allies, who were helping to get the goods through to an island nation that depended on sea-lanes for its survival. And it wasn't just the older generation that honored the Americans. As the two sailors walked farther, in the company of a self-appointed local guide, groups of girls in their early teens would run by, jump up, and tap the Americans on the back. Logue asked his guide, "What in the world did they say, and what were they doing?

"Well, you know the stars on the back of your collar?"

"Yeah."

"They lick their finger like that, and they jump up and they touch your star, and they say, 'The best

In the summer of 1942, while the first of the fast battleships were preparing for combat in the far Pacific, members of the ultimate class of American dreadnoughts were under construction back in the United States. Here, the *New Jersey* is pictured on the shipbuilding ways at the Philadelphia Navy Yard on July 8, 1942. This perspective is from amidships, looking forward toward the bow in the distance. In the foreground, one can see bulkheads in place to form below-decks compartments. The two cylindrical constructions are the barbettes for turrets one and two. Some of the turret machinery is already in place in turret two. Farther forward, deck plating can be seen on what will be the ship's forecastle.

Errant Torpedo

During the first year of World War II, Captain John McCrea was serving as naval aide to President Roosevelt. When it came time for him to go to sea, he was rewarded with one of the Navy's plum jobs for a captain. He was ordered as the first commanding officer of the *Iowa*, the lead ship of what was to be the ultimate class of American dreadnoughts ever built. (In Herman Wouk's sprawling novel *War and Remembrance*, the protagonist, Captain Pug Henry, also served as FDR's naval aide and then skipper of the *Iowa*.)

The *Iowa* went into commission on Washington's Birthday in 1943 at the New York Navy Yard and subsequently went for shakedown training in Casco Bay, Maine. On one of her trips into the bay, McCrea was slow in getting the rudder over and scraped a hole in the ship's bottom when she hit a submerged ledge of rock. The ship had to go into dry dock in the Boston Navy Yard to have the damage repaired. The skipper felt terrible about it, but he managed to retain command. Admiral Ernest King, a hard-bitten officer, was then the Chief of Naval Operations and Commander-in-Chief of the U.S. Fleet. When McCrea discussed the grounding with him, King told him that President Roosevelt had undoubtedly been informed of it. Since Roosevelt had not directed any action to be taken against McCrea, none was. It was useful to have friends in high places, and the likable McCrea received another present from Roosevelt as well. When the president was to cross the Atlantic to North Africa, thence to Tehran, Iran, for a meeting with the Allied leaders, he chose the *Iowa* for his passage.

Following his speech at the Arlington National Cemetery on Armistice Day, November 11, 1943, Roosevelt boarded his presidential yacht and rendezvoused with the *Iowa* upstream from the mouth of the Potomac River. The ship then proceeded to Hampton Roads to fill up with oil; she had discharged much of her fuel so she would ride higher out of the water and thus not scrape bottom in the Chesapeake Bay. Captain McCrea informed the president that he wanted to get his ship under way at 11:00 P.M. November 12 to head across the Atlantic because that was the time of maximum high tide, and thus the greatest clearance for the ship's bottom. But Roosevelt, who had loved the sea since his youth, recalled the old sailor's superstition against starting an important voyage on a Friday. So he asked McCrea to begin the voyage on Saturday. The *Iowa*'s anchor broke ground just after midnight on November 13 and began her momentous journey. Whether because of superstition or not, she was able to escape danger the following day.

On the sunny but windy Sunday afternoon of November 14, the battleship was steaming eastward. Her original escort had been replaced by four destroyers; the crews of these new escort ships were unaware that the president was on board the *Iowa*. Lieutenant Charles Pick was on the battleship's navigation bridge as the ships prepared for an antiaircraft gunnery drill. Pick looked down to the 01 promenade deck below, just outside the captain's cabin where Roosevelt was staying during the trip. He spotted the members of the Joint Chiefs of Staff gathered around Roosevelt, who was seated in a wheelchair, wearing a gray fedora hat, and smoking a cigarette in a holder. The officers on the bridge saw some weather balloons that had been released to serve as targets for the antiaircraft guns. Then the attention of all was riveted by an announcement over the ship's loudspeaker system: "General quarters. This ain't no drill!" The destroyers had been conducting their own exercises, and one of them, the *William D. Porter*, was simulating a torpedo attack on the battleship. However, she mistakenly launched a live, fully armed torpedo. Her crew had sent a radio message, "Torpedo on the starboard beam," to warn the battleship, which then went to full speed and turned to present as small a target as possible. Lieutenant Pick and the *Iowa*'s navigator, Commander Jack Pohl, sought to get inside but found themselves locked out of the charthouse. They heard the torpedo explode in the turbulence created by the *Iowa*'s wake, only about one hundred yards (91m) astern. Afterward, Pick returned to his normal watch station on the flag bridge. He saw the angry Admiral King glaring at the offending destroyer. Then General Hap Arnold, chief of the Army Air Forces and a fellow member of the Joint Chiefs, yanked the admiral's chain by asking, "Tell me, Ernest, does this happen often in your Navy?"

of luck to you, sir.'" To a pair of Americans who felt they were just doing their jobs, it was gratifying.

Even as some of the old battleships were operating in the Atlantic, so were some of the new ones. As long as potent German ships, such as the battleship *Tirpitz* and battle cruiser *Scharnhorst*, could menace Allied convoys, the Royal Navy kept a careful watch, and the U.S. Navy maintained new fast battleships in the Atlantic as a counter. In May 1943, the new *Alabama* and the *South Dakota*, repaired from her battle damage in the Solomons, joined up with the Royal Navy in Scapa Flow. Ensign Wayne Bundy of the *Alabama* was surprised by the accommodations he encountered when he and several fellow officers went to have dinner on board the British battleship *King George V*. In contrast to the bare decks and bulkheads on board his own ship, he was struck by the wardroom in the British ship. The deck was carpeted, and the decorations included wood paneling and drapes. The biggest surprise was the sight of a corner fireplace ablaze with a wood fire for the comfort of the British officers. The *Alabama*'s first lieutenant, responsible for damage control in his own ship, sputtered, "But, but, but— you can't do this!" One of the British officers replied, "Oh, I don't know. We look at it this way. If you get hit, you get hit. Meanwhile, you might as well be comfortable, what?"

In the months that followed, the men of the *Alabama* yearned for some of that comfort as their ship served as part of the covering force for convoys that operated north of the Arctic Circle, some on the way to the Soviet Union. Gunner's Mate Ted Cate later remembered, "Standing watch in a 5-inch (13cm) gun mount in the North Atlantic in winter is a little like sitting in your refrigerator. The bulkheads and overhead would become coated with frost from the moisture in your breath, and if it warmed up enough in daytime to melt the frost, it would rain when the mount was moved back and forth to exercise the equipment." Gunner's Mate Raymond Chartier also stood watches in a 5-inch (13cm) mount. For amusement, he and his fellow sufferers took pennies and pressed them onto the cold steel of bulkheads, where they stuck because of the moisture that had condensed and frozen.

After their deployment with the British, the *South Dakota* and *Alabama* steamed to Norfolk to spend a brief shipyard period before being dispatched to the Pacific. They could be released from the Atlantic because now the even newer *Iowa* and *New Jersey* had the "*Tirpitz* watch." For Fire Controlman Clyde Graven, it was a time of romance. He called his girlfriend Maura, who was in Louisville, Kentucky, and asked her to come immediately so they could be married. They would have a brief honeymoon in Virginia Beach before his ship had to leave again for distant waters. After the wedding on August 19, they and Graven's shipmates enjoyed a reception in a hotel ballroom, where Sophie Tucker was providing the entertainment. During a break, the singer met Maura in the ladies' room and heard about her wedding that day. Back in the ballroom later, Clyde and Maura danced in a spotlight while Tucker sang "I'll Be With You in Apple Blossom Time." It proved to be prophetic. Early the next morning, Clyde had to return to the ship at Norfolk for what he thought was a routine shifting of berths. In an experience similar to that of Ensign Fred Michaelis of the *Pennsylvania* at the beginning of the war, Clyde found that the *Alabama* was instead leaving that day for the Panama Canal and the Pacific; there would be no honeymoon in Virginia Beach. The couple didn't see each other again until Clyde arrived for advanced fire control school in Washington, D.C., in the spring of 1944— "apple blossom time."

SUPPORT FOR AMPHIBIOUS INVASIONS

Vulnerable to air attack, and too slow to steam with the fast carriers, the old battleships were essentially relegated to low-threat areas during nearly the first two years of the war. In late 1943, with carrier protection against air threat and with an increased number of oilers available to supply fuel, they finally found a suitable first-line mission with the beginning of the amphibious campaign in the Central Pacific in November 1943. There had been battles in the Solomon Islands in the south and the Aleutians in the north. Now the target was the Gilbert Islands in the center. The old battleships had two primary roles: bombardment of the islands prior to the invasion force hitting the beach, and gunfire support of soldiers and Marines once they were ashore. They weren't required to do any high-speed steaming.

In July 1943, the *Alabama* steams as part of a multinational task force leaving Scapa Flow, north of Scotland. The ships are on the way to Operation Governor off the coast of southern Norway. Their mission was to divert German attention away from the Allied invasion then taking place at Sicily in the Mediterranean. The British aircraft carrier *Illustrious* and a battleship of the King George V class follow in the column. The carrier planes overhead are Seafires and a Martlet. The latter was the British name for the American Wildcat fighter.

Instead, they would get close to the islands and unleash their big guns in concert with the smaller ones sported by cruisers and destroyers.

While Marines were assaulting the bitterly defended island of Betio (part of Tarawa Atoll) in the Gilberts on November 20, Army men were hitting nearby Makin. Included in the fire-support ships at the latter were the *Pennsylvania*, *New Mexico*, and *Mississippi*. Lieutenant (junior grade) Paul Barnes was the *Mississippi*'s officer of the deck at Makin. During the bombardment of the island, he heard a loud hiss of gas and saw flames shoot out of the

range-finder ports on either side of turret two. The turret had suffered an internal explosion, as it had in 1924. Barnes heard the report "Fire in the lower handling room of turret two." The officer of the deck realized that if the fire reached the powder magazines, the ship herself would blow up, which is was what had happened to the *Arizona* at Pearl Harbor. The commanding officer, Captain Lunsford L. Hunter, contemplated flooding the magazines. First, he sent the chief boatswain to investigate. The boatswain reported that the fire had been extinguished, but nearly everybody in the top levels of the

turret had been killed or injured by the explosion there. The other three 14-inch (36cm) turrets kept shooting. The eventual death toll was forty-three; the number killed nineteen years earlier in that turret was forty-eight. The cause was probably the same—new powder inserted into a barrel that still contained a smoldering remnant from the previous firing.

On the morning of November 20, the *Maryland*, the flagship for Rear Admiral Harry Hill, was assigned to bombard Betio Island. The ship's gunnery officer, Commander Bruce Kelley, had received orders to use

his judgment on how much to fire the 16-inch (41cm) guns, since the ship's radios were filled with vacuum tubes, and the concussion the guns produced could disrupt communications. The concussions did exactly that.

In the predawn hours, as part of the normal procedure for observing the effects of gunfire, the ship had launched an OS2U floatplane in order to have a spotter aloft during the bombardment. The plane was piloted by Lieutenant Commander Robert MacPherson; also in the plane was Aviation Radioman Robert Houle. While the aircraft was still

TOP LEFT: Until the advent of the Central Pacific island-hopping campaign in late 1943, the old, slow battle-ships could make only a limited contribution. That changed when they were called upon to provide shore bombardment and naval gunfire support of friendly troops in conjunction with amphibious assaults. Here, 14-inch (36cm) projectiles are laid out on the deck of the *New Mexico* following the re-supply of ammunition.
TOP RIGHT: The 5-inch (13cm)/25-caliber guns of the *New Mexico* prepare to fire during a bombardment of Saipan on the invasion day, June 15, 1944. These old guns were really intend-ed for antiaircraft fire—and not all that good even in that role. The fuze pot is on the left side of each mount; three projectiles were loaded into it and set with mechani-cal time fuzes. In new ships, the range and bearing were set automatically, and new radio-equipped projectiles had proximity fuzes that would set off their explosive charges when they got near enemy airplanes rather than requiring direct hits.
BOTTOM: The *Colorado* fires shore bombardment at the Gilbert Islands in November 1943.

on the catapult, Houle saw a flash on Betio and then heard a splash near the ship. The Japanese were fir-ing at the ship; the plane's exhaust flames had given the enemy gunners a target in the darkness. Once the plane was airborne, Houle had a view of the panorama of landing craft chugging their way ashore and disgorging Marines that subsequently came under withering gunfire. He saw a large red patch from the air and realized that the blood of the wounded and dead Marines was floating atop the seawater. As the plane flew at an altitude of only 300 to 400 feet (91–122m), Houle felt the Kingfisher rocked by small arms fire, then felt a hot jolt of pain where he'd been hit. MacPherson took him back to the ship for treatment. When a crane lifted the craft out of the water, men on deck could see that the main float was riddled with bullet holes, and water was pouring from it as if it were a lawn sprinkler. The plane crew had managed to survive, although many hundreds of Marines did not. The Gilberts operation proved to be costly in lives but was even-tually victorious.

In early 1944, when the *Colorado* bombarded the Marshall Islands, the next step in the Central Pacific campaign, she opened up with a broadside of 16-inch (41cm) projectiles. The aerial spotter radioed in an interesting report: "Up five miles (8km), right three islands." The ship had fired at the wrong island. Evidently, the bombardment ships still needed to make some refinements. In fact, though, that was an exception. The heavy casualties inflicted on the Marines in the Gilberts led to heavier pre-invasion bombardment in later assaults. The Japanese-held islands were subjected to a "Spruance haircut" and "Mitscher shave"—the nickname for surface and aerial bombardments led by the surface ships of Vice Admiral Raymond Spruance and carrier aircraft of Rear Admiral Marc Mitscher. The old prewar battleships were able to specialize in firing at shore targets and enemy troop concentrations, and became quite skilled. They were also the beneficiaries of reconnaissance photos and even three-dimensional terrain maps, so that gunfire directors on board ship could visualize in advance what the targets would look like from offshore. In contrast to the bloodbath at the Gilberts, the invasion of the Marshalls was a textbook success.

The liner of one of the 16-inch (41cm) guns in the *Maryland*'s turret one was extended beyond the barrel's end after the Marshalls bombardment, and the gunnery crew was concerned about possible damage to the gun. The gun was lowered, and slender Lieutenant (junior grade) John Thro crawled into the barrel with flashlight in hand to inspect for damage. While inside, crew members joked, saying such things as "If he gets stuck, we can shoot him out," and "He's in a good spot in case of an air raid." During his trip into the barrel, the young officer discovered that the liner had cracked as a result of the shooting, and the crew broke into cheers. The ship would have to go to Bremerton, Washington, to get the gun relined, and that meant Stateside liberty.

ON TO THE MARIANAS

During February of 1944, the fast carrier task force, including its screen of battleships, demonstrated the mobility and striking power that were to be its trademark throughout the inexorable island-hopping campaign toward Japan. In mid-February, carrier planes attacked the Japanese stronghold of Truk in the Caroline Islands, and the *Iowa* and *New Jersey* joined other surface warships in going after Japanese ships escaping from Truk Lagoon. A week later, the fast battleships were in the carrier screens as they approached the Mariana Islands for a softening-up strike in preparation for yet another step in the road to Japan.

In the darkness on the night of February 21–22, the ships of Task Group 58.2 came under air attack. The 5-inch (13cm) gun mounts of the *Alabama* were under radar control by Mark 37 directors and went into automatic fire when Japanese aircraft came within range. The ship maneuvered during the attack and swung to the right. The 5-inch (13cm) mounts continued to track the low-flying planes—which meant their barrels essentially remained steady as the ship rotated under them—until they finally reached the limit of their mobility. They stopped shooting because of firing cut-out cams, which were devices that prevented guns from shooting at other parts of the ship. Tragically, a man in gun mount number five on the starboard side overrode the safety feature and fired the mount's two guns directly into the back of mount number nine. The blast killed five men and injured eleven.

The debut of Iowa-class ships heralded the culmination of fast battleship development in the U.S. Navy. They had essentially the same main and secondary battery armament as the North Carolina and South Dakota classes, but were about two hundred feet longer. The extra length permitted the mounting of additional antiaircraft guns, but, above all, gave them an extra six knots of speed—to thirty-three knots.
LEFT: The *Missouri* on July 24, 1944, little more than a month after her commissioning. She was the only ship of the class to sport this curlicue camouflage pattern. It was painted over in 1945 when she went to the Pacific for operations.
BOTTOM: The new *Wisconsin* at Pearl Harbor on November 11, 1944—twenty-six years to the day after an armistice had ended World War I. She dwarfs the salvaged hull of the *Oklahoma*, which was built during World War I and knocked out of action on the first day of World War II.

The *New Jersey*, the second ship of the Iowa class, is shown shortly before her launching at the Philadelphia Navy Yard on December 7, 1942, the first anniversary of the attack on Pearl Harbor. The speakers' platform is draped with bunting, and microphones are in place at the lectern. Fore poppets are attached at the bow to help distribute weight during her backward trip into the Delaware River. The anchors and chains suspended above were used to create drag and slow her down after she built a speed of nearly twenty miles an hour going backward down the launching ways. The chains weren't sufficient for the purpose. Her momentum was such that she skidded ashore on the New Jersey side of the river, a fitting tribute, perhaps, to the state for which she had been named in 1940 by Acting Secretary of the Navy Charles Edison. When the ship was launched in 1942, Edison, son of the famous inventor Thomas Edison, was governor of New Jersey, and his wife christened the ship.

In a report written after the event, the *Alabama*'s commanding officer, Captain Fred Kirtland, stated that the man in the mount "for some unaccountable reason bypassed the safety feature." He also reported that the man had served in the gun mount since the ship was commissioned and had nine months' experience in its operation. Other members of the *Alabama*'s crew offered different explanations. Fire Controlman Harry Peaper believed that the officer in charge of the mount kept telling the crew to fire and, in his nervousness, one of the men did so by overriding the firing cut-out mechanism. Peaper was in a nearby gun director above and smelled the burning flesh of the men killed and wounded below. Gunner's Mate Ted Cate was spared because one of his shipmates, Gunner's Mate Matthew Trojan, had previously chosen to be transferred into mount nine when an opening occurred. Trojan died in the accident. Cate was listening on sound-powered telephones the night of the incident and overheard the insistent orders that the guns be fired. In later years, he offered the following, "I sincerely hope that the one that was responsible for firing the guns was able to handle the trauma associated therewith inasmuch as he was least of all responsible for the incident."

In the spring and summer of 1944, the Central Pacific amphibious offensive moved on to the islands of Saipan, Guam, and Tinian in the Marianas. As usual, the fast battleships traveled with the carriers, and the old ones were assigned to shore bombardment. On June 18, as the Japanese fleet approached to help their brethren ashore on Saipan, recently promoted Vice Admiral Lee in the *Washington* received a message from Vice Admiral Mitscher, also recently promoted. Because the fast battleships were integrated in the carrier task groups, Mitscher asked Lee if he wanted to pull them out to form a battle line and take on the Japanese heavy surface combatants that night. After discussing the situation with his staff, Lee decided against it. As his staff gunnery officer, Lieutenant Commander Ray Thompson, later explained, Lee was concerned that the battleships had not rehearsed tactically together. He had been in a night melee off Guadalcanal in late 1942 and knew how confusing it could be. And the Japanese superiority at night fighting could very well take away the advantages conferred by radar.

The following day, June 19, the fast battleships were in plenty of action as they steamed with the carriers against incoming Japanese planes. In a slaughter that came to be known as "the Great Marianas Turkey Shoot," American pilots shot down more than three hundred Japanese aircraft, and the ships' gunnery added to the total. The *South Dakota* was one of the ships in the screen, and she was hit by a 500-pound (227kg) bomb dropped from one of the Japanese planes that got through both the fighters and the antiaircraft fire. Pharmacist's Mate Ray Kanoff was at his battle station when the concussion knocked him across the compartment. The explosion from the Japanese bomb killed twenty-three men and injured another twenty-three. After he recovered from the shock, Kanoff went into action to provide first aid for the wounded, and soon the sick bay was filled to capacity. He helped to clean and dress burns and to administer blood plasma. During normal steaming, the ship's medical department dealt only with routine illnesses and injuries. On a day like June 19, sick bay was a seagoing emergency room.

During the battle for the island of Tinian, the *Colorado* was one of the older battleships called upon to provide gunfire support for the Marines ashore. The ship moved to within about 2,000 yards (1,829m) of the beach for close-in support and ended up getting blasted herself. The crew did not realize that the Japanese still had active shore batteries on the island, and the *Colorado* was peppered with twenty-two rounds of 5-inch (13cm) and 6-inch (15cm) gunfire. The incoming fire did considerable damage to the ship's topside area and produced heavy casualties. The only positive aspect was that the subsequent repair period produced an upgrade in the ship's combat capability. When the Japanese hit Pearl Harbor back in 1941, the only Pacific Fleet battleship not present was the *Colorado*, which was in the Puget Sound Navy Yard at Bremerton, Washington. Because she hadn't needed repairs at that time, Lieutenant Tom Mallison realized, she did not receive the dramatic modernization packages that went to the more badly damaged old battleships. Consequently, she went through much of the war with antiquated fire control equipment and old 5-inch (13cm)/51-caliber broadside guns. The latter could be fired only against surface targets and only off the

LEFT: Montana is the only one of the original forty-eight states for which a namesake battleship did not enter the fleet by war's end. In the early 1920s, a ship to be named *Montana* was scrapped as a result of the Washington Naval Treaty. In 1943, a new *Montana*, shown here in an artist's rendering, didn't get even that far. She and her four planned sister ships were canceled prior to the beginning of construction so the materials could be used for higher priorities. She would have been slower, at twenty-eight knots, than her predecessors of the Iowa class. Her main battery of twelve 16-inch (41cm) guns would have matched the batteries intended for the earlier *Montana* and her sisters. BOTTOM: The *Maryland* has a gaping hole in her starboard bow as the result of being hit by an aerial torpedo while anchored off Saipan on July 22, 1944. Shipyard employees at Pearl Harbor worked around the clock for thirty-four days to repair her so she could take part in the invasion of the Palau Islands in September.

RIGHT: Though she was the oldest active U.S. battleship in service during World War II, the *Arkansas* took part in one of the biggest amphibious assaults of the war. Here, German projectiles splash in the waters near the *Arkansas* as she participates in the bombardment of Omaha Beach in Normandy on June 6, 1944.
FAR RIGHT: A member of a repair crew works to patch up a hole in the side of the *Texas* after she was hit by a projectile from a German shore battery at Cherbourg, France, on June 25, 1944. The projectile was a dud that passed unexploded through the side of the ship and came to rest in a cabin on board.
OPPOSITE TOP: In an ammunition handling room in the bowels of the *Iowa*, a sailor prepares to put a powder bag into a flame-proof passing scuttle to deliver it to the compartment on the other side of the bulkhead. These passing scuttles were designed to confine the damage in the event of fire and prevent explosions.

ship's beam. When she went to Bremerton to get the damage received at Tinian repaired, she received a Mark 8 radar, new fire-control computers, and more modern 5-inch (13cm) guns that could fire at both air and surface targets.

ASSAULT ON NORMANDY

Though the Pacific theater grabbed most of the battleships during World War II, a few of the old ones—*Nevada*, *Arkansas*, and *Texas*—provided shore bombardment for the invasion of France in 1944. On June 5, the Allies sent forth a massive naval force from Southern England. The ships crossed the English Channel and put soldiers ashore the following morning on five invasion beaches on the coast of Normandy. Irvin Airey was a member of the Marine detachment on board the 1912-vintage *Arkansas*, the oldest U.S. battleship in World War II. When she was built, her hull was riveted together instead of being welded. Occasionally, when the ship was in rough seas in the North Atlantic, her hull would work back and forth. When the head of a rivet broke off, it made a loud popping sound and went skittering down the deck. As Airey explained, "You'd pull your head in real quick in case one of those things came flying around."

The long day of invasion began before dawn, and Airey was serving as gun captain of a 20-millimeter antiaircraft gun. In the darkness, he saw the flashes from German antiaircraft guns as they shot at planes arriving over the beach. Around 5:30 A.M., there was just enough daylight for the Germans to make out the *Arkansas* a few miles off Omaha Beach, and they opened up on the ship with 88-millimeter guns. The shells didn't hit, but were close enough to throw up shrapnel on deck near Airey and his gun crew. The "Arky" responded with gunfire and silenced the German 88s. After that, as the Allied troops moved ashore, the Germans shifted their gunfire from the ships to the men who were landing. The Germans commanded the heights above Omaha Beach and were able to pour down withering machine gunfire on the men as they stepped out of their landing craft. One of those was Navy Signalman Paul Fauks, who had to hunker down once he got onto the beach. If he had stood up to send visual signals, he would have been cut down quickly. He concluded his only job that day was just staying alive.

The 12-inch (30cm) guns of the *Arkansas* complemented the 14-inchers (36cm) on the *Texas* in pouring rounds out in support of troops ashore.

Rear Admiral Carlton Bryant, tactical commander in the *Texas*, was alarmed by the chaos on land. Rounds fell near the *Texas*, as they had the *Arkansas*. From his vantage point on the bridge of the *Texas*, Bryant saw a gully that the American soldiers had to move up in order to get inland. He obtained permission to fire in that sector, and it produced an immediate result. German soldiers began coming out of the gully with their hands up. On board the *Arkansas*, men didn't have a chance to get regular meals, so they ate K rations on station during that long, long day. Around dusk, a German Messerschmitt flew over the beach and headed toward the ships offshore. Airey pulled the trigger on his 20-millimeter gun and sent several rounds skyward, as did gunners in a number of other ships. The tracers produced a vivid effect in the darkening sky. The flak found its target, and the plane crashed into the water. Naturally, several ships claimed credit. Afterward Airey remarked, "I don't think I even came close to it; I was only shooting with the rest of them."

The next morning, landing craft began bringing wounded soldiers out from the beach so they could get medical treatment on board the *Arkansas* and other ships offshore. Up to then, Airey had been feeling sorry for himself because he was in such an old

ship. Once he saw his wounded countrymen, he decided his plight wasn't so bad after all. The "Arky" stayed around for a couple more weeks; by then, the soldiers had moved inland and were out of range of her guns. The following month, she provided fire support for the invasion of southern France, an operation launched from the Mediterranean. Still later, the old battleship returned to the United States, and Airey went home on leave to Baltimore. Army MPs demanded to see his leave papers, which he showed them. Then they questioned him about the battle stars on his European–North African campaign ribbon, because most Marines were in the Pacific. Irvin Airey was one Marine who wasn't—at least not until later.

THE BATTLE OF LEYTE GULF

In the two decades between the world wars, the war plans of both the Japanese and U.S. navies had contemplated a climactic battle-line gunnery duel that would take place in the Western Pacific. To prepare themselves for this eventuality, battleships of both nations had fired thousands of rounds of main battery ammunition over the course of those years. The closest that events ever came to the envisioned struggle was in the Battle of Surigao Strait, one element of the sprawling Battle of Leyte Gulf that took place in late October 1944 when the Japanese fleet contested the American invasion of the Philippines. The Japanese planned a three-pronged attack to get at American transport ships on the invasion beaches of the island of Leyte. One of those prongs had to get through Surigao Strait to reach the beachhead. Standing in the way of the Japanese force was a bombardment outfit consisting of six old battleships, eight cruisers, twenty-eight destroyers, and a flock of motor torpedo boats. It was quite a gauntlet for the Japanese to run. An additional disadvantage was that the American positions enabled them to "cross the T," that is, to steam perpendicular to the advancing Japanese, enabling the American battleships to shoot all their turrets in broadside fire, while the Japanese could shoot only their forward guns at he U.S. ships.

The battle took place during the early hours of October 25. Even as the Japanese steamed through the smaller ships, they suffered considerable dam-age. The battleship *Fuso*, which was equipped with a towering superstructure that resembled an over-grown housing development, caught destroyer-launched torpedoes and broke in two. Others steamed on toward the reception committee of bat-tleships, including the *Maryland*, *Mississippi*, and *Pennsylvania*. Also present were the *West Virginia*, *California*, and *Tennessee*, which had been equipped with the latest main battery fire control radar, the Mark 8, after their damage at Pearl Harbor. These ships did the bulk of the shooting, since they were able to acquire and lock onto the targets. At 3:52 in the morning, the *West Virginia* got off the first salvo at a range of 22,400 yards (20,483m). From their vantage points, Captain H.V. Wiley on the bridge and Lieutenant Bob Bamrucker in a fire control director, saw the explosions on the *Yamashiro* as the "Weevee's" projectiles hit home. For a long time, all Ensign Howard Sauer could do in his position topside on the *Maryland* was to serve as an admiring audience. The darkness was interrupted time and again as the guns of the *West Virginia*, *Tennessee*, and *California* erupted in convulsions of fire and sent projectiles arching through the night, tracing red trails across the sky.

It was also a night of frustration for Lieutenant Paul Barnes, who was officer of the deck in the *Mississippi*. His ship had the older Mark 3 radar, but the plotting room officer, Lieutenant J.P. O'Leary, was still able to hold a firing solution (range and bearing to the target) on one of the Japanese ships. But, in accordance with doctrine, the *Mississippi*'s skipper, Captain H.J. Redfield, directed his ship, the third in the column, to concentrate on the third ship in the Japanese line. That destroyed the fire control solution, and the ship's old fire control radar was not able to recover. As the flagship for Rear Admiral George Weyler, the *Mississippi* should have fired first. When she didn't, the other ships began pump-ing out rounds at the Japanese. When the ships later turned to a new course, the *Mississippi* and *California* nearly collided. After the ships finally

BATTLE OF SURIGAO STRAIT, OCTOBER 1944

In November 1942, in one of the earlier naval battles between the United States and Japan, the battleships *Washington* and *South Dakota* had engaged the *Kirishima* off Guadalcanal (see page 96). Nearly two years later, at Surigao Strait in the Philippines, the last-ever clash of the Titans occurred as the battle lines of the two nations came together in the narrow waters leading to Leyte Gulf. (Of the six U.S. battleships at Surigao Strait, five—the *Maryland*, *Pennsylvania*, *West Virginia*, *California*, and *Tennessee*—had been resurrected after being damaged in the attack on Pearl Harbor; the sixth, the *Mississippi*, had been in the Atlantic in December 1941, when the attack had occurred.) In October 1944, the U.S. battleships exacted a considerable measure of revenge as they and their cruisers plugged the northern end of the narrow strait between the islands of Leyte and Dinagat and completed the destruction that had been begun by a gauntlet of American torpedo boats and destroyers to the south. The Japanese lost the battleships *Fuso* and *Yamashiro* in the engagement.

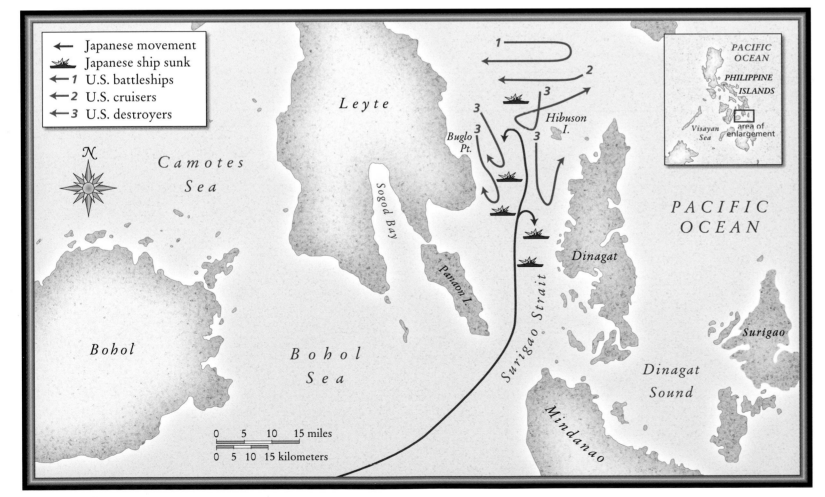

Japanese movement
Japanese ship sunk
1 U.S. battleships
2 U.S. cruisers
3 U.S. destroyers

TOP: In the fast carrier task force operations in the Pacific, the new battleships were integrated into the protective screens for the carriers, as their dozens of antiaircraft guns could provide substantial protection, especially when Japanese kamikaze tactics became part of the picture. At right, the stern of the *Missouri* is pictured at sea. On either side are gun tubs (sometimes nicknamed "back pockets") that held quadruple mounts of 40-millimeter guns. Crew members inside a ship could tell how close the enemy planes were by the sounds of the gunfire—first 5-inch (13cm), then 40-millimeter, and then 20-millimeter—as they came within range.
BOTTOM LEFT: In this wonderful shot, a group of chief petty officers enjoys the camaraderie of shipmates during time off duty. They were the senior enlisted men in the ship and provided both leadership and technical expertise for those serving under them.
BOTTOM RIGHT: Bare-chested crew members of the *New Jersey* push powder bags into the breech of a 16-inch (41cm) gun in November 1944. This is one of a series of pictures made on board Admiral William F. Halsey's Third Fleet flagship by Fenno Jacobs, a member of Edward Steichen's talented combat photography team.
OPPOSITE PAGE: The *New Jersey* refuels the destroyer *Borie* on March 16, 1945. The mobility and endurance of the fleet depended on such underway replenishment, as destroyers could carry only enough oil for a few days of maneuvering at high speeds.

came around, the *Mississippi* got off one salvo of twelve projectiles. Then firing had to cease because the destroyer *Albert W. Grant* was hit, probably by U.S. projectiles, and the admiral didn't want to risk further damage. The Japanese flagship, the battleship *Yamashiro*, was mortally wounded, but the cessation of American gunfire allowed two of her consorts to escape. The *Mogami*'s deliverance was short-lived. She was in a collision with the Japanese heavy cruiser *Nachi*, hit by gunfire from U.S. cruisers, and finally sunk by air attack after daybreak. The destroyer *Shigure* was the only survivor of the Japanese force.

Another facet of the multi-pronged attack on Leyte Gulf was the deployment of a force of battleships and cruisers that intended to steam through San Bernardino Strait in the Philippine Archipelago, and then leap upon the invasion transports that were still near the beachheads. Admiral William F. Halsey, Jr., Commander, Third Fleet, had prepared for this possibility by designating the fast battleships as Task Force 34 for a potential surface engagement. He was lured off to the north by a Japanese carrier force essentially devoid of planes. Halsey believed the

Japanese force that was planned for San Bernardino Strait had been sufficiently beaten up by attacks from carrier planes that it was headed home. Lee desired to stay behind with some of his battleships to guard the strait in the event Japanese battleships came through to attack the U.S. transports still at Leyte. He called Halsey's attention to sighting reports that indicated the Japanese force was headed toward the strait and still constituted a threat. Nevertheless, the impulsive Halsey elected to take both the carriers and Lee's fast battleships so that he would have maximum striking power. The Japanese surged through the unguarded strait and fell upon a force of destroyers, destroyer escorts, and small aircraft carriers. In response to pleas for help, Halsey reluctantly turned his force south, but didn't arrive until after the Japanese battleships had left the scene to return home. In the end, the fast battleships had steamed hundreds of miles north, then hundreds of miles south, but never got into action. Lee's flag lieutenant, Guilliaem Aertsen, felt a particular sense of frustration. This was the moment Lee had been preparing for all his professional life, and he had the ships to do the job. He also had a superior tactical situa-

tion—the ability to cross the Japanese T as the old battleships had done at Surigao. However, because of Halsey's mistake in not leaving the fast battleships behind, Lee simply wasn't given the opportunity.

KAMIKAZES

Soon after that battle, the Japanese threw still another weapon at the American ships off Leyte—kamikaze suicide planes. The Japanese had raised self-sacrifice to yet another level and had committed to a program of crashing bomb-laden aircraft into the ships, using an on-board human guidance system. On the evening of November 29, Lieutenant (junior grade) Howard Sauer was on board the *Maryland* and saw a Japanese plane suddenly emerge from a patch of sky directly overhead. He watched as the plane plunged almost straight down, executed a few last maneuvers, then crashed into turret two. Men stumbled out of the rapidly spreading flames, their faces blackened and their uniforms on fire. They ran down the deck, got the fires put out, then ran back to their battle stations. Sauer burned his hands as he threw a blazing life raft over the side.

Those who were topside saw a hole where the kamikaze's 550-pound (249kg) bomb had plunged through the deck, penetrated down several levels, and then exploded when it hit an armored deck below. It wiped out the ship's sick bay, ignited another fire, and killed thirty-one men. After the explosion, Fire Controlman Fred Vreeken hurried to the F-division berthing compartment, where the bomb had exploded, and found that his shipmates were carrying out bodies. Vreeken, a member of the F-division, had left that same compartment shortly before the crash to report to his battle station topside. Now he witnessed the shattered remains of those who had remained behind. He later described the grisly scene: "Shrapnel wounds had cut deep, bloodless gashes into their bodies. They were blown completely out of their clothes. There were parts of bodies—arms, legs—I shrank in horror. These were my friends. I felt numb. I wanted to cry, but I couldn't."

In early January 1945, U.S. forces invaded Lingayen Gulf on the island of Luzon, which had been the invasion site for the Japanese three years earlier when they had conquered the Philippines. On January 9, on board the *Mississippi*, Lieutenant Paul

Barnes went to his stateroom after the ship had been at general quarters for a long time. As he was shaving, he heard a crash, then an explosion, just forward of his room. He went to the bridge and saw that a suicide plane had crashed into a 5-inch (13cm) gun mount. The airplane's bomb had gone over the side and exploded just above the ship's waterline. Pieces of shrapnel had pierced the ship's side and traveled through the room next to Barnes's, then on into the warrant officers' mess, where they injured a few men. Outside, the devastation was far worse. Gasoline burned in pools on the deck, and men frantically threw ammunition over the side so the fire wouldn't set it off. The kamikaze's last flight had come out of the sun, so gunners didn't see him until he smashed into the battleship. Of the *Mississippi*'s crew, twenty-six men were killed and another sixty-three were either wounded or burned. As one of the injured men was being transported to a hospital ship, he held up the bandaged stump of an arm and waved to the shipmates he was leaving behind. For the dead, a bugler blew the mournful sound of taps as an honor guard buried their bodies at sea.

SUPPORT OF THE OKINAWA OPERATION

Staterooms on board battleships contained safes with combination locks that were intended to be used to store classified material. Soon after he had reported to the *Colorado* in 1943, Ensign Bob Long learned that they were also ideal hiding places for the liquor that was prohibited on board ship. He was still on board when U.S. forces invaded Okinawa on April 1, 1945. During the course of the campaign to capture the island, *Colorado* Ensign Tom Polk received the good news that his wife had just had a baby girl whom she had named Candy. The junior officers of the *Colorado* concluded that the news was as good a reason as any to celebrate. They waited until around midnight when they figured there was no longer a risk of air attack. Then they broke out the booze and had a few drinks in honor of young Candy. In the midst of their mirth, the general alarm sounded after the radar had showed unidentified aircraft approaching, so the men reported to their battle stations. Long went to the bridge to relieve the officer of the deck. His predecessor tried briefing him on

the ship's course and speed, the presence of Japanese aircraft, and so forth. After a while, he realized that his relief wasn't taking it in all that clearly. Years later, after he had completed a distinguished career as a four-star admiral, Long thought back to that moment on the bridge of the *Colorado* and reminded himself that there was a good reason for not drinking at sea.

On April 7, after they had spent six days bombarding Okinawa, the men of the *Maryland* were at morning quarters when they received news that a Japanese battleship was headed their way. Her sister had been sunk in the Philippines the previous October, and now the *Yamato*, with her 18.1-inch (46cm) guns, had been reduced to what was essentially a suicide mission to fight for the honor of what little remained of Japan's heavy surface combatants. American warships set out to intercept the incoming ship, but carrier planes got to her first, and sank her with heavy loss of life. The fight at Surigao Strait had been the last time U.S. battleships faced enemy counterparts. But the threat from aircraft remained undiminished. That evening, as the sun neared the horizon, nineteen-year-old Seaman Justin David was at his battle station, a 20-millimeter gun mount atop *Maryland*'s turret three, the high turret aft. A Japanese kamikaze bore in on that turret, unscathed by the flak delivered by the other ships in formation. For Seaman David, it was a down-the-throat shot as the plane headed directly for the turret, but the 20-millimeter rounds weren't enough to stop the incoming aircraft. It crashed into the turret and David thought to himself, "So this is what it's like to die." He was the only survivor on the turret, and men on nearby battle stations were injured as well. As he descended a ladder to the quarterdeck, his uniform was on fire, and his leg was injured by shrapnel. Wounded and burned, he received a shot of morphine and was taken to sick bay and later hospitalized.

BOMBARDMENT OF JAPAN

As spring turned into summer, American carrier forces, supported as always by battleships, launched air strikes against the Japanese home islands, augmenting those already coming from bombers based in the Marianas. The fast battleships were also peeled off from time to time to bombard the

OPPOSITE PAGE, TOP: The *Massachusetts* takes on a load of fuel from a fleet oiler.
OPPOSITE PAGE, BOTTOM: A group of battleships in dark gray camouflage paint steams together in early 1945. In the foreground is the *New Mexico*; to her left, her sister ship *Idaho*. These two and a third sister, *Mississippi*, were in the Atlantic at the time of the attack on Pearl Harbor. Both because of that and their status as the ships most recently modernized in the 1930s, they changed little in appearance during the war. By contrast, the ship at the far left is either the *Tennessee* or *California*, both of which were dramatically changed.
TOP LEFT: In the foreground, on board the *Iowa*, are the crews of 40-millimeter mounts; each mount contained four antiaircraft guns. In the background, sister ship *New Jersey* can be seen.
TOP RIGHT: The *Idaho* fires her 14-inch (36cm) guns in shore bombardment in April 1945, during the Okinawa campaign.
BOTTOM: Flak bursts fill the sky as a Japanese airplane crashes into the sea off the *Missouri*'s bow during carrier task group operations in April 1945.

RIGHT: This image, taken by Photographer's Mate Len Schmidt of the *Missouri*, is one of the most famous photos of World War II. Schmidt snapped his shutter just an instant before a kamikaze plane crashed into the starboard side of the *Missouri*'s hull on April 11, 1945. Fortunately for those on board the ship, the plane hit the hull, and its bomb did not explode. The upper half of the pilot's body and one wing of the plane wound up on the ship's deck.
OPPOSITE PAGE, TOP: The ship trails smoke after the hit, and flames can be seen below the tower foremast.
OPPOSITE PAGE, BOTTOM LEFT: The machine gun from the Japanese plane is impaled on the barrel of one of the *Missouri*'s 40-millimeter guns.
OPPOSITE PAGE, BOTTOM RIGHT: Battleship crew members stand on the aluminum wing of the Japanese plane. They later cut off pieces of the metal and saved them as souvenirs.

Japanese islands, something they could do almost with impunity because Japanese air power was so depleted.

Commander Edward J. Mathews had been a member of Willis A. Lee's Battleship Squadron Two staff. When Lee left for Maine in June to conduct anti-kamikaze tests, Rear Admiral John Shafroth took over, and Mathews became part of his staff. Mathews, along with Ellery Husted of the Pacific Fleet target staff, chose the city of Kamaishi on Honshu for the first big-gun bombardment of the Japanese home islands. It contained a steel mill that was a military target, and the mill was well up the bay from the adjacent town, and thus offered slight risk of killing townspeople. In July, the *South Dakota*, with Shafroth on board, was joined by the *Indiana* and *Massachusetts* and a number of cruisers and destroyers. "The air became solid with flying metal," Mathews later said of the bombardment. As the ships continued to rain explosives on the mill and cause considerable damage, Mathews noticed a nearby island. On it, he saw a small dog running around wildly, evidently frightened by the thunderclaps unleashed by the bombardment. In hot pursuit was a Japanese man in a kimono. He finally caught the dog, gave it a swat, and retired inside his flimsily built house for whatever sanctuary it might afford. The mill lay in ruins.

ABOVE: This grim-visaged individual is Admiral William F. Halsey, Jr., Commander, Third Fleet, shown on the flag bridge of the *New Jersey*. He had gone aboard the battleship in the summer of 1944 to direct operations before and during the invasion of the Philippines. He was famous for his fighting spirit, but his aggressiveness sometimes got him in trouble. On the one hand, he was able to speed up the timetable for the invasion of Leyte in the fall of 1944. On the other, he left San Bernardino Strait unguarded in the Battle of Leyte Gulf, a move that could have had disastrous results for the invasion forces. In December 1944 and June 1945, he led the Third Fleet into typhoons that resulted in the loss of three destroyers and damage to many more ships.

RIGHT: The *Wyoming* was commissioned as a battleship in 1912 and served in that role until being demilitarized as a result of the 1930 London Treaty on the limitation of naval armaments. She was re-designated a miscellaneous auxiliary in 1931 and thereafter served into the mid-1940s as a training ship for gunnery and for midshipman cruises. She is shown here in 1945 with 5-inch (13cm) twin mounts in place of her original turrets of 12-inch (30cm) guns. She was the flagship for Vice Admiral Willis A. Lee, Jr., in the summer of 1945 when he was doing research in Casco Bay, Maine, on how to defend against the threat of kamikazes.
BOTTOM: A much newer ship, the *Indiana*, bombards Kamaishi, Japan, north of Tokyo, on July 14, 1945. In the background, barely visible, are the battleship *Massachusetts* and a Baltimore-class heavy cruiser. This photo was taken from the third battleship in the bombardment, the *South Dakota*.

The following day, three of the newest battleships, *Iowa*, *Wisconsin*, and *Missouri*, bombarded steel production facilities at Muroran, Hokkaido, Japan's northernmost island. They used full powder charges for their 16-inch (41cm) rounds, because they were firing from ranges of around 30,000 yards (27km). The ships' spotting planes came under fire from antiaircraft batteries. Ensign Jack Barron was inside the *Missouri*'s turret two and watched the bombardment through the turret's periscope. He saw chimneys fall over and the American projectiles generally make a shambles of the facility. Many years later, long after he had left the Navy, Barron took his wife Eleanor to Muroran. He was eager to show her the devastation his ship had wrought. By that time, the damage had long since been cleared away and the plant restored, giving Mrs. Barron something to tease her husband about.

On August 9, Admiral Shafroth's bombardment force—the *South Dakota*, *Indiana*, *Massachusetts*, cruisers, and destroyers—returned once again to Kamaishi to inflict still further damage. The three dreadnoughts fired more than eight hundred rounds of 16-inch (41cm) projectiles in more than an hour and a half of shooting. Commander Robert Odening, gunnery officer of the *Massachusetts*, had to call a temporary halt near the end of the operation because of a problem in turret two. When it was solved and the turret was ready to fire, the other two battleships had completed their bombardments. Odening was given permission to shoot the remainder of the rounds allotted for the operation. As a result, the *Massachusetts* fired the first and last battleship main-battery rounds in combat during the war. She had opened hostilities with her 16-inch (41cm) guns in North Africa in November 1942, less than a week before Admiral Lee's savage night battle off Guadalcanal.

VICTORY IN THE PACIFIC

In early August, Commander Kemp Tolley, navigator of the *North Carolina*, and the crews of many other ships received a radio directive to remain some 150 miles (241km) away from the southern islands of Japan on certain dates. The order engendered all sorts of speculation about what their fellow Americans might do next. They soon found out. On August 6 and August 9, Army Air Forces B-29s

dropped atomic bombs on the cities of Hiroshima and Nagasaki. In less than a week, the Japanese government agreed to surrender. The war that had begun nearly four years earlier at Pearl Harbor was finally over. Admiral Halsey, Commander, Third Fleet, embarked in the *Missouri*, joined in the celebration. He also learned that his flagship was to be the site of the formal surrender ceremony to mark the end of hostilities. In January 1944, Margaret Truman, the daughter of Missouri's junior senator, had christened the ship upon launching at the New York Navy Yard. In April 1945, her dad became president, and so Truman chose the ship named for his state as the site of the surrender.

A large number of Allied warships made their way into Tokyo Bay in late August to attend the proceedings. The ceremony itself was held on September 2. The British battleship *Duke of York* sent a beautiful mahogany table for the signing, but it wasn't big enough to accommodate the surrender documents, so a working party rustled up a mess table from the crew's eating area and carried it to the captain's promenade deck. A green tablecloth from the officers' wardroom completed the decor. Dozens of top-ranking officers from the Allied nations were present on deck for the Sunday morning gathering. General of the Army Douglas MacArthur made an opening speech that struck an English-speaking Japanese diplomat as remarkably magnanimous. Then Japan's foreign minister, Mamoru Shigemitsu, came forward to sign on behalf of his nation, as did General Yoshijiro Umezo, chief of the Imperial General Staff. After that, General MacArthur signed to accept the surrender, followed by representatives of the various Allied nations. Carl Mydans, a photographer for *Life* magazine, had a vantage point behind the Allied delegation. He could see the faces of the defeated Japanese, but only the backs of the victors were visible. When attention was diverted, the photographer got out of the gun tub in which he was positioned and went around to the front of the Allied group. Mydans was intercepted by a husky *Missouri* Marine, who picked him up and put him back in his place. As he was being carried past, he looked at MacArthur, whom he had known for years. The general winked at him, a brief interruption of the solemn face he wore throughout the ceremony.

Once the signing was complete, the American forces unleashed a huge flock of Navy and Army Air Forces planes that flew over Tokyo Bay so low that some people were concerned they would clip the tops of the ships' masts. The sound was thunderous and drowned out all conversation. As the Japanese representatives were leaving the ship and the planes were flying over, the sun broke through the low overcast that covered the bay, and rays of sunlight spilled through and danced on the surface of the water. The image resembled that of Japan's rising-sun flag, but now the symbolism was reversed.

A member of the *Missouri*'s crew, Gunner's Mate Walt Yucka, was part of the crew taking it all in. Many years later, as he described the moment, the veteran Navy crewman became emotional once again and said, "That was the greatest thrill of my life. The war was over."

LEFT: General of the Army Douglas MacArthur reads a speech during the surrender ceremony on board the *Missouri* in Tokyo Bay on Sunday, September 2, 1945. Arrayed behind him are representatives of the various Allied nations; these men signed the surrender documents after MacArthur. BELOW: This is a wallet card given to Lieutenant Bob Balfour of the Third Fleet staff; each man on board the *Missouri* at the time of the surrender got one of the cards, which immediately became valuable souvenirs. RIGHT: Men of the *Washington* go ashore on liberty in the Panama Canal Zone while their ship was en route to Philadelphia for Navy Day celebrations in October 1945. The *Washington* compiled a notable combat record during the war. She was one of the first fast battleships in combat and served as flagship during the night battle off Guadalcanal in November 1942. She was later in many of the actions in the Central Pacific campaign while serving in the screens of fast carriers.

Chapter Seven

COLD WAR, SOMETIMES HOT

ABOVE: A crew member of the *New Jersey* cleans the muzzle of one of the ship's 16-inch (41cm) guns in September 1951 after the ship had fired on enemy installations and supply centers in Korea.
OPPOSITE PAGE: Cleaners work over the side of the *New Jersey*, right, as she and the *Missouri* sit moored to a buoy at Yokosuka, Japan, on April 6, 1953 while transferring the staff and records of the Commander, Seventh Fleet. The *New Jersey* thus became the flagship for Vice Admiral Jocko Clark, and the *Missouri* prepared to head home at the completion of her second deployment during the Korean War.

With the arrival of peace, the United States no longer needed a Navy as large as the one it had fielded during World War II. The last mission of many battleships was to serve as well-armed transport ships, bringing sailors and soldiers home from battlefields overseas. A grateful nation provided enthusiastic welcomes during celebrations in New York and San Francisco on October 27, 1945, the date celebrated

for many years as Navy Day because it was Theodore Roosevelt's birthday.

The contrast between old prewar ships and the new ones was well symbolized at the Navy Day gathering in New York City. Several dozen warships moored in the Hudson River, west of Manhattan. The newest battleship, the 887-foot (270m), 57,000-ton (51,699t) *Missouri*, was moored just astern of the next-to-oldest, *New York*, which was 573 feet (175m) long and displaced 32,000 tons (29,024t). The president ate lunch on board the ship named for his home state, sat at the table where the surrender documents had been signed the previous month, and proclaimed, "This is the happiest day of my life." Then he transferred to the destroyer *Renshaw* for a trip up and down the Hudson, receiving twenty-one-gun salutes along the way. The *Missouri*, just over a year old, was assured a place in the postwar

fleet. The *New York*, more than thirty by then, was running out of time.

BIKINI ATOMIC BOMB TESTS

Now that the atomic age had dawned, the Navy planned to turn several old battleships into targets for atomic bomb tests in the summer of 1946. By April of that year, the *New York*, now operating on a skeleton crew, had returned to the Pacific in preparation for the journey to Bikini Atoll in the Marshall Islands. Among the remaining crewmen was Ed Logue, who had reported aboard in the summer of 1941 as a machinist's mate striker. Now, nearly five years later, he was an electrician's mate first class. When the ship stopped at Pearl Harbor, Logue and his remaining shipmates left their seabags and most of their gear in a storage building, keeping with them only the few uniforms they would need on a

day-to-day basis. Then they proceeded to the site of the upcoming tests. Soon, the name "bikini" was being applied to a new style of bathing suit—this risqué two-piece suit was supposedly "explosive."

The *New York* anchored in her assigned spot among dozens of other ships, including the *Nevada*, *Pennsylvania*, and the former German cruiser *Prinz Eugen*, which had accompanied the ill-fated *Bismarck* on her famous sortie into the Atlantic in May of 1941. When it came time for the tests to begin, Logue and his shipmates moved to a transport ship to find berths. They were some twenty miles (32km) away when the first bomb, an airburst, exploded on July 1. After the wind had carried away the radiation in the air, the crew members went back aboard their ship. On July 25 came a second explosion, this one under water. It sank the *Arkansas*. Her seagoing journey, begun in 1912, had finally ended. A spout of water shot up and left radioactive debris all over the topside portion of the *New York*. When the crew members went back aboard this time, they could stay in certain places for only limited periods of time or they would be contaminated.

The *New York*'s naval service was nearly over—and so was Ed Logue's. His enlistment almost up, Logue was finally detached from the ship after more than five years on board and sent back to the United States. Had he chosen to reenlist, he could have been advanced to chief petty officer. But, like so many of his contemporaries, he decided it was time to settle down and have a family, so he became a civilian again after having served throughout the entire war.

After nearly four years of war, the citizens of the United States were eager to "bring the boys home" once peace was achieved. Just as the old battleships had brought men back from France at the end of World War I (see page 56), new battleships returned men from the Far East at the end of World War II. Here, hundreds of sailors line up on the main deck of the *Indiana* as she enters San Francisco Bay on September 29, 1945. She and the dozens of other returning warships received a tumultuous homecoming after achieving total victory over Japan. The *Indiana* remained in San Francisco to host the visitors who came aboard on Navy Day, October 27. Shortly afterward, she left for an overhaul in Bremerton, Washington. Reflecting the rapid demobilization of the U.S. armed services, she was placed in reserve in September 1946 and decommissioned in September 1947. She had been built for a useful life of perhaps twenty or twenty-five years, but naval warfare soon changed dramatically. Her active service amounted to only three and a half years.

FLOATING DIPLOMAT

In the spring of 1946, a few months before the atomic bomb tests at Bikini, the *Missouri* had been involved in a voyage that played a substantive role in the nation's postwar foreign policy of containment of communism. Before the war, it was customary that when one nation's ambassador died in the host country, the body was returned by cruiser. In 1944, the Turkish ambassador to the United States, Mehmet Munir Ertegun, died while on duty in Washington. His body was preserved at Arlington until the war's end. When no U.S. cruiser was immediately available in early 1946, the Navy chose to dispatch the *Missouri* to the Mediterranean because it fit with her operating schedule. In the spring of that year, she took Ertegun's body to Istanbul and followed with visits to Greece and Italy. Communism was gaining popularity among the governments on the rim of the Mediterranean, so the powerful presence of the *Missouri*, which by that time was the most famous ship in the world, was a useful influence in strengthening anti-communist resolve. Soon afterward, the U.S. Navy began the regular deployment of warships to the Mediterranean, a pattern that continues to this day. The "Mighty Mo" was a forerunner of the Sixth Fleet, which has now been in existence for more than half a century and still represents U.S interests in the Mediterranean.

The Turks went out of their way to make their American visitors feel welcome. The hospitality was somewhat reminiscent of that afforded to the Great White Fleet nearly forty years earlier. Prior to the visit, Turkish working parties cleaned and painted buildings in the red-light district of Istanbul, and doctors checked the local prostitutes to ensure they didn't have venereal disease. Crewmen were especially delighted when they found that the women were available, albeit briefly, without charge. Captain Roscoe Hillenkoetter, skipper of the *Missouri*, puckishly referred to the situation as "free love." Ensign Cecil Hartson wandered into the red-light district to satisfy his curiosity and remarked, "When you looked, there was a sea of white hats. It was there for the boys." Others found more innocent distractions. Seaman Tony Alessandro and his buddies went shopping in a Turkish bazaar and came away with swords, Including scimitars with curved blades.

Then they went to a movie. They expected dialogue in English with Turkish subtitles. Instead, Turkish voices had been dubbed for the American actors. Alessandro and his buddies soon got bored by the situation, and to entertain themselves, they started using their newly bought swords for duels right there in the theater. During a subsequent visit to Italy, some members of the crew visited Pope Pius XII in the Vatican, and then the ship made a stop in Morocco before heading home. The *Missouri* reached Norfolk in early May, completing her voyage as a floating diplomat.

BATTLESHIP DECOMMISSIONINGS

For the *Missouri* to make such a trip was an exception in the period shortly after the war. The U.S. Navy, which had reached its peak in manpower at the end of the war, had been reduced rapidly in size. After nearly four years of fighting, the American public wanted to "bring the boys home." Demobilization was quickly enacted, and home went hundreds of thousands of servicemen who had enlisted for the duration of the war. When they were faraway in the Pacific, some had wondered whether they would ever see home again. Now that they had a chance to leave, they did so with mixed feelings. For many, the ships had become homes, and they had developed close bonds with the buddies with whom they had endured danger. But leave they did, and many ships just couldn't operate because they didn't have sufficient manpower. Those who stayed were the career personnel, so the enlisted company had a lot of chiefs and not many Indians.

In this context, the supply of battleships in service dropped dramatically. Some of the oldest—*Arkansas*, *New York*, *Nevada*, and *Pennsylvania*—had been sent off to Bikini to serve as bomb targets. Of the pre-World War I generation, only *Texas* was saved; she was preserved as a memorial near Galveston, Texas. The *Mississippi* was converted to an ordnance test ship; her sisters *Idaho* and *New Mexico* were cut up by scrappers. The rest, one by one, were decommissioned and put into mothballs. That is, they were laid up in reserve fleets with precautions taken to minimize the aging process. Dehumidification systems were set up to cut down on internal corrosion and cathodic protection limit-

TOP LEFT: The *New York*, which had been flagship for the U.S. battleship squadron in World War I, arrives in New York City in October 1945 to help celebrate victory in World War II. She had little life remaining. The following summer she went to Bikini Atoll in the Marshall Islands to serve as a target for atomic bomb experiments. TOP RIGHT: A fireboat washes down the *New York*'s forecastle after the second bomb test, an underwater blast on July 25, 1946. BOTTOM: Helicopters were just coming into fleet service when the *Wisconsin* was part of a midshipman training cruise to Europe in the summer of 1947. Here, a Sikorsky HO3S helo delivers a man to the forecastle, as the stern is still cluttered with floatplanes and their catapults. Refueling along the *Wisconsin*'s starboard side is the destroyer *Cone*.

ed electrolysis of the external hull. Cocoons were put over gun mounts to protect them from the elements, and welders attached steel plates over openings to seal them. The population of mothballed ship sites grew steadily as members of the Tennessee, Maryland, North Carolina, and South Dakota classes went out of commission.

MIDSHIPMAN TRAINING

In the summer of 1947, only the four ships of the Iowa class remained on active service. That year, the *Wisconsin* and *New Jersey*, accompanied by two aircraft carriers and a number of smaller ships, made the first overseas midshipman training cruise since before World War II. They traveled to Great Britain and Norway. Even though the British Isles were still on desperately short rations after the privations of World War II, they eagerly shared what little they had with their American visitors. Commander Charles Duncan was on the forecastle of the *Wisconsin* to help supervise her mooring in Rosyth, Scotland, one of the ports where the American battleships had been based in World War I. As soon as his ship was shackled up to a buoy, Duncan received a two-inchthick (5cm) stack of papers with a listing of all the social events to which the American Navy men were invited. People opened their homes to the visitors and were so eager to be hospitable that, for each party, Duncan had to make up a list of people who were then ordered to attend.

OPPOSITE PAGE: The *Wisconsin* rolls heavily on a blustery day at sea during her 1947 summer cruise.

THIS PAGE: Various scenes from midshipman training cruises in the post-World War II period.

TOP LEFT: In June 1951, three boats full of midshipmen wait their turn to go alongside so the men can board the *Missouri*, which is in the background. The battleship has boat booms and accommodation ladders rigged to facilitate the process.

TOP RIGHT: On September 2, 1949, midshipmen and crew members of the *Missouri* gather topside to celebrate the fourth anniversary of the Japanese surrender. The surrender plaque is in the center of the circle on the 01-level veranda deck.

BOTTOM LEFT: Midshipmen, distinctive because of the dark blue band around their white hats, holystone wooden deck planks, an arduous process.

BOTTOM RIGHT: The *Missouri* refuels from the fleet oiler *Elkomin* during the 1948 midshipman cruise.

LEFT: Fleet tugs churn up water as they try to pull the *Missouri* off a mudbank near Norfolk, Virginia. She ran aground on January 17, 1950, and finally came afloat on the fifth rescue attempt, the morning of February 1.

RIGHT TOP: In the meantime, the Navy took a number of measures to lighten her. All her fuel was pumped out. Here, crew members remove her anchors and anchor chains.

BOTTOM RIGHT: Thousands of rounds of ammunition are taken off. Here, hundreds of 5-inch (13cm) projectiles can be seen near turret one.

This trip was, by and large, the battleship's last hurrah: the *Wisconsin* and *New Jersey* were mothballed and decommissioned in 1948, and the *Iowa* followed in 1949. In all likelihood, the *Missouri* would have gone into reserve then also, if not for one thing: this was the ship that President Truman's daughter had christened, and so the *Missouri* would remain in commission as long as he remained president. He was reelected in the fall of 1948 and began his first full term in 1949. This ensured the ship four more years of service, but she was to come to very public grief before Truman's term had gone very far.

SPECTACULAR PUBLIC GROUNDING

On December 20, 1949, the *Missouri* got a new skipper in the person of Captain William D. Brown. He had served in World War II as commanding officer of the destroyers *Gregory* and *Nicholas* and had been chief of staff for a cruiser division commander. When he took command of the "Mighty Mo," it was almost four years since he had been on active sea duty. His new command had begun during a shipyard period, but the *Missouri* was due to leave in mid-January for training in Guantánamo Bay. As she left her homeport of Norfolk, she was scheduled to run through an acoustic range that would measure the signature emitted by her propellers as part of an effort to identify ships by the noises they put into the water.

On the morning of January 17, 1950, the ship got under way from her pier and headed out to the channel, following the guidance of a harbor pilot. Captain Brown and his navigator, Lieutenant Commander Frank Morris, were on the 08 level, high in the *Missouri*'s superstructure, so they had a good perspective. The officer of the deck, Lieutenant Ed Arnold, reported to the captain that he spotted a small orange-and-white buoy. It marked the left edge of the acoustic range that the ship was supposed to run through, and so the ship should have stayed to the right. However, there was a good deal of confusion on the bridge, and both the navigator and operations officer advised Brown to steam left of the buoy. In doing so, they headed *Missouri* straight for shoal water. What's more, the skipper had the speed increased to fifteen knots, adding to the ship's

momentum as she headed in the wrong direction. Down in CIC, the men watching radar scopes saw that the ship was going the wrong way, but concluded something must be wrong with the equipment.

The quartermaster steering the ship, Bevan Travis, had been in and out of the port many times during his years on board. He tried to advise Brown that he was going the wrong way, as did the executive officer, Commander George Peckham. Brown was used to running his own show and kept the ship on course. The inevitable disaster occurred when she slid onto the underwater shoal and just kept going until she was twenty-five hundred feet (762m) inland, nearly three ship lengths. An unusually high tide at the time of the incident made the result even worse. She was hard aground in very public view. Men at the nearby Army and Air Force bases made sport of the considerable embarrassment of seeing the Navy's foremost battleship aground—literally stuck in the mud. *Missouri* was immobile and would remain so for two weeks until salvage crews could free her. A combination of removing fuel and ammunition, adding pontoons for buoyancy, and pulling with powerful tugboats was, at last, successful. On February 1, the ship finally moved free of her involuntary berth. Captain Brown was relieved of command two days later and subsequently court-martialed. His once-promising naval career was over because of a highly visible accident on a January morning.

KOREAN CONFLICT

After her superficial damage was repaired, the *Missouri* continued on to Guantánamo Bay, and in early June, began a midshipman training cruise. In late June, North Korea invaded its neighbor to the south, and the United States moved quickly to respond. Although officially labeled a "police action" and conducted under the auspices of the United Nations, the Navy was now involved in the Korean War. Not until mid-August did the *Missouri* become a player. Having since returned from Guantánamo Bay, she was in New York City with her batch of midshipmen when Ensign Lee Royal returned aboard late one night after passing a pleasant evening with a date. The officer of the deck told him it was his last good time for a while, because the ship was scheduled to leave shortly for Norfolk to resupply and

RIGHT: The outbreak of the Korean War in late June 1950 came at a time when the U.S. Navy had only one battleship, the *Missouri*, in commission. It quickly moved to bring back her sister ship, *New Jersey*, from the mothball fleet in Bayonne, New Jersey, just across the harbor from New York City. Here, crew members line up for chow in November 1950 during the reactivation of the *New Jersey*. She was recommissioned late that same month and in action off Korea six month after that.
BOTTOM: Radarman Seaman E.E. Lockley operates a radar scope in the *New Jersey*'s combat information center.

123

In the summer of 1950, the *Missouri* was hurried to Korea with the hope that she could provide bombardment support for the invasion of Inchon of September 15. She didn't quite make it, but she used her guns to great effect in the ensuing months to bombard enemy positions and support United Nations soldiers and Marines ashore in Korea. In late April 1951, the homeward-bound *Missouri* met the Korea-bound *New Jersey* in Panama. This photo was taken shortly after the *Missouri*'s return to her homeport of Norfolk, Virginia, on April 27, 1951. She is on one side of the pier. On the opposite side are the heavy cruisers *Albany* and *Macon* and the escort carrier *Siboney*.

then, on to Korea. En route to the war zone, the *Missouri* hit storms at sea in both the Atlantic and Pacific. The purpose for sending her was to have her guns available to support General MacArthur's daring invasion of Inchon on Korea's west coast in mid-September. Because of the heavy weather, she didn't quite make it in time. By the time she came near Korea, the strategic situation had soured. North Korea had overrun much of South Korea. The *Missouri*'s captain, Irving Duke, called a meeting of officers in the ship's wardroom to brief them on the situation. Ensign Royal was taken aback when he saw on a map how little territory still remained in U.N. hands. As he heard the captain's words, he thought to himself, "Going to war is bad, but going to war and getting your ass whipped is really bad."

Though she wasn't there for the Inchon landing, the *Missouri* soon made her presence felt through the effect of her 16-inch (41cm) guns. On September 15, the day of the invasion on Korea's west coast, she let loose a diversionary bombardment on the east coast at Samchock and the next day fired at Pohang. On the 17th, Lieutenant Colonel Rollins Emmerich, an Army officer, requested bombardment fire on a position held by North Korean troops. He had his corporal send a radio request to the heavy cruiser *Helena* offshore. Instead, the answer came from a *Missouri* radio transmission, "Hello, Cliffdweller, this is Battleax. We will take that mission." Projectiles rained down from the *Missouri*'s guns, some of them blasting 30-foot (9m)-wide craters in the earth when they landed. The Army officer felt the ground shake when the 16-inch (41cm) rounds exploded only a few hundred yards from his men. And so it went, through autumn and as the cold winter winds began to sweep down from the north. The *Missouri* was making a difference, and the Navy was eager to tell the world, especially after the embarrassing grounding earlier that year. So photographers and movie cameramen were invited on board to film the crew in action. One cameraman filmed a sequence in which Fire Controlman Warren Lee pulled the trigger on a firing key and unleashed a round from a big gun. That image of Lee appeared in movie theaters back in the States, first in newsreels and later spliced into a Hollywood feature titled *Retreat, Hell!*, with a plot based on the Korean War.

Integration Pioneers

One of the men who joined the *Iowa*'s crew shortly after she was recommissioned on August 25, 1951, was Lieutenant Sam Gravely, the ship's first black officer. Gravely had been commissioned as an ensign in 1944, served through the rest of World War II, then went back to civilian life. In 1949, he returned to active duty to serve as a recruiter and remained in service with the advent of the Korean War. Because of the Navy's personnel policies during World War II, he was not able to serve in a large warship with an integrated crew. He served in a small patrol craft that had a crew of black enlisted men and a white skipper. The situation had changed by the time of the Korean War, particularly in the wake of President Truman's 1948 executive order that ended official segregation in the armed services. But practice is often slow to follow policy. The Navy still had only a small number of black officers on active duty during the Korean War.

When Gravely reported to the *Iowa*, no one seemed surprised. Later, he learned that the Bureau of Personnel (BuPers) had sent a letter to the ship to warn his future shipmates that he was coming and, in effect, to pave the way for him. A few years earlier, in 1947, BuPers had asked Captain Robert Dennison, the skipper of the *Missouri*, about the prospect of assigning a black officer to that ship. Captain Dennison had politely declined, saying he thought a black officer would be better off being assigned to a less prominent ship, where he could get his feet on the ground away from the glare of attention that attended a battleship. Four years later, following the Truman edict, Gravely was accepted by his *Iowa* shipmates, although not enthusiastically welcomed. The white officer who became his roommate—a former enlisted man, not a Naval Academy graduate—was the only man who would agree to do so. As for socializing, Gravely found it convenient to go on liberty by himself. When the ship was overseas in Japan, he noticed that some Japanese women seemed to be scrutinizing him to an unusual degree. Apparently, someone had told them that he had a tail, and they wanted to see for themselves if it was true.

The situation was not entirely bleak, however. Captain William Smedberg, the *Iowa*'s commanding officer, accepted the lieutenant and made him welcome. And so did Lieutenant Commander Gene Harrell, the communication officer. Harrell said to him, "Sam, I might as well tell you now. I don't give a goddamn whether you're red, green, black, or what color you are. All I want is a radio officer, and you are it." This was exactly what Gravely wanted to hear: that he would be judged on his merits and performance, not his skin color. The two developed such a bond that Harrell later served as godfather to Gravely's first child. In 1971, when Admiral Elmo Zumwalt was Chief of Naval Operations, Sam Gravely became the first African-American selected for admiral in the history of the U.S. Navy.

The *New Jersey*'s first black officer, Ensign Louis Ivey, arrived shortly after the end of the Korean War. He had been commissioned through the NROTC program

ABOVE LEFT: Ensign Louis Ivey in the 1950s. ABOVE RIGHT: Samuel L. Gravely, Jr., in the mid-1970s as a three-star admiral. Gravely was the first black officer in the U.S. Navy to be promoted to the ranks of commander, captain, rear admiral, and vice admiral. The Navy did not have a black four-star admiral until Admiral J. Paul Reason became Commander-in-Chief, Atlantic Fleet, in 1996.

at Penn State University. He arrived on board one cold night in February 1954 and was assigned to a stateroom. When he woke the next morning, he discovered that the other officer in the room had left during the night. Then the short-time roommate requested that Ivey be assigned to a different room, which he was. Like Gravely, Ivey moved cautiously in developing relationships with shipmates. His game plan was to do his job well and then establish contacts as others warmed to him. Not all did. In one case, he had an upset stomach and went to one of the ship's doctors for treatment. The medical officer told him that he was probably having "a tough time adjusting to white man's food." Those who were especially pleased about the young officer's presence were the *New Jersey*'s black enlisted men. To them, the officer was a symbol of pride and progress. The wardroom stewards made things as easy for him as they could.

Interestingly, some of Ivey's most enjoyable times as a member of the crew came overseas. He and some fellow officers had a great time on liberty in France, where his race was not an issue—a great contrast to the ship's homeport of Norfolk, Virginia, where it was very much an issue. Unlike Gravely, Ivey did not remain for an active naval career. He entered the Naval Reserve and started medical school after his tour of duty. Subsequently, he became a respected thoracic surgeon and was a member of the traveling medical team for President Jimmy Carter.

RIGHT: Japanese workers help American crew members load a 16-inch (41cm) projectile aboard the *New Jersey* at Sasebo, Japan, in the summer of 1951. The trip from Korea to Sasebo was relatively short, so the U.S. battleships involved in the Korean War regularly went there to rearm rather than doing so at sea.
FAR RIGHT: The *New Jersey* unloads a 16-inch (41cm) round by pumping it shoreward to Korea. On the water, the blast effect from the explosion that expelled the round can be seen.

In September, even as the *Missouri* was firing at Korea, the Navy began pulling her sister ship, *New Jersey*, out of her mothball slumber at Bayonne, New Jersey. Covers came off guns and Cosmoline was stripped from propulsion machinery. On a cold November day, Fleet Admiral William Halsey was on board as his World War II flagship, the *New Jersey*, was recommissioned for active service in yet another war. Her crew was drawn from both the active fleet and from reservists who were hurriedly recalled to duty to put to use the skills they had acquired in World War II. Among them was Gunner's Mate Bob Storm, who thought he had left the Navy behind. He had been working at a good civilian job and had recently moved into a new home when the summons came. His Navy salary was a good deal lower, and having to make mortgage payments was, in Storm's colorful description, "a bitch on wheels for a while."

In March 1951, a few months after the *New Jersey*'s callup, the *Wisconsin*, too, returned to the fleet. Her skipper, Captain Thomas Burrowes, was

an experienced surface ship operator. When he took the battleship out on initial sea trials, he quickly became displeased with his navigator and asked the Bureau of Naval Personnel for a replacement. The bureau dipped down into a reserve destroyer escort, the *Tills*, and ordered her commanding officer, Lieutenant Commander Elmo "Bud" Zumwalt, to be the battleship's navigator. (Nineteen years later, Zumwalt, at age forty-nine, became the youngest Chief of Naval Operations in history.) The *Wisconsin* was due to leave shortly for Guantánamo Bay to provide shakedown training for the crew that had been assembled from a variety of sources, including reactivated naval reservists. Zumwalt did have an advantage in the fast-paced training that followed. His chief quartermaster had not liked the previous navigator and so really exerted himself to help make Zumwalt a success.

The *Wisconsin*'s first assignment after recommissioning was to make midshipman training cruises to Europe. On the way, she stopped off in New York

City and was directed to moor to buoys in the Hudson River, off 50th Street, on the city's west side. Zumwalt was concerned about the stability of the buoys and requested that the ship either go to a pier or anchor. The admiral in charge would not agree and reiterated the mooring to buoys. The *Wisconsin*'s navigator was sufficiently concerned that he maintained an underway bridge watch, as if the ship were steaming, in order to monitor her position. The next morning, following a heavy cloudburst, it became apparent to the navigation team that one of the buoys was dragging on the river bottom and taking the ship with it. No tugboats were nearby to help out, and the stern ran onto the mud, ingested some of it, and knocked out the gyrocompasses. New York newspapers made hay of the situation, of course. One of the headlines referred to the position on the riverbank as "On, Wisconsin," a play on the University of Wisconsin fight song. Zumwalt immediately began drafting a letter to document the ship's objections to mooring to the buoys. Before the letter

ever left the ship, the admiral who had given the order exonerated the *Wisconsin*'s crew.

The ship visited Scotland and France during the course of training the midshipmen. After that, the *Wisconsin* proceeded back to the United States, continued on to Hawaii for shore bombardment training, then headed to the Korean War zone. There she steamed with Task Force Seventy-Seven, the fast aircraft carriers, and she also provided naval gunfire support and shore bombardment. Still another role was as flagship for Vice Admiral Harold Martin, Commander, Seventh Fleet. The position of fleet commander at that time was traditionally held by a naval aviation admiral. Thus, Martin was not enamored of the shore bombardment work, believing that aircraft could do the bombing better. Martin sent off a message in which he expressed doubts about the efficacy of the gunfire.

Marines ashore loved the support provided by the battleship, and so returned a strong message to underscore the value of the naval gunfire, including

TOP: The only occasion on which all four ships of the Iowa class steamed in formation took place on June 7, 1954. Here, the *Iowa* leads the column.
BOTTOM LEFT: During a bombardment of Korea, Chief Gunner's Mate W. L. Stull, left, and Ensign R. H. Sprince relay an order to all guns of turret one of the *Missouri*. They are inside the booth that runs all the way across the rear of the turret, separated from the three individual rooms that house the 16-inch (41cm) guns. Beyond Ensign Sprince's head is a periscope.
BOTTOM RIGHT: In April 1953, Seaman Arthur G. Longley, left, and Gunner's Mate First Class Henry P. Castles use a power-driven rotating capstan on board the *New Jersey* to move a projectile across the deck inside the turret two barbette.

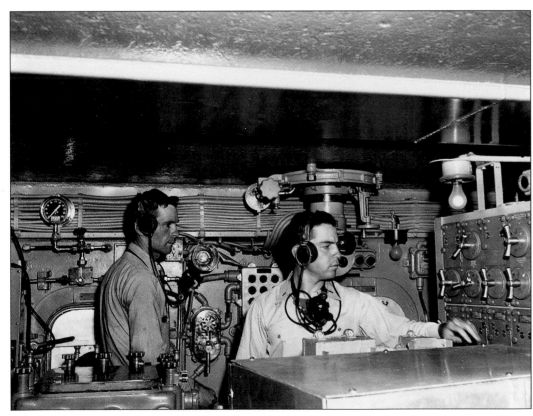

THIS PAGE: On April 5, 1952, the *Wisconsin* entered a floating dry dock, AFDB-1, at Guam as a test of overseas logistic support capabilities. During World War II, the availability of such repair facilities enabled warships to remain near the combat zone without needing to return to shipyards in the United States. By the time of the Korean War, Japan provided superb shipyard support, so the dock in Guam was no longer as vital as it had been in the earlier war. When these pictures were taken, a relic of an even earlier war was nearby. The hulk of the old *Oregon* was moored not far from the dry dock and the *Wisconsin*; it would be scrapped a few years later in Japan—more than sixty years after first going into service.

an assertion that the *Wisconsin*'s 16-inch (41cm) guns had driven a large number of Chinese soldiers out of an area with her firing. That response sent a morale surge through the ship. It also provided a strong sense of purpose. In the late 1940s, Secretary of Defense Louis Johnson had gutted the Navy's budget. Perhaps because of that, North Korea had felt emboldened to go on the attack, believing it would not be strongly opposed. Johnson had been fired a few months after the war started, and the fleet staged a renaissance as more and more ships were brought out of mothballs and sent into the fray.

One of the missions that the battleships undertook throughout the Korean War was bombardment in the mostly enclosed harbor at Wonsan, North Korea. Smaller ships, such as destroyers and cruisers, did some of the shooting with their shorter-ranged guns. Lieutenant Commander Ray Wilhite of the *New Jersey* observed, "If you're going to go in a room with a stick that's twice as long as the other guy's, you don't close to the length of his to make it a fair fight." And so the battleships used their big sticks in Wonsan. Referring to the *Wisconsin*'s bombardment in that harbor, Zumwalt later said, "I think it was a significant psychological minus to the enemy to see this huge monster operating inside waters that they had considered theirs. [Battleship bombardment] did, in truth, bring certain targets within range that it wouldn't otherwise have been able to reach, but I don't consider that that was as important as the psychological aspect." It also made a target of the *Wisconsin*. On March 15, 1952, while she was in Wonsan, the ship was hit by enemy fire for the first time. A 155-millimeter shell fired by a shore battery hit the deck near the shield for a 40-millimeter gun mount. The projectile injured three crewmen and caused superficial damage to the ship. The *Wisconsin* used her 16-inch (41cm) guns for counter-battery fire and silenced North Korean gun batteries with direct hits.

In June 1951, Captain William Smedberg had orders in hand to go to the Mediterranean and take command of the heavy cruiser *Columbus*. Before departing, he received a telephone call from the Bureau of Naval Personnel that told him he wouldn't be getting the ship after all. He was stunned and disappointed. Then came the good news; he was going to take command of the *Iowa* instead as soon as she

TOP LEFT: In the *New Jersey*'s radio central during the Korean War, radiomen listen to Morse code on their headphones and type the corresponding letters. At left, on the other side of the bulkhead, a supervisor checks through a stack of messages while a shipmate kibitzes over his shoulder.
TOP RIGHT: Crew members are packed in tiers in a berthing compartment on board the *New Jersey*. When she and her three sisters were reactivated and modernized in the 1980s, bunks of this style were replaced by "coffin racks" that were more solid in construction and equipped with privacy curtains.
BOTTOM: Three members of the *New Jersey*'s crew stand watch in main control and relay orders to other engine rooms via sound-powered telephones. Fireman John Hernandez is at the throttle; to his right are Fireman James Cronin and Fireman Robert Plank.

The old *Mississippi*, which went into commission as a battleship during World War I, makes a contribution to the modern age by serving as a test platform in the 1950s. Here, she fires a Terrier surface-to-air missile, the type that would be used in the Navy's first guided missile cruisers a few years later.

was reactivated and recommissioned at Hunters Point Naval Shipyard in San Francisco. Before he went to take up the ship, Admiral Forrest Sherman, the chief of naval operations counseled him, "Now, Smeddy, you go out there and get the *Iowa* and put her back in commission, but under no circumstances are you to run that ship aground. We don't want another *Missouri*." Captain David Tyree had received the same warning several months earlier when he put the *New Jersey* back into commission.

When the *Iowa* was ready to get under way, the shipyard commander ordered Smedberg to conduct trials within San Francisco Bay so she would be easy to rescue if the engines broke down. When he did so, the ship nearly ran aground. Shortly afterward, he visited Fleet Admiral Chester Nimitz, who had commanded the Pacific Fleet in World War II. He chastised the skipper for his unwise actions, particularly in view of the strong and tricky currents in San Francisco Bay. Smedberg protested that he was following the orders given him. Nimitz replied, "Smedberg, you've got to think of the safety of that ship. You shouldn't have done it." The lesson he learned was that some orders should be challenged, not blindly obeyed.

On April 1, 1952, the *Iowa* relieved the *Wisconsin* as Seventh Fleet flagship. One of the *Wisconsin*'s junior officers was Ensign Bill Smedberg. When the *Iowa* arrived to begin the turnover process, navigator Zumwalt saw to it that young Smedberg was in the boat that went over to meet the other battleship so he could have a reunion with his father as well. Soon, the *Iowa* got into the same bombardment routines that her three younger sisters had been performing previously. On Easter Sunday, she bombarded the North Korean port of Chongjin from early in the morning until late at night with 16-inch (41cm) rounds. Among the targets was a big gantry crane and a train of oil tank cars. When the 16-inch (41cm) projectiles hit the oil cars, the whole train blew up with a ferocious explosion that produced a large mushroom cloud—spectacular proof that the airborne spotter had gotten the fire control solution on target. Besides the spotter, the *Iowa* also had an orbiting combat air patrol of U.S. carrier fighters. Still, there was plenty of concern for Captain Smedberg and his crew. A large number of Soviet planes orbiting about forty miles (64km) to

the north was picked up by the ship's radar. The skipper's perception was that the planes were trying to scare off the battleship. That evening, the crew heard on a radio broadcast that both the *Iowa* and one of her destroyer escorts had been sunk. They were delighted to realize that this bit of propaganda was untrue.

The in-and-out rotation of battleships continued for yet another year in a war that had been essentially stalemated since the end of 1950. With the election of Dwight D. Eisenhower as president in 1952 came some impetus to end the war. A further factor was the death in early March 1953 of Soviet dictator Joseph Stalin, which resulted in a decline in outside sponsorship of North Korea. The *Missouri* was on deployment to the war zone at the time, and Stalin's death was duly noted in the ship's newspaper, edited by Lieutenant Jack Zeldes. He wrote the pithy headline that reported, "RED HEAD DEAD." Sadly, the *Missouri*'s commanding officer soon was as well. The ship fired her last bombardment mission of the war on March 25. The following morning, as Captain Warner Edsall was bringing the dreadnought in to anchor at Sasebo, Japan, he collapsed from a heart attack and fell to the deck just after giving an order to the helmsman. Commander Bob North, the exec, quickly took over the conn. The crew held a memorial service on deck the following day.

A few months later, the *New Jersey* was the duty battleship and was shooting at a heavier-than-normal pace as she joined in an effort to put pressure on the North Korean negotiating team that was involved in talks with United Nations representatives at the village of Panmunjom. On July 25, the ship was off to that favorite target city of Wonsan, where she shot 191 rounds. Two days later, the negotiators came to an agreement, and the war was over. The line of demarcation between North and South Korea was not far from where it had been when hostilities began in June 1950. But South Korea was still free and has remained so ever since.

NEW ROLE FOR AN OLD SHIP

The Korean War had given a new lease on life to the four Iowa-class battleships at a time when dreadnoughts had largely disappeared from the world's navies. But one old relic continued service in a diminished role: the *Mississippi*, which had been in

the active fleet since 1917. Following World War II, a shipyard conversion had removed her big guns and turned her into an ordnance test ship. Among her roles in the mid-1950s was serving as a test platform for the surface-to-air guided missiles that would soon be entering the active fleet on the converted cruisers *Boston* and *Canberra*.

When Lieutenant Dick Harralson reported on board the *Mississippi* in 1955 as the ship's communication officer, he brought with him an unusual background. He had served as an enlisted radioman before World War II, was captured on Corregidor in 1942, spent most of the war as a POW, and was commissioned as an ensign in 1946. One benefit of serving in an old ship with a crew much reduced from her battleship days was that the officers had loftier staterooms than they would have had in previous times (the captain was in the admiral's quarters, and so forth). Harralson enjoyed bunking in what was designated as the operations officer's cabin, which sported carpet on the deck, a porthole, a desk, a file cabinet, a table, and a bunk.

He had specialized in communications and electronics rather than in ship driving. Now he found himself on the watch bill as officer of the deck

under way—a task for which he had no experience. So he joked to himself, "I've faked it this far. Let's not quit now." He spent the night before his first watch poring over various publications, cramming for the next day's duties. Soon after Harralson took over the deck the following morning, the commanding officer, Captain Charles Martell, addressed him as "Mr. Harralson." The "Mister" in front of his name caught him up short, and he wondered, "Oh, God, what have I done?" The skipper pointed out a trawler crossing in the distance and said, "Do something." Harralson gave a rudder order to the helmsman, then heard another blast from the captain: "Blow the goddamned whistle!" And thus did Harralson learn the basics through on-the-job training—as he had learned much else in his naval service.

To conduct the test platform operations, the *Mississippi* was positioned off the Virginia Capes. An airfield ashore launched drones—full-size obsolete aircraft that were operated by remote control—and the former battleship fired off Terrier missiles, attempting to knock them down. The process was frustrating, in part because the drones were often unreliable in operation. Harralson saw very few successful shoot-downs during his time on board, but

Here, the *Mississippi* is pictured toward the end of a career that had stretched nearly forty years by the time she was decommissioned in 1956. She served as a test bed for both guns and missiles. Here, in place of what was originally a 14-inch (36cm) triple turret, she sports a 6-inch (15cm) dual-purpose gun capable of firing at both air and surface targets. The rapid-fire 6-inch (15cm) mounts were used in the light cruisers *Worcester* and *Roanoke*, but by the time they came along, the era of the all-gun cruiser was essentially over. In the late 1950s and early 1960s, missile-armed warships entered the fleet at a steadily increasing rate. During the 1950s, the Navy contemplated arming either a battleship or battle cruiser with missiles, but the idea never came to fruition.

there must have been enough to deem the tests successful. After Captain Martell left in August 1955, he became the first commanding officer of the newly recommissioned guided missile cruiser *Boston*. The following year, the former battleship *Mississippi*, which first entered service in World War I, was decommissioned and scrapped.

DREADNOUGHT FAREWELL

The *Missouri* went into mothballs at Bremerton in early 1955, with President Truman, her longtime advocate, out of the White House. Her three sisters continued in service, primarily to train midshipmen in the summertime, and also to make deployments and conduct maneuvers with other naval units. On May 6, 1956, while operating with a group of ships off the Virginia Capes, the *Wisconsin* plowed into the destroyer *Eaton* in a heavy fog. When the two ships pulled apart, the *Wisconsin*'s bow looked like a gaping mouth that had just taken a bite of steel out of the destroyer. The battleship was hustled into dry dock at the Norfolk Naval Shipyard for remedial surgery. She received a graft in the form of a sixty-eight-foot (21m) section of bow taken from the hull of the *Kentucky*, an Iowa-class battleship whose construction had begun in December 1944 and was nearly three-quarters complete when work was stopped in 1947. For a time, there had been proposals to complete her as a guided-missile ship, but those never came to fruition. Now she served as a spare-bow locker, and that much of her was finally transferred to an active ship. The quick, sixteen-day repair job got the *Wisconsin* back into action for that summer's midshipman cruise. What was left of the hull of the *Kentucky* was scrapped in 1958.

By the mid-1950s, the Navy was undergoing a technological transformation that would make it much different than it had been even a decade and a half earlier, on the eve of World War II. The big gun had been predominant then, but now the Navy was commissioning super carriers such as the USS *Forrestal*, and they had become the preeminent warships in the fleet. Moreover, jet planes had come of age in those fifteen years, and they had speeds far beyond the ability of the battleships' antiaircraft guns to respond. Thus, the battleships were no longer useful in protecting the carriers. Guided missiles

OPPOSITE PAGE: Lined up at a pier in Norfolk in the spring of 1956 are the last three battleships still in commission. Front to back, they are the *Iowa*, *Wisconsin*, and *New Jersey*. The *Wisconsin* has a bite taken out of her bow as a result of a collision on May 6, 1956 with the destroyer *Eaton*.
FAR LEFT: A close-up shows the collision damage to the *Wisconsin*, with the bow of the *New Jersey* visible in the background.
NEAR LEFT: For more than fifteen years after the conclusion of World War II, the Navy kept a number of fast battleships in mothballs for potential return to service. The ships of the Iowa class were reactivated for Korea, but the older, slower ones were not. The end of the line for the *Indiana* came in late 1963. She is shown here during the dismantling process at Richmond, California.

were increasingly becoming the weapon of choice for air defense, and the trend accelerated as more missile ships joined the fleet. Nuclear submarines became true submersibles, no longer dependent on air as the diesel boats had been. And in the Cold War atmosphere of the day, the U.S. Navy had embarked on a project to develop long-range Polaris ballistic missiles that could be launched from submerged submarines. The Navy voraciously consumed limited defense budget dollars in pursuit of such technical advances. To help pay the way, Admiral Arleigh Burke decreed the decommissioning of the remaining battleships. He was an old battleship man himself, having reported to the *Arizona* in 1923 when he was an ensign.

After having been brought back to life in the early years of the decade, one by one the three ships

were returned to the mothball state—a far less celebratory occasion. The *New Jersey*, for instance, had the life slowly drained from her in the naval shipyard annex at Bayonne, New Jersey. For bachelors such as Lieutenant (junior grade) Charles Mumford, the time in New Jersey was an opportunity to go see shows on and off Broadway. Seaman John Evans enjoyed seeing the Brooklyn Dodgers play in Ebbets Field, their last year there before moving to Los Angeles. For the married men whose families were in the ship's home port of Norfolk, some ingenuity was required. Chief Electrician's Mate Arthur Smith joined with some warrant officers in buying a used Cadillac for the trips back and forth to Virginia. To him, it was reminiscent of the type that mobsters used, but it was comfortable. And so the days dwindled down. The *New Jersey* was decommissioned in August 1957, the

Iowa in February 1958, and the *Wisconsin* the following month. With the departure of the *Wisconsin*, the U.S. Navy was without an active battleship for the first time since 1895. But the battleships were only dormant, not dead.

NEW JERSEY TO VIETNAM

The Vietnam War crept up on the American people slowly at first, then grabbed center stage with the Gulf of Tonkin incidents in 1964 and the landing of combat troops at Danang, South Vietnam, in early 1965. The Navy's biggest involvement early in the war was to provide amphibious shipping to unload troops ashore, to support the troops logistically and with naval gunfire, and to conduct a campaign of aerial attacks on North Vietnam. The latter was costly in terms of pilots and planes, producing an ever-

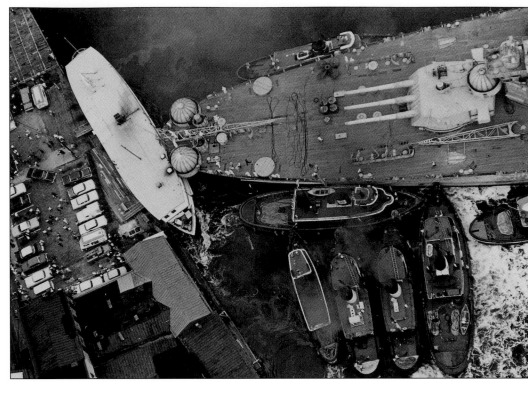

LEFT: The *New Jersey* sits in dry dock at the Philadelphia Naval Shipyard during her 1967–68 reactivation for duty in the Vietnam War. The rationale for her reactivation was that a battleship's shore bombardment of North Vietnam could replace some of the aerial bombing that was costing planes and pilots. Ironically, the U.S. government put most of North Vietnam off-limits for bombardment even before the ship was recommissioned on April 6, 1968. An embargo on bombarding the rest of Vietnam went into effect a month after the *New Jersey* reached the war zone.

RIGHT: One mothballed ship, the *North Carolina*, was saved from the scrapper's torch when she became a museum and memorial in the city of Wilmington, North Carolina. Still, her journey from the reserve fleet in Bayonne, New Jersey, to her berth near the Cape Fear River in Carolina was not entirely scot-free. As the tugs tried to put her bow into the slip where she would be moored, her stern crashed into a floating restaurant.

increasing number of prisoners of war in the hands of the North Vietnamese. One solution to the problem was to have naval bombardment take over some of the strikes delivered by aircraft. The chief of naval operations, Admiral David McDonald, wanted to recommission two heavy cruisers to use as gunships. Others, including Senator Richard Russell of Georgia, preferred the greater explosive power and longer range afforded by battleship projectiles. In early 1967, Senator Russell, a powerful committee chairman, insisted on reactivation of an Iowa-class battleship. Secretary of Defense Robert McNamara, who always had an eye on the bottom line, had resisted up to then, but new analyses were done to justify the return of a battleship. In the spring of 1967, reactivation of the *New Jersey*—considered to be in the best material condition of the four mothballed ships—began in secret at the Philadelphia Naval Shipyard. On the same day that Admiral McDonald retired as CNO, the Defense Department officially announced the reactivation.

During the autumn and winter that followed, shipyard workers gradually breathed life back into the old dreadnought, removing the dehumidification systems that had inhibited corrosion, and pulling the covers off her guns. She got updated electronics and a new threat-warning system, because the Navy was

concerned about antiship missiles, particularly in the wake of Egypt's sinking of the Israeli destroyer *Elath* with Styx missiles in October 1967. Training began for a new generation of battleship sailors, and a few from the previous generation were called back to supply their expertise in the operation of big guns and turrets.

Like the "showboat" *North Carolina* in 1941, the reborn *New Jersey* in 1968–69 was the subject of media and public attention. After loading ammunition in Norfolk, she proceeded to Long Beach, California, the port that had been the base for the ships of the old Battle Force in the years before World War II. The *New Jersey* was back, a vestigial reminder of the mighty breed that had been so preeminent before that global war. There was a traffic jam in Long Beach as people ventured to the waterfront to get a glimpse of the battleship and the former ocean liner *Queen Mary*, which was berthed nearby while being converted to a floating hotel.

Soon afterward, the ship went through extensive crew training to prepare for her role of shore bombardment in Vietnam. San Clemente Island, off the coast of southern California, took a pounding as the ship blazed away with rounds of 16-inch (41cm) and 5-inch (13cm) gunfire. On September 5, 1968, less than five months after being recommissioned in

Philadelphia, the world's only active battleship departed for war. She went first to Hawaii, then through the Philippine Archipelago, and thence to the shore of Vietnam. On the last day of the month, she unleashed her salvos of 16-inch (41cm) destruction at the southern coast of North Vietnam. For political reasons, the United State had declared most of the enemy land off-limits to bombardment just about the time the *New Jersey* was recommissioned in April. At 7:32 on the morning of September 30, the right gun of turret two spat out a 1,900-pound (862kg) high-capacity projectile, sending it in a parabolic arc toward shore. A Marine Corps TA-4 Skyhawk bomber did the spotting and made the corrections necessary for subsequent rounds to land on target. The pilot of the spotter flew toward the battleship, dipped its wings, and sent a radio message: "Welcome to the war." Retired Marine Corps Colonel Robert D. Heinl was on board that day as a newspaper reporter, and he gloried in the renaissance of battleship firepower. He had been with the fleet during World War II, when the old prewar battleships, the slow ones, had done the most precise shooting in support of amphibious landings. Now the *New Jersey* was an old ship herself, and she was shooting at the same high level of accuracy as the 1945 battleships. During the month of October, the ship ranged up and down the coast of North Vietnam.

Because of the impact the *New Jersey* was making, she was the occasional target of enemy fire from ashore. The skipper, Captain Ed Snyder, professed indifference to this threat but in truth did have some concern. On October 26, the ship was bombarding targets around the demilitarized zone that separated North and South Vietnam. Machinery Repairman Bill Sosnowski was on watch that day in the after diesel compartment, back near the stern and close to the waterline. If the ship's regular generators failed, he would have to start up emergency diesels to supply power. Other than that, he didn't really have a whole lot to do, so he put on a set of headphones and listened to a stereo set. But then he noticed the dogs—that is, the closing devices—moving on the hatch that led into the compartment. Someone was coming in. He quickly took off the headphones and hid them—just in time. In came Captain Snyder and Commander Jim Elfelt, the executive officer. The

enemy had just fired at the ship, and they wanted to know if he had heard anything. He told them he hadn't, conveniently omitting the fact that he could not have heard an impact against the hull because of his off-the-record musical entertainment.

At the end of the month, the ship received word that she was no longer permitted to fire at North Vietnam. Because of a bombing halt, probably timed to coincide with the upcoming presidential election in the United States, the entire country was off limits to bombing and shelling. A major justification for bringing the ship back from mothballs was to bombard the enemy nation, and now that mission had disappeared. For the rest of her time in Vietnam, which extended to March 1969, the *New Jersey* confined herself to firing at South Vietnam, often in support of American and South Vietnamese troops. It was, of course, a considerable benefit for the men ashore to be able to count on the big guns. Often the battleship was able to force enemy troops to back away from the coastline merely by her arrival on the scene. The North Vietnamese had seen the results of the shelling and didn't want any part of it.

The ship's respite when away from the war zone was to visit the port of Subic Bay in the Philippines. It was a sailor's paradise, a young man's fantasy realized. In the town of Olongapo, just outside the gate of the naval base, was a wide variety of entertainment. The experience usually involved one or more of three elements—music, women, and intoxicating beverages. As Ensign Chris Reed, a sage observer of the social scene, put it, "It was like a [school] dance, except that you could get drunk, and you could take the girl home." A petty officer from the battleship seconded the motion by saying of Olongapo, "It was a place where you could go, and you could get drunk. You could get yourself a girl, and she'd [even] feed you . . . all for under $10.00."

For Christmas 1968, comedian Bob Hope brought his troupe of beautiful women to entertain the crew of the world's only active battleship. The men gathered on the bow of the ship, forward of turret one, and listened to his wisecracks. Among other things, he suggested that his idea of a good time would be to go on a double date with *Playboy* publisher Hugh Hefner and take the rejects. When actress Ann-Margret said she wanted both to sing

ABOVE: En route to Vietnam, the *New Jersey* enters Pearl Harbor in September 1968. She has just swung to starboard after passing through the entrance channel, near where the *Nevada* was beached on December 7, 1941. Ford Island is in the lower right corner of the photo; the battleships were moored next to it when the Japanese attacked.
LEFT: The *New Jersey* unleashes a one-gun salvo toward Vietnam in March 1969. Because she was not able to bombard North Vietnam, the ship was used to provide gunfire support for ground troops in South Vietnam; by targeting enemies in the vicinity, she helped save American lives.

This is the *New Jersey* as she looked after being modernized in 1967–68. Still looking mostly as she had in the 1950s, she has a few noticeable changes. An antenna structure for long-range radio communications has been added to the bow. The sides of a room built to house electronic countermeasures (ECM) equipment stick out as "ears" high in the superstructure, with antennas protruding from it. The U.S. Navy took ECM quite seriously after the Egyptians sank an Israeli destroyer in the autumn of 1967. A new radio antenna arrangement is aft of the second stack. All the way at the stern, the airplane crane is a vestige of the period in World War II and shortly afterward when the ship operated catapult-equipped spotting planes. When the ship returned to commission in 1982, the stern crane had been removed.

and dance during the performance, Hope cracked, "Okay, but if I require mouth-to-mouth resuscitation, remember . . . no fellows!"

On a much more serious note, in mid-February, the men of the battleship heard something unusual after the salvo alarm—silence. The alarm, which consisted of two buzzing sounds, warned of imminent gunfire and was supposed to be followed by the roar of a 16-inch (41cm) gun. But there was a misfire in turret two. The primer in the breechblock had been fired normally, but the reduced-charge powder bag in the center gun was tilted, so the primer only ripped a portion of the bag itself and didn't ignite the black powder at the rear of the bag and thus explode all the powder. After waiting two and a half hours to see if a residual spark would explode the bag, two senior men from the turret, Lieutenant Roger Glaes and Chief Gunner's Mate Harold Sykes, entered the gun room. After pumping water into the breech, they risked their lives by opening the gun, removing the bag, and hurling it over the side into the sea. After that incident, the ship used no more reduced-powder charges during the remainder of the deployment.

Another big event followed shortly after this close call. At 1:06 A.M. on February 22, an urgent radio call came into the *New Jersey*'s combat information center from a Marine outpost ashore. A large number of enemy troops was attacking, and the Marines desperately wanted fire support from the big boy offshore. Radarman Roger Fulks was in CIC monitoring the radio transmissions and was struck by how cool the Marine radioman seemed to be in the midst of an obviously stressful situation. Because of the proximity of friendly and enemy forces, the 16-inch (41cm) guns would have made too big a hole, so the battleship opened up with her 5-inchers (13cm), firing in concert with the Coast Guard cutter *Owasco*. Over the radio, Warrant Officer Ed Flamboe heard the staccato sound of machine gun fire near the Marines. On through the night, the *New Jersey* aided the beleaguered Marines. Fire Controlman Rick Crawford was in a secondary battery plotting room watching the pattern of the 5-inch (13cm) rounds. After a while, he noticed that they formed a ring, because the Marines were surrounded. Finally, at 6:33 A.M.—nearly five and a half hours after the emergency call came in—the gunfire drove

FAR LEFT: After graduating from the Naval Academy, Ensign Bob Peniston reported to the *New Jersey* in 1946 as his first duty assignment. In January 1947, he posed with his bride Fran in front of the ship's turret one.
LEFT: In August 1969, he returned to take command of the *New Jersey* and once again posed with Fran near turret one. She died in 2000; the couple had been married for more than half a century.

away the attackers. Morning revealed that the decks were knee-deep in brass shell casings, and the paint on the 5-inch (13cm) guns had burned off the barrels, which had put out more than seventeen hundred rounds. Major Ron Smaldone, who was in command of the Marine post that night, put it well: "If it hadn't been for the *New Jersey*, they would have zapped our ass."

The ship's last firing mission of the deployment was on the night of March 31. She made one last stop at Subic Bay and then headed for Long Beach. The married men were eager to get home, especially those who had become fathers during the course of the long deployment. On April 15, when the ship was only four days from home, she received orders to head back to Japan to take station in the Sea of Japan off Korea. The North Koreans had shot down an unarmed U.S. Navy electronic surveillance plane, and the government decided to mount a show of force in readiness for possible retaliation. The crew members' families had showed up in the home port

to greet their men, but they weren't there to be greeted. The *New Jersey* milled around for a while longer off Korea before getting the order to head home a second time. In early May of 1969, she finally made it.

Now in the States, *New Jersey* spent the summer months completing two missions. The first was training to prepare the crew for a second trip to Vietnam, scheduled for that autumn. The second mission was to train a contingent of midshipmen that came aboard from the Naval Academy and from the NROTC programs of various civilian universities. This author had by then joined the crew and had the pleasure of being aboard as the battleship made port visits to Alameda, California; Tacoma, Washington; Pearl Harbor, Hawaii; and San Diego, California. The battleship was as popular as ever. During one day of general visiting at Alameda in northern California, 12,370 people came aboard. In Tacoma, the citizens had to be shuttled out by boat because the ship was anchored offshore. A young woman in a then-popu-

lar miniskirt rode a boat out to visit the ship and was accompanied by a battleship sailor she had met while he was on liberty. Hours later, after taps had sounded and the crew had gone to bed, "Miss Miniskirt" took another boat ashore; this time she was with another enlisted man, and she no longer looked as neat and tidy as when she had boarded the ship. Some of the crew members snickered as they suggested that the visitor had probably given new meaning to the battleship term "lower handling room."

The fun and games ended when the *New Jersey* pulled into Long Beach in August of 1969 to complete final preparations for returning to Vietnam. Then came the announcement that she wouldn't be going after all. The war was winding down, and it was time to cut costs. She would instead go to Bremerton, Washington, and there would be mothballed again. High expectations were crushed. Crewmen such as Lieutenant Dick Harris and Personnelman Henry Strub were among the many

A Personal View

My fascination with battleships started in the mid-1950s when I began assembling Revell plastic model kits that glued together to form miniature Iowa-class dreadnoughts. My father and I put together a *Missouri* and decorated it with sewing thread stretched as dress ship rigging, onto which we glued tiny paper signal flags. Under the Christmas tree one year, I found a model kit for the *New Jersey*. I was intrigued by the curlicue shapes of the camouflage pattern depicted on the ship's side in the painting on the box lid. Little did I know that the artist had actually depicted a camouflage design used only on the real *Missouri*, and not on her sister ship.

Fast forward more than a dozen years to a time when I was serving on board the tank landing ship *Washoe County* (LST-1165) off the coast of Vietnam. During slow night watches in the ship's combat information center, I looked through ship recognition books that showed pictures of the muscular Iowa-class ships as they had appeared when still in commission. And newspapers brought to the LST photos and stories on the reactivation of the *New Jersey* in faraway Philadelphia and then news of her wartime deployment to nearby Vietnam. Concluding that it didn't hurt to dream big, I requested reassignment to the "Big Jay." One evening in early January of 1969, I called my assignment officer in the Bureau of Personnel. The hearty voice of Lieutenant J.J. Hogan on the other end of the line brought good news: "It looks like I've got a job for you on the 'wagon.'" That was short for battlewagon, and I knew instantly what he meant. I didn't dream that night—I was too excited to sleep at all. Instead, I lay in my shipboard bunk and looked through a recent issue of the *Naval Institute Proceedings* that included a pictorial article on the *New Jersey*.

Duty on board the *New Jersey* proved to be every bit as enjoyable as I had imagined. She had been the World War II flagship of Admirals Raymond Spruance, Willis Lee, and William "Bull" Halsey. Her size and appearance were majestic. As we visited one port after another during a summer cruise, people turned out in droves to see the ship. After her crew had undergone a training stint to prepare for deployment to the gunline in Vietnam, the *New Jersey* served as the flagship for a midshipman training squadron, visiting San Francisco, Tacoma, Pearl Harbor, and San Diego. Everywhere the hospitality was marvelous, as was the public's desire to spend some time on board.

My station for underway watches was in the combat information center, or CIC. Originally intended to be a powder magazine, the space was located on the fourth deck, deep in the well-armored bowels of the ship. It was a realm of radar scopes, status boards, radio speakers, sound-powered telephones, a dead-reckoning tracer, and electronic countermeasures equipment—the latter to identify and ward off incoming missiles. Nearby were the plotting rooms, from which shipmates ran the shore bombardment operations and fired the guns. When it was time to man battle stations, the crew was summoned with a series of urgent-sounding signals: voice announcements, the bonging of the general alarm, the boatswain's pipe, and the unmistakable bugle call. The latter was a true throwback to the battleship era of long ago.

Working in the CIC, we experienced the outside world only through simulation. Our way of "seeing" the airplanes, ships, and land formations around us was by inter-

preting the phosphorescent images on our radar scopes. Or we saw vicariously through the oral descriptions provided by our shipmates who were topside and could tell us what was going on. We heard the crackling of radio transmissions as gunfire missions were executed. The sounds of the guns themselves were considerably muted by the casing of steel on all four sides, as was much of the feeling of being at sea. One night, we conducted an intership communication drill with other members of the training squadron. We heard radio announcements from the wave-tossed destroyers as their crews reported lights and windows being smashed by stormy seas. Meanwhile, the *New Jersey* plowed rock steady through those same seas. The sensation was much like that of being in a building ashore rather than on bucking waves.

There were so many little things that made the duty enjoyable. For one thing, the chow was always great. For breakfast and lunch, we could just pick a spot at a wardroom table and sit down. Dinner was a much more elaborate affair. Each of us was assigned a silver napkin ring, and for evening meals, the rings were placed on white tablecloths in precise order according to rank and seniority. Since seniority didn't change from day to day, you would sit and talk with the same fellows night after night. The only change would come when someone joined or left the ship. Because of the seating patterns, I never did get to know the ship's first lieutenant, a rugged-looking warrant boatswain named Joe Heeney. He had been in the Navy longer than I had been alive, and I figured he was the type who ate young lieutenants for breakfast. As a result, I didn't seek him out—to my sorrow. Years later, I happened to see him at a ceremony on board the *New Jersey*, introduced myself, and reminded him that we had once been shipmates. I discovered instantly that he is a warm, friendly man, and we've been in touch ever since. Camaraderie with shipmates was one of the many pleasures in serving on board the dreadnought.

The time after the evening meal brought a special pleasure when I had a chance to go out and walk on the teakwood decks (another throwback to an earlier time),

TOP: At top, the author stands in front of the forward turrets of the New Jersey at Bremerton, Washington, in October 1969.
ABOVE: Lieutenant "junior grade" Stillwell when he was serving in the crew of the *Washoe County* in 1968.

enjoy the fresh air, chat with shipmates, and watch the sun go down. And we all were thrilled to watch the ship crank up to twenty-seven knots (using only half her power plant) to get back to home port for liberty call. Having come from a fourteen-knot LST, I marveled that a ship could move that fast. In fact, this seagoing city called the *New Jersey* could push it up another six knots on full power.

Our first skipper was Captain Ed Snyder, who projected two personas. Regarding professional matters—keeping the ship sparkling in appearance, standing smart watches, being accurate in putting ordnance on target—he was demanding. On the other hand, he enjoyed being breezy or even wacky at times, and took pleasure in making flippant remarks. When asked about the threat from cruise missiles—a very real concern to the U.S. Navy at the time—he said that if one hit the ship, he would merely pipe sweepers and have the debris swept overboard. He had two of the former 40-millimeter gun tubs painted light blue inside and dubbed them swimming pools. Once he had one filled with water so he could float inside on an air mattress. The Navy demands that sailors wear hats or caps topside, but Snyder dispensed with this requirement at sea, saying the hats might blow overboard. Instead of being glued to the bridge, he liked to wander the ship and visit with the crew.

In late August of 1969, a new man came aboard to take over. He was Captain Robert Peniston, who referred to the *New Jersey* as "the big ship in my life." When he was a new midshipman at the Naval Academy in 1943, she was the first ship he ever set foot aboard. When he graduated from the academy in 1946, his first assignment as an ensign was to the *New Jersey*. Now came professional fulfillment as her commanding officer in wartime. But it was not to be. Within days of his arrival, the Navy announced that it would be mothballing and decommissioning the "Big Jay" and dozens of other warships. The Vietnam War was winding down, and it was necessary to save money. It was a sad bunch of sailors who watched the change of command ceremony, and it was a man of a different ilk who took over. I had a quarterdeck watch a few hours after we got the new skipper. Out of curiosity, I wandered back to look at one of the "swimming pools" and discovered that it had already been painted regulation gray inside. The new man was strictly by the book. Instead of taking her to Vietnam as planned, he took the ship instead to the naval shipyard at Bremerton, Washington, so she could be decommissioned. Captain Peniston spent much of his time on the bridge during that sad journey.

I made many friends on board the *New Jersey*, but none more special than the executive officer, Commander Jim Elfelt. In the typical shipboard setup, the skipper is the benevolent father figure and the exec, the duty hard-ass. Elfelt performed the job as executive officer effectively, but also with a great deal of warmth and compassion. He had a special gift for interacting with people. When Elfelt spent time with someone, he made him feel that he was the only other person in the world. The exec listened and cared. When the ship was at Bremerton and preparing to go out of commission, he wrote a note to the crew, saying he hoped that they would look him up in the future. And he meant it, as I discovered years later in Annapolis after I was working for the Naval Institute. In walked Elfelt one day, by then wearing the uniform of a rear admiral. He had just wanted to say hello to a former shipmate.

who were disappointed, but there just wasn't much they could do about it. The orders had come from someone in a far higher pay grade than theirs. The ship's new skipper, Captain Robert Peniston, had been excited over the prospect of a combat cruise; instead, he would have to preside over her reburial in the reserve fleet. He went about the job manfully, directing the crewmen to do their work carefully so that the *New Jersey* would again be ready to serve in the unlikely event that she was once again called. The decommissioning ceremony took place on a dreary, overcast day in Bremerton. In his remarks that day, Peniston captured the sentiment of the audience when he said, "The hour cometh and now is to say farewell. But, before doing so, my last order to you—battleship *New Jersey*—is rest well, yet sleep lightly, and hear the call, if again sounded, to provide 'firepower for freedom [the ship's motto].' She will hear the call, and thanks to her magnificent crew, she is ready." Afterward, he wiped tears from his eyes with a white-gloved hand as he descended the brow to go ashore for the last time.

LEFT TOP: Captain Ed Snyder throws battleship formality overboard as he relaxes on an air mattress in a "swimming pool" that was originally a 40-millimeter gun tube.
LEFT BOTTOM: The *New Jersey*'s executive officer, Commander Jim Elfelt, stands proudly with son Jimmy in September 1969 as the ship prepares to depart her home port of Long Beach for her last voyage prior to deactivation.
ABOVE: On December 17, 1969, a saddened Captain Robert Peniston leaves the ship following her decommissioning. He resolved that the ship would be mothballed carefully so she would be ready to serve if ever again called upon. Little more than a decade later, she was.

Chapter Eight

RENAISSANCE AND FINALE

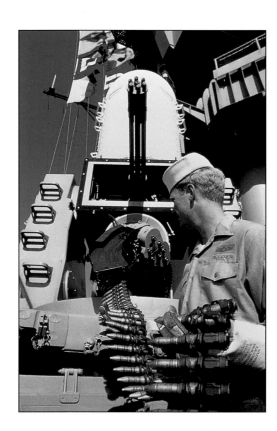

ABOVE: A sailor loads ammunition into the Vulcan/Phalanx close-in weapon system on board the *Iowa*. The abbreviation, CIWS, is pronounced *see-whiz* in shipboard lingo. It uses a six-barrel rotating Gatling-type gun to fire 20-millimeter bullets at incoming missiles. The effective range is between 500 and 1,500 yards (457.2m and 1,371.6m).
OPPOSITE PAGE: The *Wisconsin* sends a streak of fire into the sky as she fires a Tomahawk missile toward Baghdad, Iraq, on the first night of the Gulf War in January 1991.

In the years following the *New Jersey*'s decommissioning, the four Iowa-class battleships slumbered on—two at Bremerton and two in Philadelphia. The 1970s were relatively uneventful for the battleships. In 1972, when the North Vietnamese staged an Easter offensive against the south, *New Jersey* alumni, such as now—Rear Admiral Ed Snyder and Warrant Boatswain Joe Heeney, were queried about the potential for bringing the ship back into active service quickly. But interest died out as soon as it had flickered up, and the following year, the United States pulled its forces out of Vietnam. Two years later the North Vietnamese overran the south, and the war in that Southeast Asian land was at last over. Some critics called the American strategy flawed—a piecemeal commitment of troops and other assets rather than an overwhelming force that could have defeated the enemy.

It had been a limited war all along and now it was lost. The North Vietnamese had been willing to accept horrendous personnel losses in the interest of nationalism to win what was essentially a civil war against South Vietnam. Moreover, there were vast cultural differences that the Americans were never able to overcome in that localized battle against communism. More than fifty thousand Americans were killed in the struggle, and uncounted billions of dollars poured into the effort. Many Americans had actively protested or avoided the war, and a stigma against military action remained as a lingering aftertaste.

THE CARTER YEARS

In 1977, President Jimmy Carter took office and brought with him a sense of compassionate concern for human rights, coupled with a surprisingly negative view of military expenditures, given the fact that he was a Naval Academy graduate. Soviet naval forces became ever more numerous and powerful as the Cold War continued, but the Carter administration was loath to enter into an arms race. The president even vetoed a defense bill because it contained a provision for building a nuclear-powered aircraft carrier. The perception arose that United States military strength was waning, and so was the will to use it.

Other nations took advantage of this perceived weakness. In the autumn of 1979, the Soviets invaded Afghanistan and installed a puppet government. Even more threatening was the seizure of the U.S. embassy in Tehran by Iranian militants, and the capture of American diplomatic personnel. Throughout 1980, the Iranian hostage situation remained foremost in American minds, particularly with nightly telecasts that reminded viewers how long the Americans had been held. President Carter ordered a commando-type raid to rescue the captives, but it was a dismal failure. Within this context, a former fighter pilot and Pentagon official named Chuck Myers was clamoring for the reactivation of battleships, partly as an effort to rebuild dwindling military strength, and partly on behalf of a client, Martin Marietta, that had designed a drastic modernization package for each battleship. Included would have been the removal of the aft turret and the installation of missile launchers and a ski-jump flight deck on the fantail. The Navy, the Marine Corps, and some members of Congress favored the battleship reactivation plan—but the Carter administration did not.

REAGAN'S MILITARY BUILDUP

For a variety of reasons, the U.S. electorate turned Jimmy Carter out of office that autumn. The economy was woeful, inflation was staggering, and the country was viewed as weak. His Republican challenger was former California Governor Ronald Reagan, who espoused a much stronger nation, a return to a previous era of American power. When Reagan took office in 1981, his administration was intent on pursuing a military buildup. Indeed, through much of the 1980s, the money flowed toward Pentagon projects. This process was aided in no small measure by John Lehman, an activist Secretary of the Navy whose

attitude on battleships was precisely the opposite of that of the previous administration. Instead of opposing their return to the fleet, he aggressively campaigned for it. Since the *New Jersey* had been used in the Vietnam War, she was the most modern of the four ships still in mothballs, and the first chosen for return to active duty. In the summer of 1981, Congress approved funding for the initial stages of her modernization, though it was not as radical as some had hoped.

NEW JERSEY REACTIVATED

On July 27 of that year, tugboats pulled the *New Jersey* away from her berth in Bremerton for the tow to the Long Beach Naval Shipyard, where she would be reactivated and dramatically ushered into the missile age. The old ship—more than forty years had now passed since the laying of her keel—had awakened from her long slumber and was ready to heed the call that Captain Peniston had described in his decommissioning speech. At the decommissioning in 1969, Chief Personnelman Andy Lavella had lowered the American flag at the ship's fantail. He had since retired from active duty and was working in Virginia. In August 1981, he traveled across country to welcome the ship as she came into Long Beach. Thousands of others shared his sense of enthusiasm that a dreadnought would once again be part of the active fleet.

In the months to come, the shipyard put into effect a modernization package that would be pretty much standard as the battleships, one by one, rejoined the fleet during the remainder of the decade. The big guns remained the same, but four of the ten 5-inch (13cm) twin mounts were removed to make way for armored box launchers capable of firing long-range Tomahawk cruise missiles. Elsewhere in the superstructure came canister-enclosed Harpoon antiship missiles and Vulcan/Phalanx Gatling guns for use against close-in missile threats. Electronics were improved and upgraded, particularly radars and a computerized fire control system for the new missile systems.

On December 28, 1982, less than a year and a half after the reactivation began, President Reagan was on hand in Long Beach to recommission the ship. Included in the ceremony was the obligatory twenty-one-gun salute. The new skipper, Captain Bill

Because she had been modernized in 1967–68 to take part in the Vietnam War, the *New Jersey* was the first ship reactivated in the early 1980s when the Reagan administration pushed to upgrade the Navy's strength by bringing battleships back from the mothball fleet. When the *New Jersey*, shown here at dry dock at Long Beach Naval Shipyard in 1982, began the reactivation program in the summer of 1981, she had been out of active service only a dozen years. By contrast, her three sisters had been lying idle for more than twenty. Thus, they would require more extensive upgrades to return to the fleet.

None of the four ships received the radical rebuilding called for in some proposals. Each ship retained her aft turret, and there was no flight deck built on the fantail. As it was, the total cost for reactivation and modernization of the four ships was about $1.5 billion. The radical modernization would have driven the price far higher and might have imperiled congressional approval for reactivation of all four ships.

ABOVE LEFT: In nearly twelve years in mothballs, dirt collected in the seams between deck planks and provided an environment in which grass could grow.

ABOVE RIGHT: A workman lubricates a strut bearing for one of the *New Jersey*'s starboard propellers while she was dry-docked during the reactivation and modernization period in 1981–82.

LEFT: While in dry dock, the ship's underwater hull was cleaned in order to preserve it. Workmen wear protective clothing during the process. The flange protruding from the hull in the upper left corner of the photo is a portion of a bilge kill, designed to cut down on rolling while the *New Jersey* was at sea.

RIGHT: The *New Jersey*'s superstructure is covered with scaffolding as yard workers in Long Beach transform a ship designed in the 1930s and built in the 1940s into a modern weapon system capable of fighting in the 1980s.

Fogarty, asked his navigator, Lieutenant Commander Chris Johnson, to count the rounds as they were fired. As soon as the twenty-first sounded, Johnson was to lower his salute smartly so Fogarty would know that the process was complete and could move on to the next stage of the ceremony. But when the first gun went off, Johnson raised his right arm to salute, and the top button flew off the jacket of his blue uniform. That distracted him and he forgot to count. He wondered sheepishly what his new skipper would think of a new navigator who couldn't count. While he was on board, Reagan took an almost childlike delight in exploring the ship, for his enthusiasm was famous. The tour ended in Fogarty's spacious cabin on the 01 level, where the president chatted with the skipper's mother. She told Reagan that she had listened to him years earlier when he was a radio announcer in Iowa. When he inquired if she knew about a certain Prohibition-era speakeasy, she told him that she certainly did.

Soon, the *New Jersey* was involved in various training operations off the West Coast. In the spring of 1983, this writer had the privilege of returning to the ship for two weeks at sea—more than a dozen years after I had been a member of the crew. Along with hundreds of *New Jersey* men, I stood on the fantail on May 10 to observe the first-ever firing of a Tomahawk cruise missile by a battleship. On a sunny but windy afternoon, the ship was steaming near San Nicholas Island, then turned to head out to sea. The wind was throwing up waves that at times crashed onto the fantail, sending the crew scurrying. Up in the superstructure, on the starboard side, an armored box launcher was elevated so the missile could shoot across to port. When the electronic order came from a console in the combat engagement center, the Tomahawk emerged with a fiery blast from its launcher. For an instant, the missile seemed to hang in the air—long enough for me to wonder if something was amiss. But then the booster ignited as designed, and the missile soared off into the sky, trailing a plume of smoke behind. A while later, Captain Fogarty spoke to the crew on the general announcing system and reported that the Tomahawk had made a direct hit on its target in Tonopah, Nevada, about five hundred miles (805km) away. It was a remarkable increase in offensive reach for a battleship that, up to then, had

been limited to the twenty-three-mile (37km) range of her 16-inch (41cm) guns.

In June of 1983, the *New Jersey* set off on what was intended as a three-month shakedown cruise to the Western Pacific. It would be a chance to provide still more training for the crew and also afforded a chance for the men to hit some enjoyable liberty ports as a payoff for all the time they had spent going through a vast variety of drills and preparing the ship for commissioning. In Pearl Harbor, the ship rendered honors to the crew of the *Arizona*. Then it was on to the Philippines, Singapore, and Thailand. En route to Singapore, the ship crossed the equator and held the traditional hazing of the pollywogs who had not made the crossing before. The honor of playing King Neptune went to Gunner's Mate Curtis McAdams. He had first crossed the line on board the old *Nevada* in November 1943, almost forty years earlier.

ON STATION IN LEBANON

In late July, the Western Pacific portion of the cruise was abruptly aborted, and the ship was ordered to take station off Central America to support the regime in the country of El Salvador. It was a throwback to the old days of gunboat diplomacy, when a naval presence was used to aid the situation ashore. And the *New Jersey* was quite a gunboat. In fact, it was that very attribute that brought on still another change of schedule. She received orders to pass through the Panama Canal into the Atlantic. Men called home to tell their families they were headed to an undisclosed location and didn't know when they would be back. Fire Controlman Dan Clairmont called his wife in California and found she was already crying because she had heard on the news that the ship was destined for the trouble spot of Beirut, Lebanon. Soon, they were both crying at long-distance rates.

The ship proceeded to the eastern Mediterranean at high speed in order to be of possible aid in defusing hostilities in Lebanon. The chief petty officers' mess was well aft in the ship, near the propellers. The vibration at twenty-five knots was such that it made normal life difficult. Senior Chief Fire Controlman Rick Crawford observed that no one could set his coffee cup down on a table because it was shaking so much. Chief Gunner's

Mate Larry Pousson, who had been a seaman on board the ship during her Vietnam incarnation, had trouble sleeping, as did many of his shipmates. Some were often still sitting up at 2:00 or 3:00 in the morning, while others preferred to try to sleep in their offices rather than in their bunks.

Once off Beirut, the ship went into a period of watchful waiting. From their vantage point offshore, the men of the *New Jersey* observed the shooting that went on night after night in the urban battle-ground. The ship's mission was to provide gunfire support, if needed, to protect Marines who were hunkered down at the Beirut airport. In late October, a terrorist killed hundreds of the Marines with a suicide bomb. In December, Syrians shot down U.S. Navy planes involved in an air strike. In mid-December, the *New Jersey* was finally unleashed to fire her guns. The Marines were still vulnerable, so the ship had to remain on station. The deployment originally intended for three months had stretched to six with no end in sight. Naval Reservists were flown in to replace some of the crewmen and allow them to go on leave. In early February, the ship again went into action. On February 8, she fired two hundred and eighty-eight 16-inch (41cm) rounds in one day against Syrian gun positions that were shelling Beirut. It was physically exhausting work, and it also shook up the old ship. It had been a long day: the ship had fired many rounds in anger and had even reacted to a threat (which later proved groundless) that the ship was targeted for attack. Captain Rich Milligan had taken over as the new skipper shortly before the ship left Central America. When he finally got to his sea cabin in the early morning of February 9, he found that his bunk was drenched because the concussion from the firing of the big guns had broken a water pipe overhead.

REACTIVATION OF THE *IOWA* AND *MISSOURI*

Still more time passed on station, because the ship had to remain as long as the Marines did. At the time a well-known U.S. television commercial asked how one spelled relief. The answer was "R-O-L-A-I-D-S." When that same question was posed to the men of the *New Jersey*, the answer was "I-O-W-A," because her sister ship was then undergoing reactivation back in the States. When

OPPOSITE TOP: Upon going to sea in 1983 after her recommissioning, the *New Jersey* demonstrated she had new capabilities to complement the old ones. On May 10, 1983, she unleashes the first Tomahawk missile fired by a battleship, thus restoring offensive punch to battle-ships for the first time in many years.
OPPOSITE BOTTOM: Lieutenant David Glazier of the destroyer *Ingersoll* captured this shot of the *New Jersey* firing her 16-inch (41cm) guns.
RIGHT: The *Iowa* was the second of the four ships of her class to rejoin the active fleet as part of the modern-ization program. She is shown here in dry dock num-ber four in the Norfolk Naval Shipyard. Before the decade was over, the energetic work of Secretary of the Navy John Lehman had paid off. The U.S. Navy wound up with two battleships on each coast, the *Iowa* and *Wisconsin* homeported in Norfolk and the *New Jersey* and *Missouri* in Long Beach.

RIGHT: On the occasion of the recommissioning of the *Iowa* on April 28, 1984, the skipper, Captain Gerald Gneckow, accompanies Vice President George Bush and the commanding officer of the *Iowa*'s Marine detachment in inspecting the ship's Marines.

BOTTOM LEFT: As the members of the Iowa class were modernized, each ship lost four 5-inch (12.7cm) twin gun mounts amidships to make room to missile launchers. Here, the outer shield is being taken off one of the mounts following removal.

BOTTOM RIGHT: One of the key moments in bringing each ship back to life was lighting the boilers for the first time.

the Marines were finally released from their beleaguered outpost, so was the battleship. After several stops in the Mediterranean, she commenced the long journey to her home port of Long Beach, California. When she finally got back on May 5, five thousand people welcomed her. The intended three-month cruise had lasted nearly eleven months.

In that spring of 1984, Vice President George Bush was on hand when the *Iowa* was recommissioned. This marked another success for Secretary Lehman's salesmanship to Congress, and the first time more than one battleship had been in commission at the same time since the late 1950s. The men of the *Iowa* harked back to the Teddy Roosevelt era in adopting the nickname "The Big Stick" for their ship. Initially, the *Iowa* deployed to Central America and began working up the concept of the battleship battle group, an idea modeled on the aircraft carrier battle group, but intended for areas in which a lower threat was expected and thus less protection required against air and missile threats.

Two years later, on May 10, 1986, it was the *Missouri*'s turn to be recommissioned and join her sisters in active service. San Francisco was the setting on a brilliant sunny day with deep blue sky above. The commanding officer who would bring her back into the fleet was Lee Kaiss, who had asked one of the ship's enlisted men, Journalist Bill Egan,

to write a speech for the occasion. As a boy in New Jersey in October 1945, Egan had watched as the *Missouri* and dozens of other warships lined up in the Hudson River for the first post–World War II Navy Day celebration. He drew upon that experience in drafting the speech and was thrilled when he heard Kaiss open with the following words: "On October 27, 1945, when President Harry S. Truman stepped aboard USS *Missouri*, he said, 'This is the happiest day of my life.' Ladies and gentlemen, I know exactly how he felt." Also on hand for the ceremony was Margaret Truman Daniel. In January 1944, as the daughter of then-Senator Harry Truman, she had smashed a bottle of champagne across the ship's bow to christen her on the occasion of launching. Now, forty-two years later, she spoke at a banquet held for the ship's crew in San Francisco's city hall. She talked about the ship's history and what it meant to her and closed with a

statement that had the crew eating out of her hand: "Captain Kaiss and the men of the *Missouri*, there's one other thing I want to say to you. Please take good care of my baby."

In the years that followed, they did just that, although heart problems soon took Kaiss off the ship. He was replaced by Captain Al Carney, who took the *Missouri* on an around-the-world shakedown cruise that included a stop in Australia to observe the seventy-fifth anniversary of that nation's navy. Still later, she went through the Suez Canal and into the Mediterranean. She returned to Istanbul, Turkey, where she had made quite a hit in 1946. One of the men of the crew back then was Seaman John Davidson. In 1986, with a long career behind him, he had been lured back to the *Missouri* as a master chief boatswain's mate. When he had been offered an opportunity to return to his old ship, he jumped at it, explaining. "I told them I'd pay them to let me

RIGHT: In 1986, following her recommissioning, the *Missouri* made an around-the-world shakedown cruise. This imaginative shot shows her slender bow slicing through the ocean.
BOTTOM LEFT: Here, she prepares to squeeze into one of the locks of the Panama Canal. The locks are 110 feet (32.9m) wide, built at a time when battleships were much smaller. The *Missouri* and her sisters were built with a beam dimension of 108 feet (32.8m), just a foot (30cm) of clearance on either side.
BOTTOM RIGHT: The ship is in full dress during a visit to Australia during the world cruise. In the lower right corner of the picture is Prince Philip, Duke of Edinburgh, husband of Queen Elizabeth II.

serve." It turned out even better than that; the Navy paid him to do so.

As the 1980s progressed, the battleship program continued to sell in Congress. The Navy was aiming to build up its fleet to six hundred ships, and the battleships symbolized that growing strength. In 1988, the *Wisconsin* became the fourth and final ship of the class to return to active duty. Like the *Iowa*, she was based in Norfolk and operated with the Atlantic Fleet. She also deployed to the Mediterranean. With two ships now active on each coast, it was possible to set up a regular rotation of deployments. The battleships were no longer the novelty they had been at the beginning of the decade, when it was necessary for the *New Jersey* to remain on station off Lebanon for months because no other ship was available to relieve her.

BATTLESHIPS IN THE PERSIAN GULF

In 1987, another mission had grown up for the battleships in the faraway Persian Gulf. For years, Iran and Iraq had been fighting each other, and their conflict had spilled into the gulf in the form of an increasingly dangerous tanker war in which each side was attacking tankers containing the other's oil. The United States sought to keep the oil flowing by transferring a number of Kuwaiti tankers to the U.S. flag and manning them with American crews. U.S. Navy ships were called into action to escort the tankers while they were in the Persian Gulf, and larger ships operated in the Gulf of Oman in support of the mission, which was dubbed Operation Earnest Will. One of those ships was the battleship *Missouri*. In October of that year she began her first support mission. As the tankers and their escorts steamed to the Strait of Hormuz at the mouth of the gulf, the *Missouri* went with them. The smaller ships could be attacked by Iranian Silkworm missiles. The battleship's guns were in position to retaliate if necessary; their ability to do so could serve as an effective deterrent to prevent the firing of the missiles. On that first convoy trip, Machinist's Mate Bill Holland had a battle station in the alley for one of the ship's large propeller shafts. He had heard that the Iranians might try to disable the ship by firing at her propellers and shafts. At his station, he had fuel on one side and gunpowder on the other, which created

The crew of one great dreadnought honors another. The men of the *New Jersey* are manning the rail on May 24, 1986 as their ship steams into Pearl Harbor and pays tribute to the *Arizona* memorial at left. The eight battleships that were in the harbor at the time of the Japanese attack in 1941 sustained varying degrees of damage. The other seven were removed from their berths during World War II, and all except the *Oklahoma* were restored to active service. Because the *Arizona* was so badly shattered and because her hull still contained the remains of hundreds of her crew, the Navy elected to leave her in place and eventually built the white memorial that stands astride the wreck.

some disquieting thoughts. Fortunately, the Iranians chose not to attack the ship that night or any other. The deterrence was effective, though one of the tankers escorted by the battleship was hit by a Silkworm after she had made her way to the northern part of the Persian Gulf.

On July 4, 1986, the *Iowa*'s skipper, Captain Larry Seaquist, had hosted President and Mrs. Reagan on board the ship in New York Harbor to celebrate the one hundredth anniversary of the Statue of Liberty. The following year, Seaquist and the *Iowa* were half a world away to take the *Missouri*'s place in support of Operation Earnest Will. Mobility is obviously an asset for warships, as the *Iowa* demonstrated. As with the *Missouri*, the convoys got through safely on the *Iowa*'s watch. The ship carried

a crew of more than fifteen hundred, and a number of them had previous battleship service, because men moved from ship to ship during the battleship renaissance. One individual had a particularly unusual pedigree in that he was a third-generation *Iowa* man. Captain Jeffrey Bolander was the commanding officer of the ship's Marine detachment. His father had served as a junior naval officer in the crew during the 1950s, and had married the daughter of the ship's skipper, Captain Wayne Loud. It is a testament to the longevity of the ship that such an achievement was possible.

TRAGEDY IN TURRET TWO

In the spring of 1989, the *Iowa* participated in a Second Fleet training exercise in the Caribbean. On

the morning of April 19, the ship was steaming through light seas 330 miles (531km) northeast of Puerto Rico. She was due to take part in a firing exercise with her 16-inch (41cm) guns, and the commander of the Second Fleet, Vice Admiral Jerry Johnson, was on the bridge to observe, along with the ship's skipper, Captain Fred Moosally. When the crew of turret one attempted to fire the turret's left gun, it didn't go off. It was a misfire in that the primer, which was supposed to set off a charge of black powder at the rear of a large powder bag, did not do so. The center and right guns of the turret fired without any problem. Two further attempts to shoot the left gun resulted in two more misfires. Though the problem with turret one was still unresolved, it was then the turn of turret two to shoot.

Boatswain's Mate Gary Fisk operated the hoist that brought up bags of powder from the handling room below for use in the turret's center gun. Gunner's Mate Clayton Hartwig, the gun captain for that gun, was responsible for loading the powder bags into position behind the projectile. Gunner's Mate Robert Backherms, who had never before done so in a live firing, had the job of ramming the bags of powder into the breech. A hitch developed, so Gunner's Mate Richard Lawrence, who was operating the cradle over which the powder went on its way to the gun, reported by sound-powered telephone, "I have a problem here. I'm not ready yet." Shortly afterward came a second report on the telephone, this one from Senior Chief Gunner's Mate Reginald Ziegler in the turret officer's booth behind the three gun

OPPOSITE PAGE: The last battleships ever to participate in combat were the *Missouri* (here firing at night in Desert Storm) and the *Wisconsin*, shown at right. Because of Iraqi mines laid in the northern part of the Persian Gulf, the ships had only a small mine-cleared zone in which they could steam while providing shore bombardment.
RIGHT: Things went terribly wrong in turret two of the *Iowa* on the morning of April 19, 1989. Powder charges in the center gun ignited while the breech at the rear of the gun was still open, and the explosion roared back into the turret and down the powder train. Altogether, forty-seven men were killed, and the tragedy probably hastened the demise of the battleship program. Within three years, all four ships of the Iowa class were back in mothballs.
BOTTOM LEFT AND RIGHT: These photographs show the normal loading procedure for 16-inch (41cm) guns on board the *Iowa*. The huge round is brought in on a vertical hoist from the powder flats, tilted over on a cradle, and then rammed into the breech at the rear and of the gun. A rammer than pushes bags of powder in behind the projectile. Once they are in place, the breechblock is closed and locked, and the round is fired.

rooms. He said the left gun was loaded and ready, but there was still some difficulty with the center gun. Then came still another report from Lawrence, this one in an excited voice, "I'm not ready yet. I'm not ready yet."

Up on the bridge, Captain Moosally said to Admiral Johnson, "Turret two is my best crew and—" At that moment, 9:55 in the morning, an explosion erupted inside that turret. A video camera on the bridge captured the force from the center gun as its five hundred pounds (227kg) of powder went off. Before firing, the gun's breech should have been closed and sealed so that the force would exit through the muzzle. But in this case something set it off prematurely, so that much of the force went aft, into the gun room, where it killed the crew instantly. The high-pressure gases generated by the blast then spread into the rest of the turret and down the powder train that led up from below. The result was a fireball, and the ship's crew soon went to general quarters to deal with the fire. Fortunately, the design of the turrets was such that steel bulkheads separated the powder train from the magazine spaces nearby, which prevented the disaster from being even worse. As it was, forty-seven men from the crew of turret two were killed almost instantly.

The aftermath of the explosion was ugly, as the Navy instituted an investigation into the cause of the blast. Rear Admiral Richard Milligan, who had commanded the *New Jersey* off Lebanon, conducted the investigation. After taking testimony from witnesses and conducting a physical examination of the scene, Milligan issued a report that concluded the explosion was the result of a suicidal act on the part of Gunner's Mate Hartwig. It argued that he had placed an explosive charge between powder bags, causing them to go off when they were rammed into the breech of the gun. The explanation was treated with skepticism by Congress and the media. The Senate Armed Services held hearings into the matter and then arranged for the Sandia National Laboratories in New Mexico to conduct an independent investigation. It dropped powder bags onto a steel plate as a means of simulating the ramming of the bags in the gun's breech. This further investigation concluded that the explosion occurred as the result of high-speed over-ramming of the bags, complicated by the number of grains of powder in the layer nearest the

end of the bag. The Navy changed its own findings and issued an apology to the family of Gunner's Mate Hartwig.

COLD WAR BURNS OUT

While these events were taking place, the Cold War was coming to an end. Mikhail Gorbachev, general secretary of the Communist Party, instituted economic and social reforms to open up the regime in the Soviet Union, and worked to develop better relations with other countries. The Berlin Wall, which had been constructed in 1961 and served as a symbol of the Cold War division of Germany, came down in November 1989. For decades, the United States had built its defense budgets on countering the Soviet Union and other threats. Now the Soviet Union was fading away. That led to pressure in 1990 for a reduction in American defense expenditures. Among the high-profile targets were the battleships; very likely, the *Iowa's* turret explosion made them more vulnerable than they might otherwise have been. In any event, they were manpower-intensive and expensive to operate. They had been designed in an era when sailors' wages were small, particularly for men in the lower pay grades. Now, following the advent of the all-volunteer force, pay was higher, so it was much more costly to run a ship. In addition, smaller ships, such as cruisers, destroyers, and submarines, had been outfitted to carry Tomahawk cruise missiles, so that capability in the battleships was no longer so highly prized as it had been in the early 1980s. In the summer of 1990, the *Iowa* and *New Jersey* again began the inactivation process, and the Navy announced that the other two ships would follow suit the following year.

IRAQ INVADES KUWAIT

But then came an event that changed plans considerably. On August 2, three Iraqi Army divisions invaded neighboring Kuwait in the Persian Gulf. Because of a concern that the Iraqis might move on to nearby Saudi Arabia and endanger supplies of oil from the region, the United States formed a coalition with other nations and mounted a defensive effort named Operation Desert Shield. While Iraq's President Saddam Hussein failed to consolidate his gains and move on, the U.S. Navy quickly shelved its plans to decommission the two remaining battleships,

Wisconsin and *Missouri*. It also took careful precautions concerning ammunition for their 16-inch (41cm) guns to ensure there would be no repeat of the *Iowa*'s turret explosion. The *Wisconsin* was the first to arrive in the Persian Gulf, and the *Missouri* joined her on January 3, 1991.

President George Bush gave Iraq an ultimatum. Either its forces leave Kuwait by January 15, or the international coalition would take steps to liberate Kuwait by force. The buildup was over; now it was time for the combat phase, which was known as Operation Desert Storm. This would be the first combat use of the long-range Tomahawk land-attack missiles. On board the *Wisconsin*, the skipper was Captain David Bill, who headed the Tomahawk coordination team. The team planned a number of scenarios for the approximately half dozen ships equipped with the missiles. Among the considerations was ensuring that the firing ships were sufficiently separated to prevent mutual interference. In the early morning of January 17 came the countdown. The armored box launchers in the ships'

superstructures were elevated, and men in the combat engagement centers handled the electronic equipment that controlled the firing. One by one, the box launchers erupted in fountains of flame and the missiles roared off into the dark night and headed for Baghdad, Iraq's capital city. The officer of the deck in the *Missouri* that night was Lieutenant Wes Carey, who had earlier served in the *Iowa* as well. The hope that the gathering of coalition forces would cause the Iraqis to back off had failed. Now came the realization that he and his ship were at war. There was no way the missiles could be recalled now that they were on their way. And crew members began to feel a sense of fear that perhaps they would be targeted for retaliation. But Iraq was so overwhelmed that it was unable to launch any forces against the ships, especially since the coalition forces had such effective control of the surrounding airspace.

In early February, the two battleships fired their 16-inch (41cm) guns in anger for the first time since the Korean War. On February 3, the *Missouri*

Mines have been dubbed "the weapons that wait." They can be laid in secret and there they remain until exploded by passing ships. They proved a genuine concern during the Gulf War. Iraqi mines seriously damaged the Aegis cruiser *Princeton* and the amphibious assault ship *Tripoli*. Here, the *Missouri* steams in the Persian Gulf while a mine floats menacingly in the foreground. The battleship carried an explosive ordnance disposal (EOD) team to put explosive charges on the mines and blow them up in order to eliminate them as threats. On the *Missouri*'s long voyage to the Persian Gulf, the skipper, Captain Lee Kaiss, said he hoped there were two groups of people on board the ship that got plenty of rest, as their services would not be needed until later: the doctors and the EOD personnel. The latter did get a great deal of work.

shelled enemy positions at Khafji in northern Saudi Arabia. She had a new piece of equipment for spotting the fall of shot ashore. In previous wars, the spotting had been done by floatplanes or helicopters launched from battleships. These aircraft were vulnerable to enemy gunfire. Now the battleships launched unmanned remotely piloted vehicles (RPVs), which were drone aircraft fitted with television cameras and infrared sensing devices. In control rooms on board the battleships, men could measure the miss distance from a target ashore, then provide corrections to on-board plotting rooms so that subsequent rounds would be aimed to hit. The TV pictures were piped to sets throughout the giant *Missouri*, so members of her crew were able to see the results of their ship's big guns.

One night, Master Chief Fire Controlman Mark Snedeker was in the *Missouri*'s main battery plot and decided to have the RPV follow a truck that was on the Iraq-Kuwait Highway. The infrared pictures showed the truck going from place to place, evident-

ly handing out food to troops that materialized from the darkness. During the truck's two-hour trip, Snedeker recorded the places where it had stopped and thus where troops were located. Then the ship systematically fired at the positions that had been noted, no doubt causing great surprise to the victims of the nocturnal gunfire. After some time had passed, the Iraqis came to realize the connection between the appearance of the drone aircraft and the huge projectiles that followed afterward. So it was that a group of Iraqi soldiers surrendered to the *Wisconsin*'s RPV and were duly observed via television to be doing so.

In late February, the *Missouri* fired shore bombardment at southern Kuwait to create the impression that amphibious landings would take place there. It was a ruse to distract the enemy from the overland force of soldiers coming to make an attack. The ground war to recapture Kuwait began on February 24 and with it came a sustained period of shore bombardment. Early the next morning, the

ship carried out another bombardment. Captain Lee Kaiss, once again the skipper after recovering from heart trouble, saw an orange glow that grew larger and larger as it neared the ship. He realized it was a Silkworm missile headed toward the *Missouri* and ordered members of the crew to hit the deck. Down below decks, Ship's Serviceman Gregory Green thought about a variety of possibilities. He was concerned about possible damage to the ship, having to abandon ship, being captured, and wondering what the Iraqis might feed prisoners of war. Fortunately, his fears were for nought. The British destroyer *Gloucester* shot down the missile, though its trajectory was such that it probably would not have hit the American battleship. The moment of intercept appeared to those on board like a huge white flashbulb going off.

After the bombardment had gone on for several days, the *Missouri* was relieved by the *Wisconsin*, which fired a number of rounds of 16-inch (41cm) to cover the occupation of Faylakah Island off the

shores of Kuwait. On February 28, Desert Storm ended in victory for the coalition forces. The *Wisconsin* had been the last battleship ever to fire her guns in anger. Then came the long journeys home. En route, the *Missouri* stopped in Australia and at Pearl Harbor. At the latter, Journalist Gary Price, an enlisted member of the ship's public affairs staff, visited the *Arizona* visitors' center. He chatted with volunteer Dick Fiske, who had been a bugler on board the *West Virginia* when the Japanese attacked in 1941. He told Price he was going out to the *Arizona* memorial that day to express his thoughts to the long-dead crew members of that ship. Gary Price was wearing sunglasses that hid the tears in his eyes as Fiske told of his plans.

THE END OF AN ERA

The *Wisconsin* went back to her homeport of Norfolk, Virginia. In the summer of 1991, she made a final East Coast cruise and then underwent the mothballing process. She was decommissioned at the end of September. Her sister ship was granted a longer lease on life because of the upcoming fiftieth anniversary of the attack on Pearl Harbor. In late November, the *Missouri* steamed from Long Beach to Hawaii. This writer had the privilege of being on board for that final voyage. Among those with whom I chatted was Yeoman John Lewis, a Missourian who had served in the *New Jersey* in the 1980s, then had moved to the recommissioning crew of the *Missouri* in 1986. Now he was back on board for the final trip, explaining, "There are only two kinds of sailors in the Navy, those who have been on a battleship and those who wish they could."

We arrived off southern Oahu just before morning twilight on December 5. As we looked ashore from the superstructure, we could see thousands of people watching and waving. Flash cameras went off to record the last arrival in Pearl Harbor. Then the ship's bow pointed in the entrance channel. Off in the distance, the sun was just popping up over the top of crouching Diamond Head promontory. As we steamed onward, I looked off to port and saw the quays where the old battleships had been moored on December 7, 1941. Now they were painted white, with the names of those old ships marked in black letters. In my mind's eye I recalled the old black-and-white newsreels films I had seen of smoke bil-

LEFT: In the early years of the twentieth century, battleships sent aloft kite balloons, wheeled aircraft, pontoon planes, and helicopters to spot the fall of projectiles and coach succeeding rounds onto targets. In the Gulf War, the *Missouri* and *Wisconsin* employed drones with cameras on board to send pictures back to the ships. Here, a drone is recovered after flying into a net on the broad fantail of the *Missouri*.

BELOW LEFT: In the early morning of February 25, 1991, the British destroyer *Gloucester* sends up two Sea Dart missiles to intercept an Iraqi Silkworm missile headed toward the *Missouri*. This dramatic painting was done by combat artist John Roach.

RIGHT: The *Iowa* was decommissioned in September 1990, the first of the four battleships mothballed following their renaissance in the 1980s. She is shown here in a photo taken by H. M. Steele. She was then visiting Portsmouth, England, as her active duty service wound down.

In the mid-1980s, around the time this portrait of the ship's officers was made, the *New Jersey* was used to film a portion of the epic *War and Remembrance*. The television mini-series was a dramatization of a book written by Herman Wouk, the author of the World War II novel *The Caine Mutiny*. The commanding officer when this photo was taken was Captain Lew Glenn, just to the right of center, who hosted the TV people as they turned his ship briefly into a studio.

lowing up after the Japanese attack. It was an emotional moment for an old battleship sailor, especially as we neared the end of the former Battleship Row and saw the morning's first tourists making their way by boat to the *Arizona* memorial.

After the anniversary ceremony on December 7, which included a visit by President and Mrs. Bush, the *Missouri* headed back to California. She stopped at Seal Beach to off-load her ammunition. Though she hadn't fired her guns during the final voyage, she had been armed and ready. Now it was time for the next phase. Once the magazines and projectile decks were empty, the *Missouri* went into Long Beach on the evening of December 20, the last time a battleship of any nation steamed under her own power. As the old dreadnought steamed into port and approached her berth, she was greeted by a chorus of whistles and horns from the various warships in the harbor. It was a touching final tribute to the last of a mighty breed.

The era of the battleship was finally over in the U.S. Navy, ninety-six years after the commissioning of the *Texas* and *Maine* in 1895. The *Missouri*'s decommissioning followed on March 31, 1992. Hundreds of people were on hand to observe the passing of a type of ship that had served the nation well, both by achievements in combat and by virtue of a presence that embodied national power and will. Many in the crowd shed tears that day, for these great ships had a way of evoking sentiment. As Leon Tucker, a gunner's mate in the final crew of the *Missouri* so eloquently put it, "It's hard to say goodbye to yesterday."

LEFT: Because of her status as the ship where the Japanese surrender had been signed, the *Missouri* got a slightly longer lease on life than her sisters. She was retained in commission long enough to make one last sentimental visit to Hawaii to help observe the 50th anniversary of the beginning of the war that had ended on her decks. This book's author was on board when this photo was taken on December 5, 1991. She has just entered the harbor and is steaming past the *Arizona* Memorial.

BOTTOM LEFT: Members of the crew polish the surrender plaque on the 01 deck.

BOTTOM RIGHT: The last crew of the world's last battleship files off following the decommissioning ceremony on March 31, 1992. Captain Lee Kaiss had been the skipper when the *Missouri* was recommissioned in May 1986, left for a while for medical problems, and then returned to command her again. He was the skipper during Desert Storm in 1991 and then put her out of service for the final time the following year.

BATTLESHIP MEMORIALS

For general information on a wide variety of ship memorials in the United States and abroad:

Historic Naval Ships Association
c/o U.S. Naval Academy Museum
118 Maryland Avenue
Annapolis, MD 21402-5034
http://www.maritime.org/hnsa-guide.htm

Alabama **(BB-60)**
USS *Alabama* Battleship Commission
Battleship Memorial Park
2703 Battleship Parkway, PO Box 65
Mobile, AL 36601
Phone: 800/GANGWAY (800/426-4929)
Fax: 334/433-2777
E-mail: *ussalbb60@aol.com*
http://www.ussalabama.com

Arizona **(BB-39)**
USS *Arizona* Memorial
National Park Service
1 Arizona Memorial Place
Honolulu, HI 96818-3145
Phone: 808/422-2771 (recorded message: 808/422-0561)
Fax: 808/483-8608
http://members.aol.com/azmemph

Massachusetts **(BB-59)**
USS *Massachusetts* Memorial
Battleship Cove
Fall River, MA 02721
Phone: 508/678-1100
Fax: 508/674-5597
E-mail: *battleship@battleshipcove.com*
http://www.battleshipcove.com

Missouri **(BB-63)**
USS *Missouri* Memorial Association
PO Box 6339
Honolulu, HI 96818
Phone: 808/545-2263 (toll free: 888/877-6477)
Fax: 808/545-2265
E-mail: *webmaster@ussmissouri.com*
(for overnight encampments: *ljc@ussmissouri.com*)
http://www.ussmissouri.com

North Carolina **(BB-55)**
USS *North Carolina* Battleship Memorial
Box 480
Wilmington, NC 28402
Phone: 910/251-5797
Fax: 910/251-5807
E-mail: *ncbb55@aol.com*
http://www.battleshipnc.com/index.htm

New Jersey **(BB-62)**
Home Port Alliance for the USS *New Jersey*, Inc.
2500 Broadway, Drawer 18
Camden, NJ 08104
Phone: 856/966-1652

Fax: 856/966-1883
E-mail: *homeportalliance@aol.com*
http://www.battleship-newjersey.com

South Dakota **(BB-57)**
Battleship *South Dakota* Memorial
600 East Seventh Street
Sioux Falls, SD 57103
Phone: 605/367-7141
http://members.aol.com/ussdakota/ussdakota.htm

Texas **(BB-35)**
San Jacinto State Historical Park
3523 Highway 134
La Porte, TX 77571
Phone: 281/479-2411/4282 (for overnight encampments: 281/542-0684)
Fax: 281/479-4197
E-mail: *barry.ward@tpwd.state.tx.us*
http://www.usstexasbb35.com

Utah **(BB-31)**
USS *Arizona* Memorial
National Park Service
1 Arizona Memorial Place
Honolulu, HI 96818-3145
Phone: 808/422-2771 (recorded message: 808/422-0561)
Fax: 808/483-8608
http://members.home.net/wmhughes/ussutah.html

Wisconsin **(BB-64)**
Battleship *Wisconsin*
c/o Hampton Roads Naval Museum
1 Waterside Drive, Suite 248
Norfolk, VA 23510-1607
Phone: 757/322-2987
Fax: 757/445-1867
E-mail: *mmosier@nsn.cmar.navy.mil*
http://www.hrnm.navy.mil

BIBLIOGRAPHY

MEMOIRS

Barnes, Paul M. *World War II from a Battleship's Bridge*. Unpublished.

Beach, Captain Edward L., Sr., USN (Ret.). *From Annapolis to Scapa Flow*. Unpublished.

Brown, Rebecca Bundy, and Brown, Heidi Bundy, eds. *The "Mighty A" (USS* Alabama*) and the Men Who Made Her Mighty*. R. Bundy and H. Bundy, 1999.

Forrest, Commander Edgar Hull, USN (Ret.). *Change of Command: A Personal Pilgrimage*. E. Forrest, 1997.

Gore, Captain John, SC, USN (Ret.). *The Navy Years*. J. Gore, 1998.

Merritt, Captain Douglas, USNR (Ret.). *An Autobiography*. Unpublished.

O'Quin, Chief Quartermaster Herbert, USN (Ret.). *A Look Back . . . (The First Thirty-Seven Years)*. Unpublished.

Pelletier, Captain Albert J., USN (Ret.). Memoir. Unpublished.

ORAL HISTORIES

Backus, Commander Paul H., USN (Ret.). Annapolis, Md.: U.S. Naval Institute, 1995.

Bauernschmidt, Rear Admiral George W., SC, USN (Ret.). Annapolis, Md.: U.S. Naval Institute, 1991.

Bieri, Vice Admiral Bernard H., USN (Ret.). Annapolis, Md.: U.S. Naval Institute, 1997.

Cutter, Captain Slade D., USN (Ret.). Annapolis, Md.: U.S. Naval Institute, 1985.

Dennison, Admiral Robert L., USN (Ret.). Annapolis, Md.: U.S. Naval Institute, 1975.

Duncan, Admiral Charles K., USN (Ret.). Annapolis, Md.: U.S. Naval Institute, 1978.

Dyer, Captain Thomas H., USN (Ret.). Annapolis, Md.: U.S. Naval Institute, 1986.

Edwards, Captain Frederick A., Sr., USN (Ret.). Annapolis, Md.: U.S. Naval Institute, 1992.

Harralson, Lieutenant Commander Richard A., USN (Ret.). Annapolis, Md.: U.S. Naval Institute, 2000.

Hooper, Vice Admiral Edwin B., USN (Ret.). Annapolis, Md.: U.S. Naval Institute, 1978.

Hustvedt, Vice Admiral Olaf M., USN (Ret.). Annapolis, Md.: U.S. Naval Institute, 1975.

King, Vice Admiral Jerome H., Jr., USN (Ret.). Annapolis, Md.: U.S. Naval Institute, 1999.

Logue, Elda Elwood. Annapolis, Md.: U.S. Naval Institute, 1999.

Long, Admiral Robert L.J., USN (Ret.). Annapolis, Md.: U.S. Naval Institute, 1995.

McCrea, Vice Admiral John L., USN (Ret.). Annapolis, Md.: U.S. Naval Institute, 1990.

Michaelis, Admiral Frederick H., USN (Ret.). Annapolis, Md.: U.S. Naval Institute, 1996.

Pownall, Vice Admiral Charles A., USN (Ret.). Annapolis, Md.: U.S. Naval Institute, 1989.

Riley, Vice Admiral Herbert D., USN (Ret.). Annapolis, Md.: U.S. Naval Institute, 1994.

Smedberg, Vice Admiral William R. III, USN (Ret.). Annapolis, Md.: U.S. Naval Institute, 1979.

Strauss, Rear Admiral Elliott B., USN (Ret.). Annapolis, Md.: U.S. Naval Institute, 1989.

Tolley, Rear Admiral Kemp, USN (Ret.). Annapolis, Md.: U.S. Naval Institute, 1984.

Tomlinson, Captain Daniel W. IV, USNR (Ret.). Annapolis, Md.: U.S. Naval Institute, 1995.

Walker, Rear Admiral Edward K., USN (Ret.). Annapolis, Md.: U.S. Naval Institute, 1985.

BOOKS

Alden, John D. *American Steel Navy: A Photographic History of the U.S. Navy from the Introduction of the Steel Hull in 1883 to the Cruise of the Great White Fleet, 1907–1909*. Annapolis, Md.: Naval Institute Press, 1972.

Batcheller, Edgar H. *As I Remember*. New York: Vantage Press, 1995.

Buenzle, Fred J., with Day, Grove A. *Bluejacket: An Autobiography*. New York: W.W. Norton, 1939.

Clark, Charles E. *My Fifty Years in the Navy*. Boston: Little, Brown, 1917.

LEFT: Battleship *South Dakota* Memorial, Sioux Falls, South Dakota. ABOVE: *Arizona* Memorial (foreground) and *Missouri* Memorial (background, being maneuvered into place by tugboats), Pearl Harbor, Hawaii.

ABOVE: *Texas* Memorial, La Porte, Texas.

Cooling, B. Franklin. *Benjamin Franklin Tracy: Father of the Modern American Fighting Navy.* Hamden, Conn.: The Shoe String Press, 1973.

Evans, Robley D. *An Admiral's Log.* New York: D. Appleton and Company, 1910.

Friedman, Norman. *U.S. Battleships: An Illustrated Design History.* Annapolis, Md.: Naval Institute Press, 1985.

Gruner, George F. *Blue Water Beat : The Two Lives of the Battleship USS California.* Palo Alto, Calif.: Glencannon Press, 1996.

Hallstrom, Linda. *The True Story of BB 57: U.S.S. South Dakota: Queen of the Fleet.* Dallas: Taylor Publishing Co., 1987.

Hammett, Hugh B. *Hilary Abner Herbert: A Southerner Returns to the Union.* Philadelphia: American Philosophical Society, 1976.

Harris, Brayton. *The Age of the Battleship: 1890–1922.* New York: Franklin Watts, 1965.

Herget, Charles A. *Dear Shipmates.* San Diego: Grossmont Press, 1977.

Hough, Richard. *The Great Dreadnought: The Strange Story of the Mightiest Battleship of World War I.* New York: Harper & Row, 1967.

Jones, Harry A. *A Chaplain's Experience Ashore and Afloat.* New York: A.G. Sherwood and Company, 1901.

Jones, Jerry W. *U.S. Battleship Operations in World War I.* Annapolis, Md.: Naval Institute Press, 1998.

Kent, Molly. *USS Arizona's Last Band: The History of U.S. Navy Band Number 22.* Kansas City, Kans.: Silent Song Publishing, 1996.

Laning, Harris. *An Admiral's Yarn.* Edited with an introduction by Mark Russell Shulman. Newport, R.I.: Naval War College Press, 1999.

Mannix, Daniel P. III. *The Old Navy.* Edited by Daniel P. Mannix IV. New York: Macmillan, 1983.

Mason, Theodore C. *Battleship Sailor.* Annapolis, Md.: Naval Institute Press, 1982.

Matthews, Franklin. *With the Battle Fleet: Cruise of the Sixteen Battleships of the United States Atlantic Fleet from Hampton Roads to the Golden Gate, December, 1907-May, 1908.* New York: B.W. Huebsch, 1908.

Mooney, James L., ed. *Dictionary of American Naval Fighting Ships.* 8 vols. Washington, D.C.: U.S. Government Printing Office, 1959–1991.

Morison, Elting E. *Admiral Sims and the Modern American Navy.* Boston: Houghton Mifflin, 1942.

Morison, Samuel E. *History of United States Naval Operations in World War II.* 15 vols. Boston: Atlantic Little, Brown, 1947–62.

Muir, Malcolm. *The Iowa Class Battleships.* Dorset, England: Blandford Press, 1987.

Musicant, Ivan. *Battleship at War: The Epic Story of the USS Washington.* San Diego: Harcourt Brace Jovanovich, 1986.

Pater, Alan F. *United States Battleships: The History of America's Greatest Fighting Fleet.* Beverly Hills, Calif.: Monitor Book Company, 1968.

Reckner, James. *Teddy Roosevelt's Great White Fleet.* Annapolis, Md.: Naval Institute Press, 1988.

Reilly, John C., and Scheina, Robert L. *American Battleships 1886–1923: Predreadnought Design and Construction.* Annapolis, Md.: Naval Institute Press, 1980.

St. John, Philip, and Drake, Leo, eds. *USS North Carolina BB-55: The Showboat.* Paducah, Ky.: Turner Publishing Company, 1998.

Sauer, Howard. *The Last Big-Gun Naval Battle.* Palo Alto, Calif.: Glencannon Press, 1999.

Schroeder, Seaton. *A Half Century of Naval Service.* New York: D. Appleton and Company, 1922.

Schubert, Paul. *Come on Texas.* New York: Jonathan Cape & Harrison Smith, 1930.

Schwoebel, Richard L. *Explosion Aboard the Iowa.* Annapolis, Md.: Naval Institute Press, 1999.

Shulman, Mark R. *Navalism and the Emergence of American Sea Power, 1882–1893.* Annapolis, Md.: Naval Institute Press, 1995.

Sternlicht, Sanford. *McKinley's Bulldog: The Battleship* Oregon. Chicago: Nelson-Hall, 1977.

Stillwell, Paul, ed. *Assault on Normandy: First-Person Accounts from the Sea Services.* Annapolis, Md.: Naval Institute Press, 1994.

Stillwell, Paul. *Battleship* Arizona: *An Illustrated History.* Annapolis, Md.: Naval Institute Press, 1991.

Stillwell, Paul. *Battleship* Missouri: *An Illustrated History.* Annapolis: Naval Institute Press, 1996.

Stillwell, Paul. *Battleship* New Jersey: *An Illustrated History.* Annapolis, Md.: Naval Institute Press, 1986.

Sumrall, Robert F. *Iowa Class Battleships: Their Design, Weapons & Equipment.* Annapolis, Md.: Naval Institute Press, 1988.

Sweetman, Jack. *American Naval History: An Illustrated Chronology of the U.S. Navy and Marine Corps 1775-Present.* Annapolis, Md.: Naval Institute Press, 1991.

Sweetman, Jack, ed. *Great American Naval Battles.* Annapolis, Md.: Naval Institute Press, 1998.

Sweetman, Jack. *The Landing at Veracruz: 1914; the First Complete Chronicle of a Strange Encounter in April, 1914, When the United States Navy Captured and Occupied the City of Veracruz, Mexico.* Annapolis, Md.: U.S. Naval Institute, 1968.

Thompson, Charles C. II. *A Glimpse of Hell: The Explosion on the USS Iowa and its Cover-up.* New York: W.W. Norton & Company, 1999.

Tomlinson, Rodney G., ed. *A Rocky Mountain Sailor in Teddy Roosevelt's Navy: The Letters of Petty Officer Charles Fowler from the Asiatic Station, 1905–1910.* Boulder, Colo.: Westview Press, 1998.

Vreeken, Fred R., ed. *"Memoirs" Of The Crew Of The Battleship U.S.S.* Maryland, *BB46.* Salt Lake City: Publishers Press, 1990.

Weems, John Edward. *The Fate of the* Maine. New York: Henry Holt, 1958.

Wiley, Admiral Henry A., USN (Ret.). *An Admiral from Texas.* Garden City, N.Y.: Doubleday, Doran & Company, 1934.

Young, Stephen Bower. *Trapped at Pearl Harbor: Escape from Battleship Oklahoma.* Annapolis, Md.: Naval Institute Press, 1991.

ARTICLES

Alden, John D. "Whatever Happened to the Battleship *Oregon?*" Annapolis, Md.: U.S. Naval Institute Proceedings (September 1968): 146–149.

Brown, Alexander Crosby. "Launching the Battleships *Kearsarge* and *Kentucky* in 1898." Annapolis, Md.: U.S. Naval Institute Proceedings (August 1967): 158–160.

Bruce, Commander Jack D., USN (Ret.). "The Enigma of the Battleship *Nevada.*" Naval History (Winter 1991): 52–54.

De Virgilio, John F. "Japanese Thunderfish." Naval History (Winter 1991): 61–68.

Duncan, John E. "Remember the *Maine,* One More Time." Naval History (Spring 1990): 58–62.

Elliott, Major John M., USMC (Ret.). "Battleship Floatplanes." Naval History (Winter 1990): 37–40.

Long, Chief Warrant Officer Henry A., Jr., USNR (Ret.). "Tactical Exercises Ended." Naval History (Winter 1991): 41–45.

Mathews, Edward J. "Bombarding Japan." Annapolis, Md.: U.S. Naval Institute Proceedings (February 1979): 74–75.

Mason, Theodore C. "Market Street Commandos." Naval History (Summer 1990): 49–53.

McQuiston, Captain Lionel T., USN (Ret.). "Battleship Aviation." Naval History (Winter 1990): 40.

Moretz, Lawrence A. "The Battleship and Mr. Shearer." Naval History (Fall 1992): 26–30.

Muir, Malcolm, Jr. "Hard Aground on Thimble Shoal." Naval History (Fall 1991): 30–35.

Peniston, Captain Robert C., USN (Ret.). "The Big Ship in My Life." Annapolis, Md.: U.S. Naval Institute Proceedings (December 1979): 52–53.

Pick, Commander Charles F., Jr., USNR (Ret.). "Torpedo on the Starboard Beam." Annapolis, Md.: U.S. Naval Institute Proceedings (August 1970): 90–93.

Reckner, James R. "The Great White Fleet in New Zealand." Naval History (Fall 1991): 26.29.

Stillwell, Paul. "The Last Battleship." Annapolis, Md.: U.S. Naval Institute Proceedings (December 1979): 46–51.

Weller, Lieutenant Commander Oree C., CEC, USN (Ret.). "*Arizona* Survivor." Naval History (Winter 1991): 28–33.

ABOVE: *North Carolina* Battleship Memorial, Wilmington, North Carolina.

INDEX